ENCYCLOPEDIA OF CYBERCRIME

Edited by
Samuel C. McQuade, III

GREENWOOD PRESS
Westport, Connecticut • London

Library of Congress Cataloging-in-Publication Data

Encyclopedia of cybercrime / edited by Samuel C. McQuade, III.
  p. cm.
  Includes bibliographical references and index.
  ISBN 978-0-313-33974-5 (alk. paper)
1. Computer crimes—Encyclopedias. 2. Internet fraud—Encyclopedias. 3. Computer security—
Encyclopedias. 4. Internet fraud—Prevention—Encyclopedias. 5. Computer crimes—United States—
Encyclopedias. 6. Internet fraud—United States—Encyclopedias. 7. Computer security—United States
—Encyclopedias. 8. Internet fraud—United States—Prevention—Encyclopedias. I. McQuade,
Samuel C.
HV6773.E53 2009
364.16′803—dc22   2008028523

British Library Cataloguing in Publication Data is available.

Library of Congress Catalog Card Number: 2008028523
ISBN: 978-0-313-33974-5

First published in 2009

Greenwood Press, 88 Post Road West, Westport, CT 06881
An imprint of Greenwood Publishing Group, Inc.
www.greenwood.com

Printed in the United States of America

∞

The paper used in this book complies with the
Permanent Paper Standard issued by the National
Information Standards Organization (Z39.48-1984).

10 9 8 7 6 5 4 3 2 1

CONTENTS

LIST OF ENTRIES

PREFACE

There are today no more compelling sets of crime and security threats facing nations, communities, organizations, groups, families, and individuals than those encompassed by cybercrime. For over 50 years crime enabled by computing and telecommunications technologies has increasingly threatened societies as they have become reliant on information systems for sustaining modernized living. Cybercrime is not a new phenomenon, but rather an evolving one with respect to adoption of information technology (IT) for abusive and criminal purposes. Further, by virtue of the myriad ways in which IT is abused, it represents a technological shift in the nature of crime rather than a new form of criminal behavior. In other words, the nature of crime and its impacts on society are changing to the extent the Internet and other information systems, along with computers and other types of IT such as multipurpose cellular phones and PDAs, are used for illicit purposes.

Understanding and preventing cybercrime in its many forms requires basic knowledge about ways in which traditional crimes are becoming increasingly high tech and complex. Fortunately, the *Encyclopedia of Cybercrime* provides nontechnical explanations about the most important cybercrime-related issues by using simple terms in straightforward ways. A person does not need any prior education in computer science, software engineering, or network administration to understand, enjoy, and use this reference work. Indeed, the *Encyclopedia* has been specifically written with the information needs and interests of high school and undergraduate college students in mind. However, the book is written as an authoritative source of information inclusive of discussions about all major types of cybercrime offending victimization sure to be of interest to parents, teachers, security professionals, managers of organizations, and public policy officials.

This work is the first comprehensive encyclopedia to address cybercrime. Topical articles address all key areas of concern and specifically those having to do with terminology, definitions, and social constructs of crime; national infrastructure security vulnerabilities and capabilities; types of attacks to computers and information systems; computer abusers and cybercriminals; criminological, sociological, psychological, technological, and theoretical underpinnings of cybercrime; social and economic impacts of crime enabled with information technology inclusive of harms experienced by victims of cybercrimes and computer abuse; emerging and controversial issues such as online pornography, social networking, the computer hacking subculture, and potential negative effects of electronic gaming and so-called "computer addiction"; bodies and specific examples of U.S. federal laws and regulations that help to prevent cybercrimes; examples and perspectives of law enforcement, regulatory and professional member associations concerned about cybercrime and its impacts; and computer forensics as well as general investigation/prosecution of high tech crimes and attendant challenges within the United States and throughout the world. **Boldface** terms within entries are used for cross-referencing purposes.

Many entries include examples of real cybercrime cases, including some that reflect recent court rulings on major and controversial issues. Over 80 topical articles have been written by authors with many years of professional experience gained through graduate school research and employment while working in the public and private sectors. Their combined experience includes decades of managing all aspects of information systems design and security while employed for prominent corporations and government agencies. As a group they hold advanced degrees and many of the most recognized technical professional certifications currently available from leading credentialing institutions. As professionals they currently provide a full range of services pertaining to the understanding, prevention, and deterrence of information security threats and cybercrime. They exemplify real-world career paths and opportunities in constantly expanding and challenging areas of cybercrime.

ACKNOWLEDGMENTS

Many people helped bring this project to a successful conclusion after unavoidable periods of starts, stops, and delays. First is Suzanne Staszak-Silva, who served as Greenwood's project manager and primary publishing advocate for the *Encyclopedia of Cybercrime*. In the beginning Suzanne was helpful in setting out the types of topical entries needed and suggested how the work should be structured. For many months she was extraordinarily patient in guiding me through the writing process while I was recovering from major health problems. And at the end of the project she extended considerable trust and flexibility for my submitting a very solid and complete manuscript. I will always owe her a professional debt of gratitude.

I also wish to extend sincere thanks to Eric Walter who for many months served as my project coordinator. As one of my graduate students, he worked with authors to keep things moving forward when I could not, and he provided initial editing assistance to ensure topics being written about by authors were properly covered and appropriately explained. He often necessarily accomplished this and more by loyally working many hours without much guidance from me, and did so in an extremely professional and conscientious manner. In many ways he provided assistance comparable to an associate editor, and I was blessed to have his assistance.

My primary research assistant, Neel Sampat, also provided me with exceptional fact checking and writing assistance, especially as the project entered its final phases. Having grown up as a technologically savvy participant in Internet and digital youth cultures, and as an observer of the hacking subculture, Neel was able to provide important perspectives as well as original articles bound to be of special interest to younger readers of this *Encyclopedia*. His ability to use and help me use technology to research and write about cybercrime was nothing short of remarkable.

Finally, I wish to acknowledge and thank the authors, nearly all of whom I know personally. Traditionally, editors of encyclopedias like this one seek out contributing authors from far and wide to contribute their knowledge and expertise about the subject. In this case I deliberately chose a team of qualified individuals whose prior work and reputations I knew in advance. On the basis of these personal and professional relationships, I knew they could be counted on to produce solid contributions and also remain flexible as a manuscript for the emerging and complex problem of cybercrime was put into shape. I am grateful for their efforts and patience in working on this project with me. Together we have made another important contribution to societal understanding and prevention of cybercrime.

INTRODUCTION

Abuse and misuse of computer systems has existed nearly since mainframe computers were first invented during the 1940s and 1950s as a means to improve military munitions and then rocket guidance systems. As computers became more necessary for research and communications within academic institutions, military organizations, and financial institutions, pranks and pranksters inevitably came onto the scene. Originally these pranksters were mainly university students who possessed tremendous curiosity about computers and the ways in which they could be used to solve problems. Eventually, during the 1960s, with the invention of ARPANET and then the Internet, and as computers located in colleges and universities throughout the United States interconnected with those located in government agencies and businesses, pranks and the abusive use of computers and computer networks became more common and harmful. By the mid-1970s researchers began studying "computer abuse" because in those days harmful activities committed with computers were not prohibited by computer crime laws.

By the 1980s all this began to change. With more and more computers interconnected via the Internet, more abuses of computer systems drove state governments and the federal government to begin passing computer crime laws. Initially these laws focused on the growing phenomenon of computer hacking, but were soon expanded into other types of criminal behaviors. In effect, computerization made possible by inventions and innovations in computing and telecommunications technologies also made possible, if not inevitable, the concept of "computer crime." This concept, however, became outdated as computer technologies became smaller, more powerful, more affordable, and capable of performing many tasks including uploading and downloading data files on the Internet. With the emergence of the World Wide Web in 1993, along with a myriad of software applications, online content, and the beginning of high-speed/broadband Internet connections, computer crime evolved into computer-related crime and then what we know today as cybercrime.

Today computer networks are more accurately referred to as information systems. The largest information system in the world is the Internet, although there are many regions and parts to this giant network. Organizations often create and manage their own information systems and connect these to other systems and the Internet. Cybercrimes include illicit uses of information systems, computers, or other types of information technology (IT) devices such as personal digital assistants (PDAs) and cell phones. There are many forms of cybercrime that go well beyond hacking into computer systems, although that remains a problem. Modern societies must also confront identity theft, online fraud, phishing, spamming, malware, and many types of attacks launched against information systems such as denial of service attacks and those involving bot nets. All these and more forms of cybercrime are explained in the articles that follow, along with what organizations and individuals must do to protect their data and IT devices.

As you read the *Encyclopedia of Cybercrime,* remember that cybercrime now threatens more than a billion users of computers and the Internet; it is a worldwide problem that is becoming more technologically complex and difficult to manage with each passing day; and it is costing consumers billions of dollars each year and is not going away anytime soon. If you wish to remain safe online, you must educate yourself about cybercrime and ways to prevent it. Finally, you must also chose to use information systems, computers, and other types of IT devices responsibly. Doing so is your duty as a citizen of our increasingly interconnected world. This encyclopedia can help. Enjoy these entries and use this reference work to your advantage.

CHRONOLOGY OF SELECTED CYBERCRIME-RELATED EVENTS

1600 Choice theory came about through the thinking and writing of Cesare Beccaria in the mid-seventeenth Century, and it is still widely relied on to explain why people break laws against many types of traditional crime and cybercrime. *See* **Theories of Cybercrime**

1789 Copyright protection was legalized to empower creators, "To promote the progress of science and useful arts, by securing for limited times to authors and inventors the exclusive right to their respective writings and discoveries." *See* **Copyright Infringement**

1800 Beginning in the nineteenth century new scientific methods lead to discoveries having to do with trait theory. *See* **Theories of Cybercrime**

1900 In the twentieth century several additional general theories of crime came into being. One of these was social process theory, which posits that people commit crime as the result of how they are raised, educated, and acculturated in society. *See* **Theories of Cybercrime**

1903 Originally known as the Bureau of Corporations, the FTC was created on February 14, 1903, under legislation sought by President Theodore Roosevelt to guard against price fixing by corporate cartels.

1914 Congress reconstituted the Bureau of Corporations into the FTC with enactment of the *Federal Trade Commission and Clayton Act*. *See* **Regulatory Agencies with Cybercrime Oversight Responsibilities**

1923	Interpol is established as an international crime information organization. *See* **Interpol**
1929	October 24, Black Thursday. The Stock Market crashed starting the Great Depression, which ultimately led to banking reforms including the establishment of the Securities Exchange Commission (SEC) as authorized by Congress in the *Securities Act of 1933* and *Securities Exchange Act of 1934. See* **Regulatory Agencies with Cybercrime Oversight Responsibilities**
1932	Enigma was deconstructed originally by a Polish mathematician, Marian Rejewski, in 1932, who was able to decipher a pattern and method of encryption allowing the evolution of Enigma to be tracked. *See* **Cryptography and Encryption**
1933	Convention on Rights and Duties of States (inter-American); December 26, 1933. *See* **International Cybercrime Laws and Agreements**
	Federal Deposit Insurance Corporation (FDIC) created in response to the thousands of bank failures that occurred in the 1920s and early 1930s. *See* **Regulatory Agencies with Cybercrime Oversight Responsibilities**
1934	Federal Communications Commission (FCC) established by the *Communications Act of 1934* as an independent agency of the federal government, directly responsible to Congress. *See* **Regulatory Agencies with Cybercrime Oversight Responsibilities**
1937	"SPAM" was first coined (and trademarked) in 1937 as the brand name of a canned pork product that is still made by the Hormel Foods Corporation. *See* **Spam**
1939	World War II begins with Germany's invasion of Poland and sets the stage for computer research and development leading to innovations in munitions and rocket and missile guidance systems.
1945	World War II ends with Germany and Japan surrendering to allied nations. The United Nations is founded in the aftermath.
1950s	Students attending Massachusetts Institute of Technology (MIT) establish the basis for what eventually would emerge as the hacker subculture. *See* **Hacking and the Hacker Subculture**
1958	The *Federal Aviation Act of 1958* created the Federal Aviation Agency (forerunner to the FAA). *See* **Regulatory Agencies with Cybercrime Oversight Responsibilities**
1960	PLATO is developed and considered to be the first online educational community. *See* **Gaming Online**
1963	The term "cyber culture" first appears in the Oxford English Dictionary. *See* **Cyber/Internet Culture**

1967   Federal Aviation Agency, changed to the FAA in 1967 when it became a part of the U.S. Department of Transportation. *See* **Regulatory Agencies with Cybercrime Oversight Responsibilities**

1969   ARPANET is created by connecting the mainframe computers at Stanford Research Institute, the University of California–Santa Barbara, the University of California–Los Angeles (UCLA), and the University of Utah. *See* **ARPANET**

1972   Atari's Pong is released, considered the first true video game. *See* **Gaming Online**

1974   Congress created the Commodity Futures Trading Commission (CFTC) as an independent agency with a mandate relating to that of the SEC, to regulate commodity futures and option markets in the United States. *See* **Regulatory Agencies with Cybercrime Oversight Responsibilities**

U.S. Nuclear Regulatory Commission is established as an independent agency to regulate civilian use of nuclear materials as authorized by the *Energy Reorganization Act of 1974*. *See* **Regulatory Agencies with Cybercrime Oversight Responsibilities**

1975   Dungeons and Dragons is created by Gary Gygax and Dave Arneson is released, one of the first fantasy role-playing games originally designed for tabletop play. *See* **Gaming Online**

Congress creates the Federal Election Commission (FEC) to administer and enforce the *Federal Election Campaign Act (FECA)*, the statute that governs the financing of federal elections. *See* **Regulatory Agencies with Cybercrime Oversight Responsibilities**

1976   *Copyright Act of 1976* grants exclusive rights to a copyright owner, including the following: (1) the right to reproduce the work; (2) rights to create and reproduce other works based on the original piece; (3) the right to distribute copies; (4) rights to perform the work publicly; and (5) the right to display and transmit the work in a public place. *See* **Copyright Infringement**

In a 1976 Congressional Committee to Study Governmental Operations with Respect to Intelligence Activities (i.e., the Church Committee), examples of the Federal Government's illegal domestic spying are revealed. *See* **Government Intelligence Gathering**

1978   The *Foreign Intelligence Surveillance Act (1978)* creates a secret court to review wiretap and other requests of law enforcement agencies in cases that threaten national security. *See* **Laws, Privacy Protections**

1980s   Public key encryption was first conceived of in the mid-1980s. *See* **Cryptography and Encryption**

Leetspeak makes its first appearance in the mid-1980s. *See* **Leetspeak**

Malware begins plaguing information systems, which initially are not illegal and considered malicious computer abuse pranks. *See* **Malware Incidents**

1982   "Cyberspace" first appears in print, but author William Gibson popularized the word and concept of cyberspace with his 1984 book *Neuromancer*. *See* **Cyberspace**

1983   MILNET splinters from ARPANET, founded as the dedicated Military Network. *See* **ARPANET**

The protocol (set of communications rules) known as TCP/IP became the main networking protocol of ARPANET and continues to be used as the technical basis of data exchange on the Internet. *See* **Botnets, Zombies, and Remote Control Attacks**

1984   Steven Levy publishes his 1984 book titled, *Hackers: Heroes of the Computer Revolution*, which described the "Hacker Ethic." *See* **Hacking and the Hacker Subculture**

The National Center for Missing and Exploited Children (NCMEC) is founded under a Congressional Mandate. *See* **National Center for Missing and Exploited Children**

1985   Razor 1911 forms to become what is widely considered to be the oldest surviving warez group. *See* **Warez Groups**

1986   *Federal Computer Fraud and Abuse Act* is passed (18 USC 1030), the first computer criminal law in the United States.

The *Electronic Communications Privacy Act of 1986* (an update to the *Wiretap Act* codified at 18 U.S.C. Section 2701-2711) is passed. *See* **Government Intelligence Gathering**

1988   CERT/CC® was formed by the Defense Advanced Research Projects Agency (DARPA) in November of 1988. *See* **Computer Emergency Response Team**

The Internet is commercialized. *See* **Computerization**
Robert Morris Jr., a doctoral (PhD) candidate at Cornell University, releases the first Internet worm. *See* **Cybercriminals, Famous**

The *Digital Millennium Copyright Act* (1988). *See* **Laws, Privacy Protections**

1989   SANS Institute is founded as a cooperative research and education organization. *See* **Careers in Investigating and Preventing Cybercrime**

1990   ARPANET is disbanded. *See* **ARPANET**

Bot programs are developed by users of Internet Relay Chat (IRC). *See* **Botnets, Zombies, and Remote Control Attacks**

Personal computers (PCs) become a mainstream commodity. *See* **Computer Forensics**

Electronic Frontier Foundation is founded by Mitch Kapor, John Perry Barlow, and John Gilmore. *See* **Electronic Frontier Foundation**

Kevin Poulsen, a skilled computer and telephone network hacker, and two accomplices manipulate a telephone network to win a "call in" radio contest hosted by KIIS-FM in Los Angeles, California. *See* **Cybercriminals, Famous**

Controversial Operation Sundevil investigation by U.S. Secret Service. *See* **Government Intelligence Gathering**

Network Centric Warfare develops at the end of the Cold War conflict between United States and Union of Soviet Socialist Republics (USSR). *See* **Network Centric Warfare**

1991   The Computer Crime and Intellectual Property Section (CCIPS) was established in 1991 as the Computer Crime Unit within the U.S. Department of Justice, with three prosecuting attorneys. *See* **Computer Crime and Intellectual Property Section**

Pretty Good Privacy (PGP) computer program was developed by Philip Zimmerman for encryption emails and other electronic communications. *See* **Cryptography and Encryption**

The terms "identity theft" and "identity fraud" are not believed to have been used in print until 1991. *See* **Identity Theft**

Operation Desert Storm, First Gulf War. *See* **Network Centric Warfare**

1993   ID Software's DOOM is released, becoming the first modern multiplayer game. *See* **Gaming Online**

1994   The *Violent Crime Control and Law Enforcement Assistance Act* (1994). *See* **Laws, Privacy Protections**

Landmark court case *United States v. LaMacchia* centers on cybercrime involving $1 million in lost revenue through distributing copyrighted software on the Internet. *See* **United States v. LaMacchia**

1995   Known as "America's Most Wanted Computer Outlaw," Kevin Mitnick is apprehended in Raleigh, North Carolina. *See* **Cybercriminals, Famous**

At this point there were 16 million users of the Internet. *See* **Internet**

1996   The *Health Insurance Portability and Accountability Act of 1996* (HIPAA) is legislated and signed into law by President Bill Clinton. *See* **Computer Emergency Response Team**

Council of Europe's Committee on Crime Problems (CDPC) began studying and drafting a proposed Convention on Cybercrime. *See* **Council of Europe Convention on Cybercrime**

Economic Espionage Act of 1996 gives law enforcement greater means to investigate and prosecute corporate espionage. *See* **Corporate Espionage**

The U.S. President's Commission on Critical Infrastructure Protection (PCCIP) addressed national vulnerabilities associated with interdependent technological systems. *See* **Critical Information Infrastructure**

Internet2 is founded as a nonprofit organization. The purpose of Internet2 is to discover the full potential of Internet technology and further promote collaboration and innovation. *See* **Internet**

1997   "Cyberterrorism" enunciated by Mark Pollitt. *See* **Cyberterrorism**

The *No Electronic Theft Act of 1997* makes it illegal for anyone in the United States other than the copyright holder, assignees, or their agents to distribute copyrighted software over the Internet. *See* **Laws, Privacy Protection;** *United States v. LaMacchia*

1998   *Identity Theft and Assumption Deterrence Act* (U.S. Public Law 105-318) criminalizes identity theft. *See* **Identity Theft**

Domain Name System (DNS) is created as the universal resource locator (URL) for all Web sites. *See* **Internet**

1999   Various tools such as Trinoo, Tribal Flood Network, Stacheldraht, and Shaft developed to carry out distributed denial of service (DDOS). *See* **Botnets, Zombies, and Remote Control Attacks**

Anticybersquatting Consumer Protection Act (ACPA) enacted to assist copyright and trademark holders in disputes regarding the registration of domain names. *See* **Cybersquatting**

David Smith releases the Melissa Worm by using a stolen America Online account to post a message promising access to pornographic Web sites on the Alt.sex newsgroup. *See* **Malware Incidents**

2000   DDOS tools merged with worms and rootkits in order to automate the multiple compromise systems to launch further attacks. *See* **Botnets, Zombies, and Remote Control Attacks**

Emergence of peer-to-peer (p2p) networks and other file-sharing programs enables people to share and download music for free, resulting in loss of royalties for artists. *See* **Copyright Infringement**

The family of the musician Jimi Hendrix pursued legal action against Denny Hammerton, the registrant of the domain name "jimihendrix.com." *See* **Cybersquatting**

Hacker launched Denial of Service (DOS) attacks against Yahoo, CNN.com, Amazon, Buy.com, and eBay, which severely limited their access to the Web sites of these companies. *See* **Cyberterrorism**

Programming student in the Philippine Islands releases the ILOVEYOU Worm causing significant damage to computers running Microsoft Windows. *See* **Malware Incidents**

Y2K (Year 2000) bug expected to knock out computer systems throughout the world due to a programming flaw involving the assignment of dates that used only six bits (00/00/00) instead of eight bits (00/00/0000) to represent a month, day, and year.

2000, A&M Records and several other record labels sue p2p firm, Napster. *See* **Napster**

2001   The completed Council of Europe Convention on Cybercrime was opened for initial signature by participating nations in Budapest, Hungary. *See* **Council of Europe Convention on Cybercrime**

September 11 aircraft hijacking terrorist attacks against World Trade Center and Pentagon kill 3,000 people and result in United States "war on terrorism" and unprecedented monitoring of cyberspace for possible illegal activities. *See* **Cyberterrorism**

"Digital natives" and "digital immigrants" described by Marc Prensky. *See* **Digital Youth Culture and Social Networking**

USA PATRIOT Act is signed into law on October 26, 2001.

Code Red released onto the Internet as a means to exploit a flaw in Microsoft IIS (Web page) servers. *See* **Malware Incidents**

Warez group known as Drink or Die (DoD) disbanded after an anti-online piracy campaign. *See* **Warez Groups**

Operation Buccaneer carried out by the U.S. Department of Justice. *See* **Warez Groups**

2002   U.S. export controls of "strong encryption" relaxed. *See* **Cryptography and Encryption**

Denial of service (DOS) attack cripples seven servers integral to Internet functioning. *See* **Cyberterrorism**

2003   Federal Trade Commission reveals that over 27 million Americans have been victims of identity theft in the preceding five years. *See* **Identity Theft**

2003   *CAN-SPAM Act See* **Laws, Privacy Protection; SPAM**
Malware known as Slammer infects 90 ercent of the computers vulnerable to its attack method within ten minutes. *See* **Malware Incidents**

2004   National Center for Missing and Exploited Children logs 39 percent one-year increase in number of reported incidents of child pornography. *See* **Child Pornography**

The CISSP program earned the American National Standards Institute (ANSI) ISO/IEC Standard 17024:2003 accreditation, the first information technology (IT) certification to have done so. *See* **Certified Information Systems Security Professional Standard**

Major earthquake and tsunamis lead to widespread disaster relief fraud on Internet. *See* **Fraudulent Schemes and Theft Online**

Economic losses within the United States attributable to Spam estimated at over $21 billion. *See* **Spam**

2005   Qui Chengwei, age 41, stabbed to death fellow online gamer Zhu Caoyuan in Shanghai, China, for selling a virtual cyber-sword that the men had previously jointly won in an online auction. *See* **Gaming Online**

College students in the United States begin using Internet II to pirate music, movies, and software. *See* **Internet**

Landmark court case *Metro-Goldwyn-Mayer Studios, Inc., et al. v. Grokster, Ltd., et al.* effectively changes ways in which p2p firms can operate so as not to infringe on copyright. *See* **MGM et al. v. Grokster Ltd. et al.**

ChoicePoint, one of the largest data collectors and resellers in the United States, pays $10 million in civil penalties and $5 million for consumer redress due to an unprecedented data breach. *See* **Privacy**

2006   Congress approves President George Bush to sign Council of Europe Convention on Cybercrime. *See* **Council of Europe Convention on Cybercrime**

Thirteen-year-old Megan Meier commits suicide allegedly because of online harassment. *See* **Cyber Bullying, Threats, Harassment, and Stalking**

Government Accountability Office (GAO) reports that the Federal Emergency Management Agency (FEMA) was duped into erroneously paying out over $1 billion in disaster relief to alleged victims of the Katrina and Rita hurricanes that struck the Gulf Coast in 2005. *See* **Fraudulent Schemes and Theft Online**

America Online (AOL) accidentally releases Internet search data of 658,000 customers. *See* **Privacy**

2007   Austrian authorities uncover international organized child pornography ring involving over 2,300 people from 77 countries who used standard point-of-sale systems to pay for and view videos of children being sexually abused. *See* **Child Pornography**

Forty-three countries had signed the International Convention on Cybercrime, and 21 nations had ratified it. *See* **Council of Europe Convention on Cybercrime**

Computer servers believed to be located in Russia used to launch cyber attacks against critical information infrastructure of Estonia. *See* **Cyberterrorism**

The Consumer Reports National Research Center, on the basis of survey of more than 2,000 households with Internet access, estimated that in the two years prior to the study U.S. consumers lost $7 billion as the result of computer viruses, spyware, and phishing schemes. *See* **Social and Economic Impacts of Cybercrime**

Researchers at the Rochester Institute of Technology (RIT) launch world's largest cybercrime victimization and offending survey involving over 40,000 K–12 students. Findings verify a considerable number of cybercrimes are committed by and among adolescents. *See* **Social and Economic Impacts of Cybercrime**

Nucleus Research estimated that the costs of spam exceeded $71 billion worldwide. *See* **Spam**

2008   There are approximately 1.5 billion individual users of the Internet. *See* **Computerization**

An undersea telecommunications cable in the Mediterranean Sea is severed, slowing Internet access dramatically in India, Pakistan, Sri Lanka, and several nations in the Middle East. *See* **Critical Information Infrastructure**

Hackers successfully disrupt electrical power grids in several U.S. cities. *See* **Cyberterrorism**

A

ACADEMIC MISCONDUCT

Academic misconduct occurs whenever students cheat on classroom assignments or exams. There are many ways in which this occurs that involve computers or other types of portable information technology devices, such as personal digital assistants (PDAs) and cellular phones that are capable of storing digital files, remotely searching **Internet** Web sites, sending text, or receiving messages. To help prevent such abuses, academic institutions are increasingly creating and enforcing *acceptable use policies* that govern the purposes and ways in which school computer resources or those used on campuses may be used.

Another prevalent way in which academic misconduct takes place is when students or another author, such as a teacher or school administrator, does not properly cite the use of text or an image from another author's work. Using the exact words of someone else's text without adding quotation marks and an in-text citation to show ownership is **copyright infringement** as well as being *plagiarism*. Paraphrasing (i.e., expressing others' ideas in one's own words) while not giving an author credit for his or her original ideas with an in-text citation also constitutes plagiarism and copyright infringement. Changing a few words around in a sentence or paragraph is not acceptable paraphrasing. Instead, an author who uses written ideas of other people must do so by completely rewriting the material in his or her own words. When someone does not properly cite another person's work by using quotation marks when quoting word-for-word passages or when rewriting ideas not of their own original thinking, readers may (and should) assume the work is of that person. If it is not actually his original work, it is plagiarism, a form of stealing (RIT Libraries, 2003).

Students frequently use the Internet to do homework assignments and research information for term papers. Some students actually purchase papers written by other authors to use as their own, or they copy and paste large amounts of text and patch them together to create a paper that is handed in to the teacher or professor. In the latter types of cases, students unfortunately may not realize that a lot of information posted on the Internet may actually belong to someone else, that it can only be used with advance permission, and that, at the very least, it needs to be properly cited, paraphrased, or quoted.

Plagiarism also occurs when a student submits the same paper (or a large amount of the text) for more than one class assignment without permission from the teachers in each of the classes. This is called "double dipping." Students using parts of a previous class assignment in another class project must accurately cite or quote to identify the prior use of the information (Roig, n.d.). To correctly use information, students need to research and find acknowledged and accurate resources, combining them by using paraphrases to create and complete an assignment.

As more students have access to the Internet's extensive resources, school teachers and college/university faculty have become concerned that students have the ability to copy and paste and to use information from a vast supply of information. This problem may be worsened by international students who come to study in the United States but have not been taught copyright guidelines relating to their academic studies in America and how to avoid copyright infringement under U.S. laws. While some U.S. copyright laws are the same or similar to those in some countries, there are also many differences in laws among other nations. Since teachers have the responsibility to award grades and degrees based on original and honestly created student work, they need to ensure that students are doing their own work in accordance with academic standards and applicable copyright laws.

In early 2000, faculty began using the newly available plagiarism-detection tool, Turnitin. A Web-based tool, Turnitin takes a student paper that is uploaded into its database, it creates a digitized algorithm of the paper, and Web-bots circulate it around the Internet to check for exact matches of text. A report is generated that shows a list of Web site sources, i.e., universal resource locations ("URLs") from where the information was found, providing links that can be checked for any instances of possible copyright infringement. If there is any plagiarism found, the teacher and student will often review the paper together, creating a valuable learning experience. The use of Turnitin has been controversial because digital copies of papers submitted are automatically retained for future comparison. Students have complained this constitutes a copyright violation of their original works because they did not given permission for their paper(s) to be used in this way. However, students actually retain the copyright to their papers and their ownership is protected to guard against other people (including other students) using the paper for illicit purposes at a later date.

Suggested Readings: Buehler, M. (2007, March). Turnitin: Friend, not foe. *Reporter Magazine, 56*(23), 13; RIT Libraries. (2003). *Copyright & plagiarism tutorials.* Rochester Institute of Technology (RIT) Web site: http://wally.rit.edu/instruction/dl/cptutorial/; Roig, M. (n.d.). *Avoiding plagiarism, self-plagiarism, and other questionable writing practices: A guide to ethical writing.* St. John Fisher Web site: http://facpub.stjohns.edu/~roigm/plagiarism/Academic%20self%20plagiarism.html.

Marianne Buehler

ADDICTION, ONLINE

Addiction is usually defined by the relationship between the individual and his or her visible behaviors. The severity of addiction can usually be determined by its impact on various areas of an individual's life, including heath, finances, career, and relationships with family, friends, and society. Given the reports of obsession by individuals with computer technology and the **Internet**, it does not require a great leap in logic to regard seemingly all-consuming behavior as a form of addiction. Let us examine the evidence for computer and Internet misuse or abuse. We frequently hear that our primary instinct is self-preservation. We are wired (no pun intended) to act in our self-interests, and we generally consider this behavior as normal, and hopefully acceptable, by society. Yet when confronted with the choice, we may act irrationally and embrace behaviors that provide immediate pleasure, even when faced with negative consequences.

Take the example of a hard core gamer. Some of these individuals appear totally absorbed in their favorite games. These people might be described as "zoning out," perhaps even forgoing basic needs such as food, elimination of bodily waste, and sleep. Failure to recognize and respond to the real world environment, as when one is preoccupied with electronic games, may be an indicator of addiction. Consider the case of Kim Kyung-jae. The Republic of South Korea consists of approximately 50 million citizens, approximately half of whom are connected to the Internet. Of that number, approximately 10 million individuals utilize broadband connections to access the Net. There are approximately 25,000 Internet cafés in the country, the majority of which are open 24 hours every day. South Korean police were called to one such café to investigate the death of 24-year-old Kim Kyung-jae. Witnesses informed the police that he had been constantly playing games on a computer for about 84 hours, without taking any breaks to eat, sleep, or use the restroom. Kim Kyung-jae had become so engrossed in the computer game that he failed to attend to the most basic bodily functions that kept him alive. Although deaths related to electronic gaming are very rare, similar cases have been reported.

Arousal patterns are another indicator of addiction. People can become aroused by numerous activities, and each individual has his own unique method of gaining satisfaction. Therefore, some people will use alcohol, drugs, sex, gambling, or many other forms of entertainment to stimulate and sustain arousal. Millions of other people maintain arousal by playing electronic games. All of these and many other methods have the capacity to generate pleasurable responses within the brain and central nervous system. Consider further that gaming activities are often available in noisy and busy environments designed to promote attraction and interest. Accompanying these influences are internal human drives toward pleasure and the relief of boredom, tempered by the propensity among individuals to engage in risk-taking behaviors. Sometimes this can result in people seeking opportunities for immediate stimulation, whatever that something is that gives them the "rush" or "fix" they desire.

For some people the risks of stimulating experiences are proportional to potential rewards: the greater the risk, the greater the reward. This notion is fundamental in classical criminology thinking, which posits that criminals mentally weigh the possible benefits of crime against the severity, swiftness, and certainty of punishment they will face if they get caught. By extension, people may express and/or stimulate themselves through greater risk-taking adventures, even those causing harmful consequences or (more rarely) affecting personal survival. This is the pathway to addictive behaviors. At some point, the individual loses his ability to distinguish appropriate and life-sustaining choices, instead choosing actions that provide an immediate thrill. With regard to computer-based addictions, a person may become so aroused by the competition and adventure of an electronic game that his esteem and self-worth are defined by his ability to master each new technological challenge the gaming environment provides. Some computer hackers have reportedly broken into very secure information systems simply for the thrill of it. This obsessive behavior largely goes unobserved by the participant or is met by an internal promise to never go that far again. Eventually, the potential for sustained arousal is all that the individual can think of, and he loses the ability to make constructive and healthy choices. This is the nature and scope of addiction, and it can impair the ability to act in an individual's own best interests.

According to arousal theory, individuals who want to maintain a certain level of excitement will pursue activities that sustain their interest and enthusiasm, even at the cost of committing crimes. However, individuals differ in their ability and desire to become aroused. Not every person who prefers high arousal activity will pursue criminal activities as a method of sustaining their arousal. However, some individuals do appear to lack the capacity to distinguish between helpful and unhelpful life-sustaining behaviors. Within the privacy of our homes or business environments, we are largely free to mask Internet-driven activities that feed our need for stimulation. The "gaming fix" experienced by some Internet users may best highlight this, but an addiction to online pornography may have more damaging psychological, social, or financial consequences. Individuals may find that online pornography has become essential to satisfying sexual needs. In time it can replace the need for interpersonal contact, particularly given the large variations of stimulating materials available to viewers of such content.

Consider that as the individual becomes more focused upon this type of stimulation, he may lose the ability to distinguish between an actual need versus a strong desire. For these individuals, the desire may become indistinguishable from and mistaken as a need, dominating all alternative methods of stimulation. An individual starts to lose his basis for maintaining sexually intimate relationships with another person, and instead hides behind his online persona. Indeed, some individuals use the anonymity granted by computers to satisfy their violent or sex-related desires. Cyber stalkers implement strategies and fantasies of controlling others, using computer technology to bully, harass, threaten, or abuse others. One would think the increase in applications used to detect such predators would be a deterrent from acting on these impulses. However, individuals who have embraced addictive behavioral patterns may have lost their ability to act in a manner that demonstrates understanding of these dangers or at the very least discounts or disregards possibilities of being found out.

Now consider less drastic but equally self-harming abuses of computer technology: An individual uses an employer's computer system to pursue gaming, gambling, or pornography, or just to track a pending sale at an online auction site. He is using these resources for personal gain and/or arousal, while exposing the network to the possible introduction of **malware**. Similarly, an individual computer programmer may use his skills to write a script for hacking into the company's computer. While there may not be intent to inflict harm, these actions represent an individual's effort to overcome boredom by hacking into the system. The stimulation, whether emotional or physiological, is similar to the satisfaction derived by individuals who are playing computer games. Similarly, a gifted high school student who is bored with the activities of his computer programming class may write his own malware. By first attacking the vulnerable school computer system, and then moving on to more advanced systems for the challenge they represent, the student may eventually explore vulnerabilities within corporate or government systems.

These hypothetical scenarios illustrate the scope of potential for abuse. They are not representative of the consequences associated with the enhanced need for arousal and/or stimulation. Many individuals who have begun a pattern of addictive behavior have said, "I can stop any time I want…I just don't want to stop right now." However, the individual who rationalizes his impulsive and excessive behavior cannot stop without incurring discomfort, irritability, or more severe consequences. When this happens, the individual may experience denial, a central characteristic of addictive behavior.

The American Psychiatric Association has yet to formally recognize Internet addiction disorder as a mental disorder in its *Diagnostic and Statistical Manual of Mental Disorders—Revised IV* (DSM-R-IV). Additionally, some experts argue that there is not enough empirical evidence to determine whether computer or Internet addiction is its own (primary) disorder or if such behavior is instead due to other, more basic, addictions or disorders (See Shaffer et al., 2000). Nevertheless, an individual's irrational and obsessive behaviors associated with computer use appear to be a way of increasing arousal and reducing tension. When these behaviors replace normal life activities in the face of serious consequences, mental health professionals recommend that the individual get help in dealing with his impaired thinking and self-destructive behaviors.

Suggested Readings: American Psychiatric Association. (1994). *Diagnostic and statistical manual of mental disorders* (4th ed.). Washington, DC: Author; Belluck, P. (1996, December 1). Stuck on the Web; The symptoms of Internet addiction. *The New York Times,* Sunday, Late Edition—Final, section 4, page 5, column 1, Week in Review Desk. Retrieved electronically from LexisNexis Academic Database; CIA—The world factbook—United States. *Central Intelligence Agency.* Retrieved May 15, 2007, from https://www.cia.gov/library/publications/the-world-factbook/geos/us.html; DeAngelis, T. (2000, April). Is Internet addiction real? *Monitor on Psychology, 31*(4). Retrieved May 10, 2007, from http://www.apa.org/monitor/apr00/addiction.html; Frequently asked questions. *Center for Internet Addiction Recovery.* Retrieved April 15, 2007, from http://www.netaddiction.com/faq.htm; Kershaw, S. (2005, December 1). Hooked on the Web: Help is on the way. *The New York Times,* Sunday, Late Edition—Final, section G, page 1, column 1, Thursday Styles. Retrieved electronically from LexisNexis Academic Database; McQuade, S. (2006). *Understanding and managing cybercrime* (150–152). Boston, MA: Pearson/Allyn and Bacon; Shaffer, H.J., Hall, M.N., & Vanderbilt, J. (2000). Computer addiction: A critical consideration. *American Journal of Orthopsychiatry 70*(2), 162–168; Yang, D.J. (2000, January 17). Craving your next Web fix. *U.S. News & World Report, 128*(2). Retrieved electronically from Academic Search Premier Database.

Kelly Socia and Kevin J. McCarthy

ADULT ENTERTAINMENT AND PORNOGRAPHY

Online sex-related crimes are prominent in today's high tech and computerized world. This reality stems from the fact that humans are sexual beings with natural and compelling sex drives "satisfied in a variety [of] ways including through fantasizing about romantic encounters and sexual activities" (McQuade, 2006, pp. 242–243). Explicit descriptions and depictions of people engaged in sexual activities have existed in many societies throughout the ages through incorporation into literature, art, music, architecture, and other areas of culture. Eventually these underpinnings, along with legalized prostitution in many locations throughout the world, became the basis for what

is now commonly referred to as the *adult entertainment industry.* This industry is estimated to generate $10 billion annually from just the sale of *pornography* in the form of
sexually explicit books, magazines, and movies along with sex paraphernalia.

The **Internet** and World Wide Web forever changed the nature of, extent of, and
access to sources of adult entertainment and pornography. In the early 1990s standardized Web browsers such as Microsoft's Internet Explorer and Netscape Navigator,
along with online communities like CompuServe and America Online, enabled the
adult entertainment industry to expand its marketing and distribution of pornography. Computers, specialized software, webcams, digital photography equipment,
and other information processing technologies also greatly contributed to capabilities
of the adult entertainment industry. Previously, such technologies accessing nondigital
forms of pornographic sex stories, photographs, and movies was limited to adult
entertainment specialty stores and mail order. By and large, adult entertainment
including pornography was out of the public view and required special effort to view.
However, facilitated with rapidly increasing broadband Internet connections, thousands of adult content vendors now maintain millions of Web sites that cater to adults
seeking various forms of pornography such as galleries of sexually suggestive or
explicit photographs, downloadable DVDs, and even real-time sex chat and online
sexual encounters.

The Web has also created multiple venues for consenting adults to directly engage
each other in online sexual conversations via chat rooms, instant messenger programs,
and streaming video. Initial contacts in these manners prompt some adults to access
additional commercial Web sites offering discreet casual sexual encounters between
singles, married couples, and people who favor alternative lifestyles and various
fetishes. Much of this content and many of these activities are accessible through
standardized credit card payment systems. However, a considerable amount of pornography is available free of charge and is often used to advertise other sex-related
products and adult entertainment services.

Sometimes pornographic Web sites contain adware, spyware, or other forms of
malware that automatically sends visitors pop-up advertisements or unwanted email
(i.e., **spam**) of a sexual nature. Malware unknowingly acquired by visitors to pornographic Web sites may also facilitate unscrupulous adult entertainment vendors
engaging in other forms of **cybercrime**. As a result of its association with criminal
activities, including illegal prostitution, **child pornography**, and human sex trafficking and slavery, the adult entertainment industry has historically been mired in moral,
political, and legal controversy. This is especially true in the United States where millions of people regard pornography as repulsive and especially harmful to young
women and children who may be forced into or naively entangled in content production. Some critics of the adult entertainment industry also believe that online pornography is the leading source of all Internet data and may contribute to marital infidelity.
Surfing the adult world on the Internet has given those normally kept in check by
cultural traditions and personal inhibitions a false sense of security as they readily
and secretly access online pornography from the privacy their homes. Some adults
act upon their sexual fantasies and desires without truly understanding the ramifications of their actions. For example, people who indiscreetly access pornography from
public places using portable electronic devices or even while using computers in their
places of employment are often chastised or worse.

Parents as a group are generally very concerned about their children inadvertently
or intentionally accessing pornography when using the Internet. The current

proliferation of free pornography and the ease of accessing it cannot always be controlled by using content filtering software. Survey research conducted by the Rochester Institute of Technology in New York State in 2007–2008 involving over 5,000 second- and third-grade students revealed that approximately 10 percent of children surveyed had been asked private things about their own body or were told or shown private things about the bodies of other people while they were using the Internet. Yet for millions of people throughout the world, the adult entertainment industry provides positive ways to explore their sexuality in ways viewed as not being harmful. Perhaps this is why so many countries around the world allow if not embrace products and services provided by the adult entertainment industry. As technology continues to rapidly evolve, the adult entertainment industry will continue to pose moral and legal challenges to human conceptions of ethical conduct online.

Suggested Readings: Fogel, J. (2003). *Addictive and sexual behavior on the Internet.* Paper presented at the 111th Annual Meeting of the American Psychological Association. See http://www.medscape.com/viewarticle/471656; Lane, F.I.S. (2000). *Obscene profits: The entrepreneurs of pornography in the cyber age.* New York: Routledge; Lucich, J.P. (2007). *Cyberlies—When finding the truth matters.* StarPath Books, LLC; McQuade, S.C. (2006). Online pornography. In *Understanding and managing cybercrime* (Section 7.2.4, 242–247). Boston: Pearson Education, Inc.

Michael J. Kozak

ARPANET

In the late 1960s under the initial guidance of J.C.R. Licklider, researchers, scientists, and engineers throughout the United States were commissioned by the U.S. Department of Defense to create a way for people separated over long distances to communicate using computers. The resulting computer network, known as "ARPANET" (Advanced Research Project Agency Network), became the predecessor of the modern **Internet** and World Wide Web. ARPANET was initially activated in 1969 by connecting the mainframe computers of Stanford Research Institute, the University of California–Santa Barbara, the University of California–Los Angeles (UCLA), and the University of Utah. Within two years, 15 other universities and research institutes across the United States had also connected to each others' computers using ARPANET. ARPANET marked a transition in computing from stand-alone machines capable of complex mathematical calculations to devices that also enabled communication between individual computer users and the organizations they worked in. All of this was accomplished during the Cold War and space race between the United States and former Union of Soviet Socialists Republic (i.e., the USSR, a nation consisting of modern day Russia and several smaller countries in Eastern Europe).

ARPANET pioneered the use of packet switching technology that allows for data to be separated into bytes consisting of eight digits (1s and 0s). Bytes are capable of being sent electronically from one computer or computing device to another in digital string messages that are sent via available telephone wires or wireless cellular phone satellite connections. This process allows people using computers or mobile IT devices made by different manufacturers and with different operating systems to communicate. *Packet switching* is now the dominant technological basis for the exchange of digitized text, audio, and graphical content on the World Wide Web. In 1983 the protocol (set of communications rules) known as TCP/IP became the main networking protocol of ARPANET and continues to be used for the Internet today. The military portion of ARPANET was also split off into its own network known as MILNET (Military Network) in 1983. APRANET itself was disbanded in 1990, but not before the technology developed and expanded into other, newer networks like USENET, BITNET, and the National Science Foundation's NSFNET. By the early 1990s these and other networks made possible Internet communications for commercial purposes.

Suggested Readings: Internet history from ARPANET to broadband. (2007). *Congressional Digest* [serial online], *86*(2), 35–64; Leiner, B., Cerf, V., Clark, D., Kahn, R., Kleinrock, L., Lynch, D., Postel, J., Roberts, L., & Wolff, S. (n.d.). *Internet Society: A brief history of the Internet.* Internet Society Web page available at www.isoc.org/internet/history/brief.shtml.

Eric Walter

ATTACK VECTORS

Attack vectors are methods used to gain unauthorized access to information systems. They can also be thought of as "possible angles of attack" based on computer or security systems vulnerabilities identified by **cybercriminals**. Identifying and implementing attack vectors can also refer to ongoing planning and implementing of combinations of **social engineering** tactics, **cybercrimes**, and network abuse, including, for example, exploitation of known security flaws in computer operating systems and software applications. Attack vectors may also involve automated placing of payloads such as **malware** or a keystroke logger program onto a victim's computer to facilitate additional cybercrimes. Ultimately attack vectors help cybercriminals to gain unauthorized access to information systems.

Attack vector motivations are as varied as cybercrimes and cybercriminals, who often resort to methods they are most familiar with and capable of carrying out. This is equivalent to a traditional criminal's modus operandi ("M.O."), which police investigators often try to identify in order to determine who may be responsible for a series of similar crimes. Cybercriminals with software programming skills may favor the creation and distribution of malware. However, computer crackers and hackers, respectively, may prefer to identify passwords and gain unauthorized access to information systems. But these types of cybercriminals and attack vectors are not mutually exclusive—a single cybercriminal may employ any number of attack vectors when planning and carrying out various forms of information systems abuse and online crime. Of course, traditional criminal intentions such as acquiring money, accessing valuable data, using extortion, damaging reputations, and exacting revenge may also factor into the motivations of cybercriminals and the attack vectors they employ in particular situations.

Cybercrimes are increasing in number and complexity. This reality reflects increasingly sophisticated attack vectors. Operating systems vulnerabilities continue to be a major source of attack vectors, including those such as Windows, Mac OS X, and Unix. According to the SANS Institute, cybercriminals also employ SQL injection to trick a software application into running unauthorized queries against its back-end database. With SQL injection, an attacker can gain complete control of a database, stealing or altering its contents at will. This tactic has been used to steal millions of credit card account numbers in several high-profile hacking incidents. What is more, with numerous incidents of large-scale data losses in recent years, cybercriminals may have already established vast archives of personal information they can use to carry out future identify theft or other types of financial crimes.

Attack vectors may also include emails with malware attachments, scams, hoaxes in which false information security alerts cause users to delete files critical to system operation, online lottery and auction frauds, and **phishing** schemes that direct unsuspecting users to counterfeit Web pages. Thereafter users are directed to enter their username, password, and personal financial account information typically to validate or help secure an online account of some kind. Many other types of attacks rely on these and other attack vectors, along with a mix of network and application vulnerabilities. Computer worms search out other vulnerable systems in search of an easy infection. Malicious macros can be placed in common word processing applications to infect a system. Instant messages can also be used with spoofed URLs and application vulnerabilities to exploit unwary computer users. New telephone technologies such as voice over IP (VOIP) can also be a source of attack whereby telephone-connect line minutes can be resold or attacks launched against traditional phone networks. Open ports, weak passwords, weak firewall rules, nonuse of encryption software, and **denial of service attacks** can also become part of a cybercriminal's attack vector.

Suggested Readings: Claburn, T. (2007). Spam made up 94% of all email in December. *Information Week* Web page, http://www.informationweek.com/showArticle.jhtml ?articleID=197001430; McQuade, S.C. (2006). IT-enabled abuse, attacks and crime. In *Understanding and managing cybercrime* (Chap. 3). Boston: Pearson Education, Inc.; SANS Institute. (2007). *Top 20 Internet security attack targets (2006 annual update).* SANS Web page, http://www.sans.org/top20/; SANS Institute Press Update. (2007). *2006 annual update of attack targets shows marked increase in targeted attacks and a human error joins the top 20.* SANS Web page, available at http://www.sans.org/ top20/2006/press_release.pdf?portal=05f0c036c9e04e014be379370ec0e37f.

Paul Lepkowski

B

BANKING ONLINE

Widespread availability of **Internet** access has granted millions of consumers the ability to manage their finances remotely and purchase items from the convenience of their homes and other locations. This ability is steadily changing the technological ways in which online financial transactions occur, as well as the overall amount and sales value of items purchased online. Many experts now believe that the monetary value of online purchases may one day exceed that of products physically sold in retail stores. In recent years online banking has grown, and it is now estimated that by 2010 a total of $31 billion in online transactions will occur each year, in contrast to $7 billion at automatic teller machines (ATMs). To stay ahead of the curve, banks are working to find ways to secure their networks from hackers. As with online banking, e-commerce has grown significantly. Countless retailers have made their products available for online shopping as a way to increase sales. In the United States, e-commerce accounts for approximately $144 billion in annual sales. Banks, credit unions, insurance firms, stock brokerage firms, and even gambling vendors (including online state lottery agencies) now offer the ability to acquire loans, make purchases including investments, or transfer money in some form. Throughout the world ATMs now make it possible for people to deposit, withdraw, or transfer funds between financial accounts with ease.

Although online banking provides convenience and seems to underscore either promise or fears about the potential for a world in which cash may no longer be needed, there are serious security concerns associated with transferring data online when the data represent "real money." These risks range from people hacking into computerized financial accounts and cracking encryption codes designed to keep such data secure to **identity theft**, **phishing** scams, other forms of fraud, and the spread of **malware** as the result of unwary consumers not protecting their own data and computer systems or financial institutions doing likewise.

Other concerns have to do with online financial services not being readily available or experiencing technical difficulties that impinge of the ability of consumers to make fund transfers when desired or needed. Ideally, online transactions require people to sign in to a controlled information system with a specific user name and password that grants access to one or more financial accounts (e.g., savings, checking, credit, debit, loan, stock trading, etc.). Once logged into the system, digital command instructions will pass through various levels of *firewalls* within the controlled Web site environment. All financial account information including digital funds transactions are further protected through triple-level encryption as determined by agencies of the U.S. Department of the Treasury and U.S. Department of Commerce, which oversee and help set security and other technology standards for computerized financial exchanges. Ultimately, the perception and actual success of online banking and commerce depends on trust by everyone involved.

Suggested Readings: Frances, C. (2004, November 7). Cahoot security lapse raises doubts about internet banking. *The Sunday Times,* p. 3; Kunkel, T.M. (2007, October). Banking on "cyber liability" coverage. *Best's Review, 108*(6), 100; Mullaney, T.J. (2004, June 28). Best buys: The net. *Business Week, 3889,* 116.

Daniel Cator

BOTNETS, ZOMBIES, AND REMOTE CONTROL ATTACKS

"*Bot networks,*" or *botnets,* are collections of computers that have traditionally been under the control of a single entity, usually without the knowledge or consent of the owners or users of those computers. Individually affected computers are running software known as a "bot" (from "robot"), and these infected computers are often referred to as "bots" or "zombies." Botnets are used by the controlling entity, sometimes known as a "botherd" or "botherder," to perform one or more functions on computers owned or used by other people. Expert botherds are able to distribute functions across individual computers running a bot (such as cracking passwords) or have them work in concert (e.g., engaging in a denial of service attack).

Bot programs were initially created in the early 1990s by Internet Relay Chat (IRC) users to provide automated responses while they were away from their computers, to attack and defend control of IRC channels, as well as to perform other tasks. By 1999, various tools such as Trinoo, Tribal Flood Network, Stacheldraht, and Shaft were developed to engage in distributed **denial of service (DDOS) attacks**, often against IRC servers. In 2000, these DDOS tools were merged with *worms* and *rootkits* in order to automate the rapid compromise of systems used to launch attacks. By 2002, the IRC control functionality of the original bots was merged with these tools, and bots became a general purpose platform for compromising systems, taking control of them, and using them for a variety of tasks beyond DDOS. The DDOS capability became less common as bots began to be used by criminals for economic gain.

Some botnets have begun to use other communications mechanisms besides IRC, including *peer-to-peer (p2p)* protocols that eliminate dependence upon a *botnet controller* at the expense of losing the ability to send commands simultaneously to all bots. Botnets have also become one of the primary tools of criminal activity used on the **Internet**, and botnet activity is often motivated by the desire of **cybercriminals** to make money. Botnets provide a technology infrastructure that, in conjunction with a creative division of labor, disperses risks faced by online criminals, allowing them to grow their operations to larger scales with minimal fear of being identified, arrested, and prosecuted.

An information system can be compromised with bot software by any mechanism used for distributing **malware**, such as through email that contains a compromised attachment or that entices a user into visiting a Web page that exploits vulnerabilities in a Web browser. Malicious code installed on compromised popular servers, in p2p delivered content, or by a worm that exploits vulnerabilities in software can also be used in conjunction with bots to attack information systems. When a system is compromised with bot software, it will usually perform a number of initial actions, such as downloading more up-to-date versions of software, testing the bandwidth of its host computer Internet connection, and "phoning home" to a server to register itself with a "botnet controller" or *command and control (C&C) server*. It may also install spyware or adware in order to generate advertising revenue through an affiliate program, to the benefit of the botnet owner. If a bandwidth test is performed and shows that the bot is installed on a machine with a low bandwidth connection, such as a telephone dial-up connection, the bot may be programmed not to connect to the botnet controller.

A bot's connection to a botnet controller, most commonly using the IRC protocol, is used by the controller to issue commands to the bot and receive data in response. These commands may cause a bot to send out **spam** or **phishing** emails, disseminate worms or viruses, spread the bot software itself, launch denial of service attacks against Web sites for extortion, start services such as proxies or remote access ability (a backdoor) on the computer, search the computer for private information such as passwords and financial information, intercept communications and log keystrokes to find such information, or cooperate in parallel computing efforts with other bots on tasks such as cracking passwords, manipulating online polls, or engaging in "click fraud" against online advertising programs.

Bots will often continue to monitor for and execute commands it is given via the botnet controller until either the owner of the computer identifies and removes the malware or the botnet controller itself is shut down, usually by its upstream *Internet Service Provider (ISP)*. When a botnet controller is shut down, the bot may attempt to contact a secondary server or be modified to do so via a backdoor connection used by the owner of the botnet, in which case the cycle starts over again.

Criminal activity using botnets has been split into multiple roles, where different individuals and groups can participate in separate tasks. This allows specialization both in particular activities and for the dispersal of risk. Some of the common roles include: (1) writing the malware used to compromise systems; (2) compromising popular Web servers and using them to deploy that malware; (3) collecting bots into botnets (the "botherder" role); (4) using botnet-provided services to distribute data (such as spam or malware), collecting data (such as financial account information and passwords), or processing information (such as password cracking); (5) selling captured account information; (6) using captured account information to engage in credit card fraud or to create forged ATM cards; (7) using forged ATM cards to empty bank accounts; and (7) laundering the proceeds of credit card fraud by reselling purchased items.

Botnets and the division of criminal activity into these distinct roles provide a mechanism for putting distance between the criminal and the crime. The individuals who perform the riskiest tasks, such as laundering the proceeds of credit card fraud or collecting cash from ATMs with forged cards, may be recruited over the Internet and deceived into participating by claims that they are performing a legitimate service. Those who capture financial account information and provide botnet services, on the other hand, need not come in personal contact with their victims or the customers who purchase from them.

The main defense against botnets is proactive prevention against system compromises. This can be accomplished by keeping systems patched against vulnerabilities and using layered defenses such as firewalls, intrusion prevention, and antivirus software. Most bots are installed on the Windows systems of home users rather than on information systems used by commercial organizations because home users are more likely to have unpatched and less protected computer systems. Once a system has been compromised with a bot, it or its botnet controller may be detected by network security monitoring by ISPs. Oftentimes ISPs shut down botnet controllers by filtering or "blackholing" their traffic, which prevents commands from being sent to the individual bots. They may also quarantine or shut down service for customers whose systems are infected with bots, as indicated by behavior such as the generation of spam or hosting of "phishing" Web sites.

One of the most effective means of tracking botnets is by allowing *honeypots* or systems on honeynets to become infected with malware, then reverse engineering that malware to determine how it works, and using client software that simulates a bot-infected system to collect information from a botnet controller. Some bot software tests whether it is running in a virtualized environment and includes obfuscated and encrypted code in order to make reverse engineering more difficult. Criminal prosecutions of users of botnets have been relatively rare, but the FBI's public announcement of "Operation Bot Roast" on June 13, 2007, included the names of three individuals arrested and charged with crimes involving botnets (Federal Bureau of Investigation, 2007).

Suggested Readings: Abad, C. (2005). The economy of phishing. *First Monday, 10*(9). Web page, http://firstmonday.org/issues/issue10_9/abad/index.html; Bächer, P., Holz, T., Kötter, M., & Wicherski, G. (2005). *Know your enemy: Tracking botnets.* Honeynet Project. Available at http://www.honeynet.org/papers/bots/; Berinato, S. (2007, September). Inside the global hacking service economy. *CSO,* pp. 20–32. Available at http://www.cio.com/article/135500; Dittrich, D. (2005, March). *Evolution: Rise of the bots.* Information Security Web page, http://searchsecurity.techtarget.com/tip/ 1,289483,sid14_gci1068914,00.html; Federal Bureau of Investigation. (2007, June 13). *Over 1 million potential victims of botnet cyber crime.* FBI Web page http:// www.fbi.gov/pressrel/pressrel07/botnet061307.htm; Grizzard, J.B., et al. (April, 2007). *Peer-to-peer botnets: Overview and case study.* HotBots '07 conference paper. Available at http://www.usenix.org/events/hotbots07/tech/full_papers/grizzard/grizzard_html; Krebs, B. (2006, March 21) Bringing botnets out of the shadows. *Washingtonpost.com* Web page. Available at http://www.washingtonpost.com/wp-dyn/content/article/2006/ 03/21/AR2006032100279.html; Menezes, J. (2007, July 25) Why we're losing the botnet battle. *Network World* Web page. Available at http://www.networkworld.com/news/ 2007/072507-why-were-losing-the-botnet.html.

James Lippard

C

CAREERS IN INVESTIGATING AND PREVENTING CYBERCRIME

Career opportunities in areas of investigating and preventing **cybercrime** are increasing as new forms of cybercrime emerge, as traditional crimes involve more reliance on the **Internet** and information technologies (IT), and as **critical information infrastructure** and organizations also increasingly rely on IT. Simply put, **computerization** has created more opportunities for cybercrime, which requires more professionals throughout society being needed to combat it. Career opportunities now include specializations within law enforcement, the security industry, legal professions, technology R&D, information systems administration, accounting/internal auditing, IT device retail sales, education and professional training, and community services connected with prevention and public awareness activities of nonprofit organizations. In addition, there exist increasing consulting opportunities for qualified individuals who are oftentimes employed by firms that specialize in providing network design, data protection, and security solutions.

Examples of positions now offered and maintained by organizations include, but are not limited to the following:

(1) high tech crime investigator (law enforcement);
(2) assistant district attorney (ADA) specializing in prosecuting computer crimes and **intellectual property** cases (law enforcement);
(3) information security officer (government agency or private sector firm);
(4) chief information officer (CIO) (all types of organizations);
(5) director of audits and information technology assessments (accounting/consulting firms and other large organizations);
(6) information technology scientist or R&D technician (universities and government-funded laboratories);
(7) computer crime professor (colleges and universities);
(8) media enrichment/technology teacher (primary and secondary education);

(9) salesperson/manager (in retail outlets that sell commercial and retail computing and telecommunications equipment;

(10) security software designer (within the private software development industry);

(11) intelligence/data analyst (in certain government agencies and private sector firms); and

(12) training coordinator/instructor (within government, private, and nonprofit organizations).

In 2008 the vast majority of employment opportunities having to do with investigating and preventing cybercrime were in rather large government agencies and corporations, especially those subject to federal regulations requiring policies, procedures, and training of personnel in matters relating to protecting information systems and data (see encyclopedia entry on **Laws, Information Security Requirements**). However, thousands of other organizations are steadily upgrading technologies, adopting new policies and procedures, and training personnel in order to prevent cybercrime. This bodes well for people interested in developing a career that focuses on investigating and preventing cybercrime. Qualifications to obtain a position often require three or more years of professional experience in a related field, a four-year bachelor's degree from a college or university, and professional certifications or validation of having completed one or more technical training courses. (See the encyclopedia entry on **Certifications** for specific examples.) Of course, aspiring attorneys, whether planning for employment in the criminal prosecution/defense arena, in corporate-related law, or social/privacy activist organizations will need to possess a law degree and pass the bar exam in states they intend to practice within. It is also advised that individuals seeking management or executive positions possess a master's degree inclusive of education in areas such as business administration, public policy, accounting, information systems administration, and security technology management.

It is also advisable when beginning and advancing within one's career to establish membership in a professional association. For example, the High Technology Crime Investigators Association (HTCIA) is a national and international professional membership organization with chapters located throughout the world. Members of HTCIA include

> police officers, investigators, attorneys, management and security professionals who specialize in cybercrime cases....Area chapters often maintain active restricted online chat forums for their members who discuss emerging cybercrime-related issues. Some chapters also archive information about various types of cybercrimes and information security issues....[The HTCIA] has developed a professional code of ethics for high tech crime investigators, and shares investigative and research findings with its membership and the public in certain unrestricted situations. (McQuade, 2006, p. 340)

Other important professional membership organizations include the **Information Systems Security Association** (ISSA)® (see separate entry) and Infrared, the Federal Bureau of Investigation (FBI) program to protect critical infrastructure by promoting communication and collaboration among organizations throughout society.

Suggested Readings: Balkin, J.M., Eddan, K., Grimmelmann, J., Kozlovski, N., & Wagman S. (eds.). (2007). *Cybercrime: Digital cops in a networked environment (Ex machina: law, technology, and society).* New York: New York University Press; High Technology Crime Investigators Association. (2008). International High Technology Crime Investigators Association (HTCIA) Home Page. Retrieved from http://www.htcia.org/;

Information Systems Security Association. (2008). Information Systems Security Association (ISSA) Home Page. Retrieved from http://www.issa.org/; InfraGard. (2008). InfraGard Home Page. Retrieved from http://www.infragard.net/; McMillan, T. (2007). *Change your career: Computer Network security as your new profession (Change your career)*. New York: Kaplan Publishing; Office of Personnel Management. (2008). United States Office of Personnel Management (OPM) Home Page. Retrieved from http://www.opm.gov/; SysAdmin, Audit, Network, Security Institute. (2008). SysAdmin, Audit, Network, Security Institute (SANS) Institute Home Page. Retrieved from http://www.sans.org/.

Samuel C. McQuade, III

CERTIFICATIONS

Employment opportunities for IT professionals with security expertise exist in government, private, and nonprofit sectors. Individuals who hold one or more professional certifications in combination with college degrees and employment experience are often able to qualify for more and higher paying job opportunities. Several, but not all, potentially important certifications provided by professional membership associations, information technology (IT) developers, and training institutions are described below. Several of these relate directly to information security expertise needed to protect information systems from cybercrime. IT professionals who have earned these and other recognized certificates will often list the abbreviations of these on their business cards, organizational letterhead, and resume as a way of advertising their qualifications.

Professional certification programs are not without critics. Criticisms include that examination and the testing processes may include high fees and questions that cover information security or other important topics broadly rather than in-depth. Examinations may not measure a level of detailed knowledge that information security professionals are expected to have in the modern age of **cybercrime**. The exam may also include questions related to outdated information or technology. This is worrisome to professionals who work in organizations that still utilize legacy technology. A reverse problem has to do with dated examination questions that often are made up or periodically reviewed by senior professionals who are most familiar with older technologies. Some people may also believe that examination questions are unnecessarily tricky and detract from the actual subject material that needs to be demonstrated.

The best certification organizations overcome such concerns by having examination questions and processes regularly reviewed by a wide number and variety of qualified persons through a process commonly known as "peer review." All things considered, professional certifications are an important means of ensuring that people entrusted to protect information systems from cybercrime are qualified to do so.

Certified Computing Professional

The Certified Computing Professional (CCP) certification is a general purpose credential that combines three previously separate credentials conferred by the Institute for Certification of Computing Professionals (ICCP), which are the following: (1) the Certificate in Data Processing (CDP), (2) Certified Computer Programmer (CCP), and (3) Certified Systems Professional (CSP). The new CCP is awarded to individuals who pass the examination, meet or exceed professional employment experience, and comply with the Code of Ethics, Conduct and Good Practice established by the ICCP.

Certified Fraud Examiner

The Certified Fraud Examiner (CFE) program is an accrediting process for individuals dedicated to the detection, investigation, and deterrence of fraud. The training and certification program is administered by the Association of Certified Fraud Examiners. It aids individuals in establishing expertise to resolve cases alleging all forms of fraud whether committed online and with or without aid of information systems. Before applying to become a CFE, candidates must first become associate members of the Association of Certified Fraud Examiners. They must also hold the equivalent of a bachelor's degree from a recognized college or university, plus two years of professional experience related to detecting and deterring fraud. Finally, candidates for the CFE credential must pass the Uniform CFE Examination.

Certified Identity Theft Risk Management Specialist

As of 2008 the Certified Identity Theft Risk Management Specialist (CITRMS®) certification program was the only dedicated professional training program in the United States to be developed specifically for professionals specializing in identify theft fraud prevention. People who seek the CITRMS certification are dedicated to educating and assisting organizations and individuals within the general public with identify theft issues. Professionals qualifying to apply for this certification are typically employed in financial services, mortgage and real estate firms, law enforcement, and other government agencies. They serve in many positions including as attorneys, certified public accountants (CPAs), financial advisors, administrators, and consultants.

Certified Information Systems Security Professional

Policies and procedures for earning the **Certified Information Systems Security Professional (CISSP)** certification are governed by the International Information Systems Security Certification Consortium (commonly known as "ISC²"). In June 2004, the CISSP program earned the American National Standards Institute (ANSI) ISO/IEC Standard 17024:2003 accreditation, the first information technology (IT) certification to have done so. It is formally approved by the U.S. Department of Defense (DoD) in both their Information Assurance Technical (IAT) and Managerial (IAM) categories. The CISSP has been adopted as a baseline for the U.S. National Security Agency's Information Systems Security Engineering Professional (ISSEP) program, which extends the CISSP standard significantly. However, the CISSP credential is for most information security professionals used to indicate their essential awareness and technical competencies in matters pertaining to information systems security.

Earning the CISSP credential involves considerable preparation to understand ten "domain areas" of knowledge. To be eligible to take the CISSP exam, a minimum of three years of full-time work experience is mandated in one or more of the ten domain areas in addition to any education obtained (at least one year in the professional field). The first three domains address security management, access control, and technology for securing data. The next three domains address the design and implementation of security architecture across infrastructure components. And the last four domains have to do with various aspects of integrating information security with other organization issues, such as legal and ethical contexts, physical security, and business continuity planning. There are currently three major concentrations in the CISSP standard, which are as follows: (1) Information Systems Security Architecture Professional (ISSAP), (2) Information Systems Security Engineering Professional (ISSEP), and (3) Information Systems Security Management Professional (ISSMP). The CISSP credential is valid for only three years, after which it can be renewed by examination or by a candidate substantiating that he has earned at least 120 Continuing Professional Education (CPE) course hour credits.

Certified Information Security Manager

The Certified Information Security Manager (CISM) certificate is awarded by the Information Systems Audit and Control Association. It is designed for experienced information security professionals and focused on physical and cyber risks to data stored on information systems and media. Professionals who seek this credential also by virtue of their managerial roles within organizations need to be aware of "big picture" issues, even though they may also be involved in technical security and information systems design and administrative issues. Requirements of the CISM include passing the CISM examination, adhering to professional ethics established by the Information Systems Audit and Control Association, a minimum of five years of professional experience related to information security and three years of information security management work experience in three or more specialty areas.

Certified Information Systems Auditor

The Certified Information Systems Auditor (CISA) designation is awarded by the Information Systems Audit and Control Association to individuals with professional interests in auditing of information systems policies and procedures for control and security purposes. People earning the CISA credential have successfully completed the CISA examination, adhere to professional ethics established by the Information Systems Audit and Control Association, have at least five years of professional experience auditing information systems or other professional experience, and agree to comply with continuing education expectations.

Certified Information Technology Professional

The American Institute of Certified Public Accountants (AICPA) offers the Certified Information Technology Professional (CITP) credential, which recognizes Certified Public Accountants with IT ability to identify problems and potential solutions having to do with combinations of business practices and information technology systems. Unlike some certifications that emphasize the importance of only technical skills, the CITP credential requires applicants to demonstrate knowledge and technical abilities across wide ranging business management and technology practices, including but not limited to strategic technology planning, IT architecture, enablement of business processes, compliance with government regulations, project management, information systems management, and information systems security, reliability, and control. To qualify as a CITP a person must already be a Certified Public Accountant and member of the American Institute of Certified Public Accountants. They must also substantiate they have significant professional experience in organizational settings and a pattern of professional development in topical areas over at least five years preceding their CITP examination.

Certified Internal Auditor

The Institute of Internal Auditors (IIA) offers a Certified Internal Auditor (CIA) certificate that requires candidates to demonstrate expert ability to identify risks of internal fraud, misuse of data, and abuse of information systems and then recommend appropriate policy, program, and financial accounting remedies. Professionals who qualify for the CIA credential have extensive knowledge of auditing standards and sound accounting practices, as well as knowledge pertaining to management principles and controls, information technology, and emerging strategies to improve business firms and government agencies.

Certified Protection Professional

To address concerns about threats to information systems and cybercrime, the American Society for Industrial Security (ASIS) International administers the Certified Protection Professional (CPP) program. Professionals seeking this distinction have demonstrated considerable knowledge of security threats posed by cybercrime as well as solution strategies based on proven and sound organizational practices. In general, the CPP credential demonstrates commitment to the security profession, instills more skills and knowledge, prepares individuals for more employment opportunities and job responsibilities commensurate with higher earnings potential, and enhances achievement potential and professional image.

CISCO Systems, Inc. Certifications

Cisco Systems, Inc. is a supplier of computer networking equipment and a resource for people whose responsibility includes design, development, or administration of information systems. Cisco provides three levels of certification for information technology professionals with separate learning tracks to meet the needs of the individual. This means there are several paths to a certification from Cisco, each requiring passing one or more exams that incorporate demonstration of knowledge and skills. Specific certifications pertain to the following: (1) Network installation and support (CCNA/CCNP), (2) network engineering and design (CCDA/CCDP), (3) communications and service (CCIP), and (4) Cisco Qualified Specialist.

Global Information Assurance Certification

The SANS Institute Global Information Assurance Certification (GIAC) Training and Certification Program is designed for professionals who are or will be managing and protecting important information systems including components of national **critical information infrastructure**. Content included in GIAC training course topics were with input from information security professionals including over 100 members of the SANS Institute faculty and other experienced security practitioners. Their combined opinions, knowledge, and expertise continue to provide an expert source for updating GIAC training courses. The GIAC certification program consists of three levels of training, including: (1) Information Security Kick Start, (2) Level One Security Essentials, and (3) Level Two Subject Area Modules. Courses are provided in-person and/or online.

Microsoft Corporation Certifications

Microsoft Corporation in collaboration with professional training schools and businesses offers several technical certifications that pertain to its products and broader issues relevant to information systems security. Given the large number of organizations and individuals who use computers equipped with Microsoft operating systems, applications, and compatible software, several technical certificate programs are widely recognized. For more information on current Microsoft certification programs visit the Microsoft Certification Web page.

Professional in Critical Infrastructure Protection

The Professional in Critical Infrastructure Protection (PCIP—formerly CCISP) credential is especially sought by security professionals who are responsible for protecting critical infrastructure resources that are associated with production, delivery, and/or functioning of electrical power, oil and gas facilities, financial services institutions, telecommunications networks, transportation assets, and Supervisory Control and Data Acquisition (SCADA) systems used to monitor and control large industrial complexes. As explained throughout this encyclopedia, information security threats and various forms of cybercrime are now a major concern for **information assurance** and functioning of information systems including the **Internet**. Cybercrimes and threats to information systems including those depended upon for national security are becoming increasingly more common and complex. The PCIP credential prepares information security managers for emerging challenges posed by **malware**, computer hackers, and cyberterrorists. It is administered by the Critical Infrastructure Institute. PCIP certified professionals will have demonstrated knowledge and skills required for designing, maintaining, and managing security needs of critical infrastructure facilities. For authenticity purposes people who receive the PCIP credential are listed with a unique certification number maintained in a secure database.

Symantec Certifications

Symantec Corporation offers four levels of certification for security professionals, including: (1) Symantec Product Specialist (SPS) that proves knowledge of a specific Symantec product, (2) Symantec Technology Architect (STA) to substantiate a person's knowledge and experience in one of four different areas of security, (3) Symantec Certified Security Engineer (SCSE) that demonstrates both (1) and (2) above, and (4) Symantec Certified Security Practitioner (SCSP) for all four defined areas of security disciplines plus all related Symantec products.

Suggested Readings: *Certification Magazine, Certmag.* (2008). *Certification Magazine salary survey 2006.* Retrieved from *Certification Magazine* Web site: http://www.certmag.com/images/CM1206_salSurveyFig1.jpg; Grimes, J. (2005). *Information assurance workforce improvement program.* DoD 8570.01-M. Washington, DC: Government Printing Office; Harris, S. (2002). *Mike Meyers' CISSP(R) certification passport.* New York: McGraw-Hill Osborne Media; International Information Systems Security Certification Consortium, ICS2. (2008). *Frequently asked questions, application requirements.* Retrieved from ICS2 Web site: https://www.isc2.org/cgi-bin/content.cgi?category=1186.

Samuel C. McQuade, III and Neel Sampat

CERTIFIED INFORMATION SYSTEMS SECURITY PROFESSIONAL STANDARD

The Certified Information Systems Security Profession (CISSP) is an independent information security certification process governed by the International Information Systems Security Certification Consortium (commonly known as "ISC^2"). In June 2004, the CISSP program earned the American National Standards Institute (ANSI) ISO/IEC Standard 17024:2003 accreditation, the first information technology (IT) certification to have done so. It is formally approved by the U.S. Department of Defense (DoD) in both their Information Assurance Technical (IAT) and Managerial (IAM) categories. The CISSP has been adopted as a baseline for the U.S. National Security Agency's Information Systems Security Engineering Professional (ISSEP) program, which extends the CISSP standard significantly. However, the CISSP credential is for most information security professionals used to indicate their essential awareness and technical competencies in matters pertaining to information systems security.

Earning the CISSP credential involves considerable preparation to understand ten "domain areas" of knowledge. To be eligible to take the CISSP exam, a minimum of three years of full-time work experience is mandated in one or more of the ten domain areas in addition to any education obtained (at least one year in the professional field). The first three domains address security management, access control, and technology for securing data. The next three domains address the design and implementation of security architecture across infrastructure components. And the last four domains have to do with various aspects of integrating information security with other organization issues, such as legal and ethical contexts, physical security, and business continuity planning.

There are currently three major concentrations in the CISSP standard, which are the following: (1) Information Systems Security Architecture Professional (ISSAP), (2) Information Systems Security Engineering Professional (ISSEP), and (3) Information Systems Security Management Professional (ISSMP). These knowledge concentration areas are in addition to the CISSP base certification and read such as CISSP-ISSAP for someone who holds a concentration in architecture.

The CISSP credential is valid for only three years, after which it can be renewed by examination or by a candidate substantiating that he has earned at least 120 Continuing Professional Education (CPE) course hour credits. To maintain the CISSP certification, a candidate must either present the 120 CPE credits or retake the exam and pay the annual membership fee, which as of 2007 was $85 per year. Program changes that took effect in early 2008 required that a person seeking renewal must have at least 20 CPE credits merely to register in order to qualify and pay the annual CISSP membership fee.

CPEs can be earned several ways, including by taking relevant courses offered by colleges or universities, attending professional conferences and training seminars, teaching other professionals in particular subject areas, undertaking volunteer work, authoring books or articles in academic or professional publications, and so forth. Most of these activities are valued as the equivalent of 1 CPE for each hour spent. However, preparing training materials for others is usually weighted at 4 CPEs for each hour spent, publishing articles is worth as much as 10 CPEs, and authoring a book may be valued at as high as 40 CPEs.

Employment opportunities for IT professionals with security expertise exist in government, private, and nonprofit sectors. Individuals who hold the CISSP credential are often in high demand by employers because the knowledge and skill required to earn and to maintain the CISSP credential must be continually demonstrated. In 2005, *Certification Magazine* surveyed 35,167 IT professionals in 170 countries regarding their salary compensation. The survey found that CISSPs led their list of professional certificates ranked by salary, with individuals holding the Certified Information Systems Security Management Professional (CISSP-ISSMP) drawing the highest average salary at $116,970 annually. Individuals who held the Certified Information Systems Security Architecture Professional (CISSP-ISSAP) certificates reportedly earned $111,870 per year. A 2006 *Certification Magazine* salary survey also ranked the CISSP credential highly at $94,070 per year, and ranked CISSP concentration certifications as the top best paid credentials in IT, with CISSP-ISSAPs averaging at $114,210 per year and CISSP-ISSMP at $111,280 per year.

Criticisms of the CISSP exam and the testing process include high exam fees and questions that cover information security topics broadly rather than in-depth. As such, the exam may not measure a level of detailed knowledge that information security professionals are expected to have in the modern age of **cybercrime**. The exam also may include questions related to outdated information, which may indicate that many organizations still utilize legacy technology, or that individuals who periodically review examination questions are most familiar with older technologies. The CISSP test is formulated so that candidates must respond in the best choice answer method from a group of correct answers. Many people believe that the questions are unnecessarily tricky and detract from the actual subject material. Nonetheless, the CISSP is a valued credential for information security professionals, and the organization that maintains this standard makes a valuable contribution to the enhancement of information security systems and prevention of cybercrime.

Suggested Readings: Grimes, J. (2005). *Information Assurance Workforce Improvement Program.* DoD 8570.01-M. Washington, DC: Government Printing Office; *Certification Magazine, Certmag.* (2008). *Certification Magazine salary survey 2006.* Retrieved from *Certification Magazine* Web site:http://www.certmag.com/images/ CM1206_salSurveyFig1.jpg; Harris, S. (2002). *Mike Meyers' CISSP(R) certification passport.* New York: McGraw-Hill Osborne Media; International Information Systems Security Certification Consortium, ICS2. (2008). *Frequently asked questions, application requirements.* Retrieved from ICS2 Web site: https://www.isc2.org/cgi-bin/ content.cgi?category=1186.

Neel Sampat

CHILD PORNOGRAPHY

"Pornography" is a broad term generally applied to sexually graphic content. Prior to the advent of the World Wide Web, pornography appeared in some "adults only" magazines, books, and movies that were usually sold by retail or mail order establishments not widely advertised or readily accessible to the public. However, the **Internet** now includes millions of Web pages that describe or show human beings engaged in sexually explicit poses and activities. Much of this "**adult entertainment**" can now be purchased via commercial Web sites or accessed online for no charge. Throughout American history the existence and accessibility of pornography in all its forms has been morally, socially, and legally controversial.

Child pornography includes sexually explicit or suggestive images of non-adults. For example, photos or movies that contain nude images of boys or girls engaged in sexual activities with each other or with adults is child pornography. To help protect youth from being exposed to and harmed by the making of child pornography, most countries strongly condemn its creation, distribution, or possession. The United States and several other countries expressly prohibit all forms of child pornography, and criminal courts routinely impose harsh prison sentences on law violators.

Many people who engage in child pornography crimes are pedophiles—adult sexual offenders who seek out inappropriate physical interactions with children. And today's pedophile profile has little if any socioeconomic boundaries. Pedophiles come from all walks of life and social status. The **National Center for Missing and Exploited Children** (NCMEC) closely associates the existence of pedophilia (i.e., extrafamilial-child-sexual molestation) with child pornography, online enticement of children for sexual acts, and obscene materials of a sexual nature being sent to children. In 2004 the NCMEC logged a 39 percent one-year increase in the creation, possession, and distribution of child pornography. The astounding growth of child pornography available on the World Wide Web has the public and law enforcement officials concerned. What was once illegal contraband and hard to obtain is now easily available to anyone, including youth, simply by using a computer or other Internet access device. And even more disturbing is that its appeal appears to be growing exponentially throughout the world in an organized manner.

Child pornographers are becoming more proficient at using these same tools to create and market their merchandise worldwide through peer-to-peer networks, newsgroups, and Internet Relay Chats. A particularly sinister method of creating child pornography involves holographic images that depict unreal (digital) youth without clothes on and/or engaged in illegal sexual activities. Compounding these problems is the reality that a large portion of child pornography available on the World Wide Web is believed to come from organized criminal elements located in Eastern European countries. Many of these organizations operate in areas of the world that do not have strong child pornography laws, where law enforcement resources are comparatively limited, and from where they can leverage the power of the Internet to market their illicit materials.

The investigation and prosecution of child pornographers is further hindered by the ability of offenders to conceal their real identity online. In 2007 Austrian authorities uncovered a major international organized child pornography ring involving over 2,300 people from 77 countries who used standard point-of-sale systems to pay for and view videos of children being sexually abused. Many of these individuals took extreme precautions to hide their true identities on the World Wide Web. Many local, state, and national police and child protection agencies, including the NCMEC, the Federal Bureau of Investigation (FBI), and the international police organization called **Interpol** are now actively working to combat child pornography and child-sex crimes that occur both online and offline.

Suggested Readings: *Austrian police uncover global child porn ring.* (2007, February 7). See MSNBC News Services Web page: http://www.msnbc.msn.com/id/17022345/; Foley, J. (2005, February 14). Technology and the fight against child porn. *Information Week;* Taylor, M., & Quayle, E. (2003). *Child pornography: An Internet crime.* New York: Brunner-Routledge; National Center for Missing and Exploited Children

Web site http://www.missingkids.com/ and especially http://www.missingkids.com/ missingkids/servlet/PageServlet?LanguageCountry=en_US&PageId=218.

Michael J. Kozak

COMPUTER CRIME AND INTELLECTUAL PROPERTY SECTION

The U.S. Department of Justice's Computer Crime and Intellectual Property Section (CCIPS) is a part of the Department that prosecutes federal cybercrime laws on behalf of the U.S. government, along with U.S. Attorney's Offices in 96 districts located around the country. The CCIPS leads the Department's effort to combat computer and intellectual property crimes worldwide. In addition, CCIPS serves as the Department's expert on the confluence of law enforcement and emerging technologies, especially those related to the collection of electronic evidence. **Cybercrimes** that originate in the U.S. districts, territories, or states and are determined to be prosecuted as federal crimes will be investigated by federal agents and readied for trial by CCIPS lawyers and lawyers from the U.S. Attorney's Offices around the country. Cases may be referred by state or local law enforcement agencies for prosecution by federal authorities, or initiated and investigated solely by federal agents or with involvement of state and local officers. CCIPS also collaborates with other federal, state, and local level government agencies, the private sector, academic institutions, and its counterparts in other countries.

Section attorneys work to improve the domestic and international information infrastructure in legal, technological, and operational ways (see encyclopedia entry on **Information Assurance**) needed to pursue network criminals most effectively. The Section's enforcement responsibilities against **intellectual property (IP)** crimes are substantial and growing as **pirating** and *economic espionage* for *trade secrets* increase. IP has become one of the principal engines of the U.S. economy, making it a prime target of choice for **cybercriminals** despite its being protected as copyrighted materials, trademarks, patents, or trade secrets. Section attorneys prosecute IP crimes and promote and support the investigation and prosecution of such offenses in the United States and abroad. As part of these initiatives, Section attorneys are responsible for resolving unique legal issues raised by emerging technologies. Attorneys in the Section:

- Investigate and prosecute cases involving intellectual property violations and attacks on computers and computer networks;
- Advise prosecutors and law enforcement agents on high tech issues;
- Speak to a variety of audiences and train investigators and other prosecutors;
- Propose, write, and advise on legislation relating to computer and intellectual property crimes and to the collection of electronic evidence;
- Lead international efforts to promote effective cooperation to address the threats of computer and intellectual property crime; and
- Draft policies and monographs addressing significant issues relating to its responsibilities.

CCIPS was originally founded in 1991 as the "DoJ Computer Crime Unit." In 1996 it was upgraded to Section status and now has dozens of dedicated staff, including prosecutors and technical experts who focus nearly exclusively on crimes involving the illegal use of computers or other IT enabled devices. The Section also conducts follow-up investigations, provides legal training, litigates cases, and, as indicated above, supports large-scale national and international investigations. The Section can also help in proposing new legislation for enactment by Congress and regulations promulgated by **regulatory agencies** that also help to investigate and prevent cybercrime. The Section participates in the international G-8 subgroup on high tech crime and conveys public information about cybercrime as a means of raising awareness and supporting cybercrime **prevention education**.

Federal computer crime prosecutors, both at CCIPS and in the U.S. Attorney's Offices, have prosecuted numerous major cybercrime cases, many of which can be read about on the Section's Web page at http://www.cybercrime.gov/cc.html. For example, on March 14, 2008, Robert Alan Soloway, 28, the owner of Newport Internet Marketing Corporation (NIM) of Seattle, Washington, pleaded guilty in U.S. District Court in Seattle, Washington, to mail fraud, fraud in connection with electronic mail, and willful failure to file a tax return. Soloway was indicted in May 2007 and dubbed the "spam king" by the investigators involved. Between November 2003 and May 2007 Soloway reportedly operated NIM, which offered email software and services. His products created a means for **spam** to be distributed over the **Internet**. Soloway made a number of false and fraudulent claims about the products and services on the firm's Web site. Among them was a claim that the email addresses used for the products and services were "opt-in" email addresses, implying that the owners of the email addresses had consented to the receipt of the marketing emails. The Web site promised a satisfaction guarantee with a full refund to customers who did make purchases. However, customers later complained about the goods and services they had purchased and alleged they were threatened with additional financial charges and referral to a collection agency if they did not pay what they owed.

On March 6, 2008, Robert Matthew Bentley, 21, Panama City, Florida, pleaded guilty to conspiracy to commit computer fraud and other fraud. Bentley was indicted by a federal grand jury in Pensacola, Florida, in November 2007. The case originated in December 2006 when the London Metropolitan Police Computer Crime Unit requested assistance from the United States Secret Service after European representatives of Newell Rubbermaid Corporation reported being the victim of a computer intrusion. Bentley agreed to a detailed factual summary filed at the time of his guilty plea outlining his role in the computer intrusions. Other unnamed co-conspirators implicated reportedly infected hundreds of computers in Europe with *adware* that cost tens of thousands of dollars to detect and neutralize. Bentley and others reportedly received payment through a Western European based operation called Dollar Revenue for their unauthorized intrusions and placement of the adware. Bentley used computers in the Northern District of Florida to accomplish the intrusions and to receive payment.

As a final example, Hario Tandiwidjojo, 28, an illegal alien from Indonesia, admitted hacking into business kiosks at hotels and stealing credit card information that he used to obtain credit. On March 3, 2008, he was sentenced to 10 months in federal prison and ordered to pay $34,266 in restitution, following his pleading guilty to one count of unauthorized access to a protected computer to conduct fraud. Tandiwidjojo admitted that he hacked into approximately 60 computers operated by Showcase Business Centers, Inc. Tandiwidjojo reportedly bypassed four password checks that Showcase Business Centers had in place on their computers, using passwords he obtained while employed by a company that serviced the business kiosks. After hacking into the computers, Tandiwidjojo installed malicious software that allowed him to intercept data such as credit card information from customers who used the business kiosks. The malicious software transferred the stolen customer data to a Web site that Tandiwidjojo controlled, which then enabled him to make fraudulent charges to the stolen credit card accounts.

Suggested Readings: Computer Crime and Intellectual Property Section. (2007). *Prosecuting computer crimes.* Washington, DC: U.S. Department of Justice. Available at http://www.cybercrime.gov/ccmanual/index.html; Computer and Intellectual Property Section–Criminal Division. (2002). *Searching and seizing computers and obtaining electronic evidence in criminal investigations.* Washington, DC: U.S. Department of Justice. Available at http://www.cybercrime.gov/s&smanual2002.htm; Hugh, S.A. (2006). *Computer and intellectual property crime: Federal and state law.* Arlington, VA: BNA Books; Toren, P. (2003). *Intellectual property and computer crimes (intellectual property law and business crimes series).* New York: Law Journal Press; United States Department of Justice. (2008). *Computer Crime & Intellectual Property Section.* Retrieved from USDOJ Web site: http://www.justice.gov/criminal/cybercrime/ccnews.html.

Samuel C. McQuade, III

COMPUTER EMERGENCY RESPONSE TEAM

Computerization and the rise of international **cybercrimes** has given rise to the creation of one or more Computer Emergency Response Teams (CERT) in several countries. The lead U.S. CERT in the United States is located in Pittsburgh, Pennsylvania, at the Carnegie-Mellon University's Software Engineering Institute (SEI). Known as the CERT Coordination Center (CERT/CC®), its mission is to detect, track, and report on new forms of **malware** and other threats to information security. At least annually CERT/CC® publishes reports that alert information security professionals working in government agencies, academic institutions, and businesses about emerging online threats to information systems. CERT also employs experts capable of providing emergency technical assistance in situations involving major cybercrimes and threats to **critical information infrastructure**.

CERT/CC® was formed by the Defense Advanced Research Projects Agency (DARPA) in November 1988. In the wake of the infamous *Morris Worm* released onto the **Internet**, the Center focused its efforts on anticipating future trends related to malicious software and information systems exploitation. The stated intent of its creator, Robert Morris Jr., was to provide a demonstration of several types of systems vulnerabilities, which proved in combination capable of infecting not one or even a few computers but a major portion of the Internet located in the United States. The effect slowed or shut down thousands of computers and amounted to the Internet's first **denial of service attack**. Officials at DARPA realized ways in which future malware like the Morris Worm could threaten the Internet and therefore the need for a permanent, trusted and available organization to provide for coordinated threat analysis and response.

CERT/CC® was charged with developing research capabilities in the area of security analysis and education capability in the areas of incident prevention and handling.

From the beginning CERT/CC® was envisioned to be a multidisciplinary resource consisting of computer scientists, software engineers, professional communicators, educators, legal experts, and those skilled in management and policy formulation. As the Internet expanded, other nations recognized the wisdom of establishing CERT teams. It also had a critical role in establishing the Forum of Incident Response and Security Teams (FIRST), which includes CERT teams from corporations and universities, along with CERTs from countries such as the ones in Germany and Australia. There are many similarities among these organizations. Many have an internal group of professionals that comprise a computer security incident response team (CSIRT). According to cert.org (2008), a CSIRT "is a service organization that is responsible for receiving, reviewing, and responding to computer security incident reports and activity. Their services are usually performed for a defined constituency that could be a parent entity such as a corporation, governmental, or educational organization; a region or country; a research network; or a paid client." A CSIRT can be formally or informally organized depending on threats posed by an unfolding cybercrime situation.

Professionals often refer to CERTs and CSIRTs as being one and the same thing. However, internal CSIRTs, especially in the early days, were usually established after a major cybercrime event. Often an organization would organize and respond with an ad hoc team, and later evaluate the need for a permanent team. Some of those teams would be centrally organized and funded, leading and coordinating responses to subsequent computer security incidents. Slowness of organizing internal incident response teams has periodically attracted the attention of U.S. legislators, resulting in federal laws and regulations pertaining to the establishment of CSIRTs by organizations in particular service sectors. For example, the *Health Insurance Portability and Accountability Act of 1996* (HIPAA) requires certain health care organizations to establish security incident response procedures in order to help protect private medical records of patients. Similarly, federal laws and regulations require management of information system–related risks in the financial services sectors.

The SysAdmin, Audit, Networking, and Security ("SANS") Institute defines the following six steps of computer security incident handling, all of which have generally been adopted by CERTs and CSIRTs: (1) *Preparation* that begins with a mind-set that even the best defenses may fail at some point and that adequately trained and resourced experts are required to implement and manage information systems security within organizations; (2) *Identification* of cybercrime attack threats such as malware; (3) *Containment* of cybercrime attack impacts on information systems; (4) *Eradication,* which means to neutralize and remove malware that has infected information systems; (5) *Recovery* to restore the functioning and security of information systems; and (6) *Discovery of lessons learned,* which refers to debriefing processes about computer security incidents and extends to technological upgrades, personnel training, and improving policies, programs, and practices to improve upon the above in future cyber attack situations.

The CERT/CC® now provides a reliable, trusted, 24-hour, single point of contact during computer security incident emergencies. CERT/CC® professionals facilitate communication among experts working to solve security problems, and provide critical assistance for identifying and correcting vulnerabilities in computer systems. They also maintain close ties with research activities and initiate proactive measures to increase awareness and understanding of information security issues. CERT/CC® provides worldwide leadership for software assurance, secure information systems, organizational/enterprise security, coordinated incident response capabilities, and personnel training.

Suggested Readings: Alberts, C., et al. (2004, October). *Defining incident management processes for CSIRTs: A work in progress.* Available at http://www.cert.org/archive/pdf/04tr015.pdf; CERT Charter. (1988). *Meet CERT.* Available at http://www.cert.org/meet_cert/meetcertcc.html; GLBA Safeguards Rule. (2002, May 23). Available at http://www.ftc.gov/os/2002/05/67fr36585.pdf; Grance, T., et al. (2004, January). *Computer security incident handling guide.* NIST Special Publication 800-61. Available at http://csrc.nist.gov/publications/nistpubs/800-61/sp800-61.pdf; HIPAA Security Rule. (2003, February 20). Available at http://www.cms.hhs.gov/SecurityStandard/Downloads/securityfinalrule.pdf; Osborne, T.R. (2001, July 3). *Building an Incident Response Program To Suit Your Business.* Available at https://www2.sansorg/reading_room/whitepapers/incident/627.php; Page, B. (1988). *A report on the internet worm.* Retrieved November 22, 2007, from http://ftp.cerias.purdue.edu/pub/doc/morris_worm/worm.paper.

Jim Moore

COMPUTER FORENSICS

"Computer forensics" is a generic term that refers to the search, recovery, and preservation of digital evidence found on information systems while investigating criminal or civil cases. Information systems include any number of stand-alone or networked computers and other electronic devices, including portable media such as cell phones, PDAs, flash drives, CDs, DVDs, pagers, video games, MP3 players, and so forth. As a law enforcement, private investigation, and scientific discipline, computer forensics began during the early 1990s as personal computers (PCs) became popular among business and residential users. The misuse of PCs to violate acceptable use policies, violate computer crime laws, or harm people in other ways led to the onset of computer forensics and advancements within this field. Law enforcement in particular needed policies, procedures, and tools to identify, collect, and preserve digital evidence of various types of **cybercrimes** increasingly being committed by criminals.

Whereas most forensic processes are comparative in nature (i.e., involving comparison of evidentiary patterns against known samples of fingerprints, DNA, ballistics tests, controlled substances, and tool marks, etc.), computer forensics consists mainly of searching for evidence and artifacts that indicate use, possession, or ownership of digital evidence. For this reason computer forensics is like archeology insofar as the examiner is looking for evidence and artifacts that provide information from the past about who possessed, owned, and used certain things (i.e., computerized files) and for what purposes. And like sciences underlying information technology (e.g., mathematics, physics, electronics, and chemistry), the scientific nature of computer forensics relies upon tested and verified processes recognized in courts of law for identifying and protecting incriminating data.

Securing and processing digital evidence requires special knowledge and tools to ensure that evidence is properly maintained for future presentation in a court of law. These tools consist of hardware devices and software designed to prevent changes to digital evidence being examined. These tools allow for duplication of digital evidence in a format that can be safely examined and allow for examination of data at a level that ordinary users cannot see. Many of these special software tools were originally stand-alone programs or applications that performed a narrowly focused task.

Improvements in this technology now combine computer forensic tools into a suite of software capable of performing a multitude of examination and recovery tasks.

Locating, securing, analyzing, and presenting digital evidence in court or other official hearings requires special knowledge and skills in using hardware and software tools. These tools allow investigators to duplicate incriminating evidence so it can be safely examined without the risk of accidentally damaging or destroying the original data. The tools not only provide protection to the data but allow for examination of the data at a level that the ordinary users cannot view or manipulate. Early software tools used by computer forensics experts were stand-alone software applications that performed narrowly focused types of analysis. Today many of those programs are combined into a suite of software tools capable of performing a multitude of examination and recovery tasks.

Suggested Readings: McQuade, S.C. (2006). Investigating and prosecuting cybercrime. In *Understanding and managing cybercrime* (pp. 331–403). Boston: Pearson Education, Inc.; Reith, M., et al. (2002, Fall). An examination of digital forensic models. *International Journal of Digital Evidence, 1*(3); Scientific Working Group on Digital Evidence. (2007, November 5). Available at http://68.156.151.124/index.html.

Joseph F. Hennekey

COMPUTERIZATION

"Computerization" refers to worldwide technology integration and adoption of computers and other electronic IT devices, along with the **Internet**, to support the activities that people do in the course of their daily lives. A person who uses a computer online exemplifies computerization, as do millions of other people who use any type of IT device. Thus, computerization generally has to do with the integration of IT devices and computerized systems into communications, transportation, manufacturing, military weaponry, entertainment systems, and virtually all other technological areas of modern life. The process of computerization began in the late 1940s with the invention of modern computers to provide munitions guidance systems for the U.S. military. However, it was not until 1969 with the invention of the Advanced Research Project Agency Network (**ARPANET**) that computerization as we now understand it really began to expand. This is because ARPANET pioneered packet switching technology, which began the basis for the Internet in 1983, its commercialization in 1988, and finally the World Wide Web in 1991. Over this period of time, extending half a century, what began as a small number of mainframe computers evolved into personal computers (PCs) that have been widely adopted for academic, government, business, nonprofit organization, and individual user purposes.

Today over 1 billion computers exist on the Earth, with approximately 1.5 billion individual users of the Internet. The adoption of computers and other IT devices enhances Internet usage, and vice versa. High-speed (broadband) Internet connectivity expansion also drives computer, IT, and Internet technology adoption and utilization by individuals and organizations throughout the world. Utilization of the Internet expanded nearly 275 percent from 2000 to 2008. In North America alone approximately 72 percent of the domestic population (244 million out of 337 million people) now use the Internet regularly. North America represents approximately 18 percent of worldwide Internet users. And there are currently over 100 million

Web sites existing on the World Wide Web, with thousands of new Web sites created everyday.

Growth of computer and IT device users and the Internet also stems from how much easier these technologies are to use. Long gone are the days in which a user needed to understand programming in order to use computers. Originally, computers were built with bulky vacuum tubes and comparatively crude electronic components by today's standards. Consequently, these "mainframe" machines with their computer punch-card readers and their printing components would literally take up very large or several rooms within a building. Each mainframe computer cost millions of dollars. Today digital computers, IT devices, and plug-in media/components are increasingly smaller, portable, and much more affordable. They have faster processing speeds, greater memory, and increasingly more built-in functions. For example, Apple's iPhone and iPod touch devices are media players that also have Internet browsing and communication abilities. Several manufacturers are integrating personal digital assistant (PDA) and cellular phone capabilities, and it is difficult to purchase a cell phone without a built-in digital camera.

Suggested Readings: Alakeson, V., Aldrich, T., Goodman, J., & Jorgensen, B. (2004). *Making the Net work: Sustainable development in a digital society.* Sterling, VA: Stylus Publishing; Ifrah, G. (2002). *The universal history of computing: From the abacus to the quantum computer.* San Francisco, CA: Wiley Publishers; Miniwatts Marketing Group. (2008, March). World Internet Usage Statistics Web site: http://www .internetworldstats.com/stats.htm; Okin, J.R. (2005). *The Internet revolution: The not-for-dummies guide to the history, technology, and use of the Internet.* Winter Harbor, ME: Ironbound Press; Walton, M. (2006, November 1). *Web reaches new milestone: 100 million sites.* CNN Web site: http://www.cnn.com/2006/TECH/internet/11/01/ 100millionwebsites/index.html.

Samuel C. McQuade, III and Neel Sampat

COPYRIGHT INFRINGEMENT

Written into the U.S. Constitution in 1789, copyright protection has been legalized to empower creators, "To promote the progress of science and useful arts, by securing for limited times to authors and inventors the exclusive right to their respective writings and discoveries." The copyright protection of scientists' discoveries and authors' creative works are authorized by this clause to benefit our society by supporting innovation and limited time copyright protection. When a unique expression of an idea is created into a tangible format where it can be read, viewed, or heard, it is automatically copyrighted. Registering with the U.S. Copyright Office is not necessary, although it does add a higher level of copyright protection for someone who plans on commercially using his/her own work.

Copyright infringement occurs when a person other than the owner of the **intellectual property** uses a piece of work, such as from an article, text in a book, an image, information, software, or music from the **Internet**, in a way that does not give credit or pay royalties to the creator. As such, copyright infringement in relation to any form of intellectual property is possible, including patents, trademarks, and trade secrets. Here is an example of the commercial, for profit use of an item and how its copyright can be violated: the musician Bruce Springsteen and his recording company officially copyright his music, thus protecting his rights to make a living and those of the company to profit by receiving royalties from the fans who purchase Springsteen's music. However, in 2000, new *file-sharing* software available on the Internet enabled people to download and share music for free, resulting in the music artist and his record label losing substantial profits from users not paying for the music.

Under pressure from the Recording Industry Association of America (RIAA), the Motion Picture Association of America (MPAA), the Software Business Alliance (SBA), and other lobbying organizations concerned about the pirating of music, movies, and software, the U.S. Congress and federal courts have steadily strengthened laws protecting these kinds of intellectual property. This is resulting in a crackdown on companies that create or make available *peer-to-peer* services specifically with intent to defraud copyright holders. Several thousands of these people have been successfully caught, prosecuted, and fined for copyright infringement, and some of the worst violators have even received prison sentences under U.S. law.

Copyright infringement can be avoided by being aware of copyright owners' legal rights. The *U.S. Copyright Act of 1976* grants exclusive rights to a copyright owner, including: (1) the right to reproduce the work; (2) rights to create and reproduce other works based on the original piece; (3) the right to distribute copies; (4) rights to perform the work publicly; and (5) the right to display and transmit the work in a public place.

One of the exceptions to copyright owners' exclusive rights is the "fair use provision." Fair use is primarily applied in an academic setting where a large majority of intellectual property is used for educational purposes. There are four factors to be considered when making a determination of fair use: (1) *Purpose and character of use.* Is it commercial (for profit) or educational (teaching, research, comment, or criticism)? Also, does the transformation from the original work add something new with a different purpose or is it basically a copy of the original? (2) *Nature of copyrighted work.* Some works are more deserving of copyright protection than others. Is the item creative or is it factual? The more creative an item is the more protection it has. Facts or ideas cannot be copyrighted. (3) *Relative amount.* The amount of the item used and its value of importance to the whole are taken into account. Is more of the item going to be used than necessary? (4) *Effect upon potential market.* Will the use harm the current or potential market for the material(s) used? Does the use affect future income for the original owner? When determining fair use, all of the factors do not necessarily need to be in favor of the use. One needs to weigh and balance the four factors to evaluate in which direction the use fits.

Materials in the *public domain* (i.e., available to everyone online, in libraries, and through common knowledge) are not protected by copyright and may be freely used. This occurs when either the copyright term for the item has expired, the author failed to formalize copyright regulations when copyright law changed, or the work was created by the U.S. government. All works, such as movies, music, art, books, journal articles, etc., created prior to 1923, are also in the public domain. When these public domain materials are freely used, they still need to be cited to give the original author credit (see encyclopedia entry titled **Scientific and Professional Misconduct**). Some believe that everything on the World Wide Web is in the public domain and is free to be used in whatever way a person decides. With the free and available use of the Internet, online creative material has flourished and grown exponentially. It is very easy for someone other than the owner-creator to copy and paste text, images, and other materials for further use. Copyright infringement laws and guidelines apply to resources on the Internet as they do to a book, article, video, or music.

Suggested Readings: McQuade, S.C. (2006). The social and economic impacts of cybercrime. In *Understanding and managing cybercrime* (pp. 295–301). Boston: Pearson Education, Inc.; Parloff, R. (2003, September). Killer app. *Fortune, 148*(4), 111–116, ABI Inform/Proquest Direct; "We the people," Celebrating the Constitution. (n.d.). United States Senate Web site: http://www.senate.gov/.

Marianne Buehler

CORPORATE ESPIONAGE

Corporate espionage typically involves spying for business, manufacturing, or industrial information to help competing firms gain an economic advantage. Also known as *economic espionage,* this type of crime may also be committed by individual spies hired by competing firms or unethical insider employees. Motivations include but are not limited to financial profit for individuals or companies involved. For example, employees who may have been bribed or wish to settle a grudge against a firm's management are sometimes motivated to steal, destroy, or leak information in order to profit from and/or damage the reputation of their company. Sometimes researchers and senior managers recruited to competing firms will attempt to take trade secrets with them to their new jobs. In fact, recruiting experts for hire is sometimes rooted in unscrupulous intentions to learn what secrets they know and how a new employer can benefit from this information.

For all these reasons corporate espionage frequently involves theft of **intellectual property**, especially *trade secrets* related to chemical formulas, agricultural innovations, manufacturing processes, details of a new product being planned, its intended release date and marketing plan, client data, or other information affecting a company's stock market value. Any unauthorized access to or release of such information can give a competing firm a significant economic advantage. When it comes to **cybercrime**, corporate espionage may also involve manipulation or *sabotage* of hardware, software, and information saved in either digital or hard copy forms. Corporate spies increasingly use these tactics along with the stealing of trade secrets in today's extremely competitive and computerized global economy.

In today's global marketplace a corporation's reputation and trademark brand recognition may also be a prime target of sabotage combined with corporate espionage. For example, damaging manufacturing apparatus or facilities may delay or prevent a product from being produced on time or at particular locations. Sabotage may be overcome by reconstruction, outsourcing, or transferring product lines, but a brand name or corporate image that has been tainted by poor quality, questionable, or possibly hazardous materials causing physical harm through injury can result in long-term financial damage or even bankruptcy. Consider a 1982 case of product tampering: although it was never proven that corporate sabotage was the objective, tainting of the pain reliever Tylenol sold in grocery stores stirred a media sensation and caused many people not to buy the product for fear of being poisoned. This resulted in significant financial hardship for the manufacturer, Johnson & Johnson, and had a ripple effect throughout the pharmaceutical industry that resulted in the tamper-proof packaging we see today on bottles of pills and other medical products sold in stores.

Stealing of proprietary information and the associated damage to corporate reputations annually result in billions of dollars in losses and/or illicit gains that sometimes cause businesses that are victimized to fail or, conversely, allow unscrupulous businesses to succeed although as the result of violating cybercrime laws. Economic espionage and sabotage have become weapons of choice for some companies and even countries that pursue unfair economic advantages in violation of crime and international laws. State sponsored acts of economic espionage and sabotage can have a significant impact across global industries and regions of the world, affecting trade agreements and treaties to curb the financing of terrorism. Recognizing that corporate espionage can also threaten economic national security, President William Clinton signed the *Economic Espionage Act of 1996* (Title 18 U.S.C. §1831-1839) into law, giving law enforcement officials greater means to investigate and prosecute this type of crime. In 1998 the law was used to prosecute David T. Krumrei, who after gaining access to information about a secret floor lamination (coating) process, tried to sell it first to FBI agents in a sting operation and later to a competing firm located in Australia. In the following year Krumrei pleaded guilty to violating the *Economic Espionage Act.* He was sentenced to two years imprisonment and ordered to pay $10,000 in restitution.

Stealing corporate secrets is not new; however, the digital age has made information much easier to obtain, store on compact devices and media, and transfer physically as well as over the **Internet** to buyers located throughout the world. Small electronic devices with storage capabilities and Internet up/downloading capabilities, along with miniature computer storage media like stick drives, make smuggling valuable information out of facilities easy unless this is carefully controlled. Digital technology that facilitates hacking and surveillance of computer network activity along with monitoring movement of people and electronic eavesdropping add to espionage threats now faced by many companies. Nevertheless, some of the most effective security techniques involve relatively simple low-tech procedures like providing routine information systems security updates, requiring that documents be shredded before being recycled or disposed of, prohibiting anyone from searching through trash bins (i.e., "dumpster diving"), and guarding against **social engineering**, bribery, and even blackmail of employees entrusted with secret information.

Suggested Readings: Halligan, R.M., Esq. (2007). *Reported criminal arrests and convictions under the Economic Espionage Act of 1996.* Available at http://my.execpc.com/~mhallign/indict.html#_Toc9924969; *United States v. David T. Krumrei.* (2001, July 26). 258 F.3d 535; U.S. Department of Justice Web page: http://www.usdoj.gov/criminal/cybercrime/usamay2001_6.htm; Freeh, L.J. (1998). *Statement of FBI Director Louis Freeh before the Senate Select Committee on Intelligence, January 28.* Available at http://www.yale.edu/lawweb/avalon/terrorism/t_0011.htm

Joseph F. Hennekey

COUNCIL OF EUROPE CONVENTION ON CYBERCRIME

In November 1996, the Council of Europe's Committee on Crime Problems (CDPC) began studying and drafting a proposed Convention on Cybercrime. ("Explanatory Report," *Convention on Cybercrime,* part II, para. 7.) Five years later, the completed Convention was opened for initial signature initiating nations on November 23, 2001, in Budapest, Hungary. The United States was one of 30 countries that initially signed the treaty, but it did not take force until July 1, 2004. On November 17, 2003, President George W. Bush sent the Convention to the U.S. Senate for its review and to proceed through the approval process to be ratified. On April 4, 2006, Congress approved of the United States joining the international Convention on Cybercrime. As of October 2007, 43 countries had signed the Convention, and 21 nations had ratified it.

The Convention on Cybercrime is the most comprehensive international treaty yet to define, prevent, and prosecute **cybercrimes**. As with all criminal laws in the United States, the document specifically defines (in Article 1) many terms so that nations implementing the agreement, as well as countries contemplating future signing of the Convention, understand exactly what is referred to in the document. The Convention outlines criminal offenses that participating countries must add to their criminal code. One set of offenses concerns the "confidentiality, integrity, and availability of computer data and systems." (*Convention on Cybercrime,* Chapter II, Section 1, articles 2–8.) These offenses include illegal access, interception, and interference of data; interference with information systems; misuse of information technology (IT) devices; and computer-related forgery and fraud. Additional sets of offenses proscribed pertain to **Internet** content (**child pornography**), **copyright infringement**, and aiding and abetting (articles 9–11). Article 12 addresses corporate liability and article 13 addresses adoption of appropriate criminal sanctions.

The Convention requires that participating countries adjust or augment their criminal and legal procedures to permit investigation of the cybercrimes indicated above, while retaining whatever additional computer laws member countries already have in place. Of particular concern is the preservation and real-time collection of computer data, and the legal ability of law enforcement authorities and others to demand the production of data, and to search, seize, or intercept data. (These issues are addressed in Chapter II, Section 2, articles 14–21 of the Convention.) The final article in Chapter II of the Convention requires participating countries to take whatever measures are needed to establish jurisdiction over proscribed offenses when they are committed within their borders or territories, or on ships and aircraft registered in that country, which are normally considered as national territory.

The main purpose of multilateral agreements such as the Convention on Cybercrime is to encourage and develop means of improving and streamlining international cooperation. The Convention on Cybercrime addresses international cooperation concretely in terms of extradition, or moving **cybercriminals** from one country to another, and more generally in laying out the basic principles and procedures of cybercrime law. These principles and procedures are collectively called Mutual Legal Assistance (MLAT). The Convention adds the offenses listed above to those for which extradition can be requested. Chapter III, Section 1, article 24 provides the equivalent of a formal extradition treaty between two countries that do not already have such an agreement, but only for the offenses listed in the Convention.

The remainder of Chapter III lists and describes in detail the types of actions that make up MLAT and how countries participating in the Convention are obligated to incorporate them into existing laws, and how these actions can be used in the absence of existing agreements between countries. Specific provisions include requesting and providing expedited preservation or disclosure of stored computer or traffic data; assistance in seizing and securing data; accessing—without a specific request—open source stored data in another country; and assistance in real-time collection and interception of data. The final article of substance (article 35) requires participating countries to designate a point of contact available at all times to provide immediate investigative or procedural assistance.

An international agreement such as the Convention on Cybercrime enters into force when a certain number of countries have agreed to be legally bound by its provisions. By signing the Convention, a country expresses its interest in implementing the convention. Ratification of the Convention means that a country has agreed to be legally bound by the provisions of the Convention and to incorporate it into its legal system. As will be seen below, countries signing and/or ratifying the Convention may add statements, known as declarations or reservations. These statements are sometimes clarifications, such as designating a contact for mutual assistance, or they may state that the ratifying country may apply a differing interpretation of a particular offense. (For some examples, see *Convention on Cybercrime,* List of Declarations…, status as of October 16, 2007.)

When drafting the Convention, the CDPC also considered criminalizing racist and xenophobic Internet content, subjecting its production and dissemination to the same enforcement and mutual assistance standards as child pornography. Although it was not included in the Convention, a protocol (amendment) "concerning the criminalisation of acts of a racist and xenophobic nature committed through computer systems" to the Convention was drafted and opened for signature on January 28, 2003. The protocol entered into force on March 1, 2006, and criminalizes the following uses of computers and the Internet: Dissemination of racist and xenophobic content through computer systems; the use of computer systems for making racist and xenophobic motivated threats and insults; the use of computer systems for "grossly" denying, minimizing, or justifying of genocide or crimes against humanity; and aiding or abetting the above. (See Additional Protocol to the Convention on Cybercrime, concerning the criminalization of acts of a racist and xenophobic nature committed through computer systems, status as of October 16, 2007.)

The Convention on Cybercrime and the Additional Protocol may serve as a model for a broader use of international agreements against cybercrime. There may be questions concerning **privacy**, the security of commercial data, and the costs of complying with information requests from law enforcement, but the idea of expanding the reach of international law to combat cybercrime must be seriously examined and, if possible, implemented.

Suggested Readings: Council of Europe. (2003, January 28). *Additional Protocol to the Convention on cybercrime, concerning the criminalisation of acts of a racist and xenophobic nature committed through computer systems.* European Treaty Series No. 189. Strasbourg, France. Retrieved from http://conventions.coe.int/Treaty/en/Treaties/Html/189.htm; Council of Europe. (2007). Chart of signatures and ratifications: Status as of 16/10/07. *Additional Protocol to the Convention on cybercrime, concerning the criminalisation of acts of a racist and xenophobic nature committed through computer systems.* European Treaty Series No. 189. Strasbourg, France; Council of Europe. (2007). Chart of signatures and ratifications: Status as of 16/10/07. *Convention on Cybercrime.* European Treaty Series No. 185. Budapest, Hungary, November 23, 2001. Retrieved from http://conventions.coe.int/Treaty/Commun/ChercheSig.asp?NT=185&CM =8&DF=10/16/2007&CL=ENG; Council of Europe. (2001, November 23). *Convention on Cybercrime.* European Treaty Series No. 185. Budapest, Hungary. Retrieved from http://conventions.coe.int/Treaty/en/Treaties/Html/185.htm); Council of Europe. (2001, November 23). Explanatory report. *Convention on Cybercrime.* European Treaty Series No. 185. Budapest, Hungary. Available at http://conventions .coe.int/Treaty/EN/Reports/Html/185.htm; Council of Europe. (2001, November 23). List of declarations, reservations, and other communications: 16/10/07. *Convention on Cybercrime.* European Treaty Series No. 185. Budapest, Hungary. Available at http://conventions.coe.int/Treaty/Commun/ListeDeclarations.asp?NT=185&CM=8 &DF=10/16/2007&CL=ENG&VL=1; Council of Europe. Treaties glossary of terms. Available at http://conventions.coe.int/Treaty/EN/v3Glossary.asp; U.S. Department of Justice. Computer Crime & Intellectual Property Section Web page: http://www .usdoj.gov/criminal/cybercrime/COEFAQs.htm.

Thomas Schiller

CRITICAL INFORMATION INFRASTRUCTURE

In 1996 the U.S. President's Commission on Critical Infrastructure Protection (PCCIP) addressed national vulnerabilities associated with interdependent techno-logical systems. It described **critical infrastructure** as being combinations of physical and cyber assets vital to national economic well-being and security. Critical informa-tion infrastructures are essentially wired and wireless telecommunications subcompo-nents of critical infrastructure that have generally to do with **computerization** and the reality that since the early 1980s the Internet and other major computerized telecom-munications networks have transformed the ways in which people all over the world communicate and conduct their lives. When you download music or a movie, research something online, use a GPS device, or communicate using a computer or other type of IT device, you are normally using the World Wide Web. But this is pos-sible only because of electrically powered computerized telecommunications systems. Take away electric power or the Internet and many of the electronic devices you may be accustomed to using, such as a computer or cell phone, cannot function interac-tively with devices being used by other people.

Computerized nations now depend on electrical power and computerized telecom-munications systems for many things like communications, transportation, and manufacturing as well as for education, financial services, and national defense. The U.S. national information infrastructure, for example, also supports emergency police and fire services, the online capabilities of libraries and research institutions, health care administration, monitoring of the environment, and radio and television services. Consequently, when critical information infrastructure malfunctions or is disrupted for any reason, such as can occur as the result of a major **malware** or **denial of service attacks**, tasks or objectives may be impossible to accomplish.

U.S. critical information infrastructure relies on a limited number of large computer networks for the exchange of data, including the **Internet**, *Internet II,* and *MILNET.* Each of these networks is composed of wired and wireless telecommunica-tions systems and uses different protocols for *packet switching* to transmit or receive data between devices. Each network also employs different information security stan-dards and has different data/server exchange capacities. Although each system is rea-sonably safeguarded and has technological redundancies to guard against catastrophic failure, they are all subject to malfunctioning and disruption. Cyber attacks occur in many ways that can involve online combined with offline activities. On January 30, 2008, an undersea telecommunications cable in the Mediterranean Sea was severed, slowing Internet access dramatically for businesses and people in India, Pakistan, and Sri Lanka, along with several nations in the Middle East. In the following weeks, four more underwater cables were cut, two of which were severed in several places. Damage resulted in severe Internet bandwidth losses within these countries; however, Iran completely lost its Internet connectivity for approximately five days. Clearly the loss of cabling, even if only temporary, can have major disruptive effects on people and organizations that depend on critical information infrastructure.

In the wake of the PCCIP report efforts were made by various cabinet level offices to establish a National Infrastructure Protection Center (NIPC) that was to become established within the Federal Bureau of Investigation (FBI). However, following the terrorist events in September 2001, NIPC responsibilities eventually shifted primarily to the U.S. Department of Homeland Security. Currently the U.S. Department of Homeland Security manages the Protected Critical Infrastructure Information (PCII) Program, which is intended to enhance information sharing between private organizations and government agencies. Specific program objectives include: (1) analyzing and securing critical infrastructure and protected systems, (2) identifying vulnerabilities and developing risk assessment tools and methods, and (3) strengthening recovery preparedness measures that can be implemented following an attack on critical information infrastructure assets. Much of the work undertaken by PCII is not available to the public because it could potentially be used by criminals or terrorists to launch major attacks against physical or cyber infrastructure specifically targeted to disrupt key functions relied on by society (e.g., communications, financial services, transportation, manufacturing, national defense, and so forth). Consequently, PCII information is not applicable to state and local disclosure laws, and it cannot be used for purposes of civil litigation or for regulatory oversight.

Also funded by the U.S. Department of Homeland Security and the U.S. Commerce Commission National Institute for Standards and Technology (NIST) is the Institute for Information Infrastructure Protection (I3P). I3P is a consortium of national cyber security institutions, including academic research centers, government laboratories, and nonprofit organizations. It was founded in September 2001 following hijacked aircraft terrorism attacks against the World Trade Center in New York, the Pentagon in Washington, D.C., and United Flight 93 that crash-landed two miles north of Shanksville, Pennsylvania. I3P's mission is to help meet a need for improved research and development (R&D) to protect the United States' information infrastructure against catastrophic failures. Its main role is to coordinate a national cyber security R&D program and help build bridges between academia, industry, and government.

The U.S. government in partnerships with private sector firms continually monitors threats to the Internet and critical information infrastructure. The federal government in combination with the Internet Corporation for Assigned Names and Numbers periodically reviews international policies for assigning *Internet domain names* and the *Domain Name Server system*. For example, consideration has been given to not allowing definitions or protocols pertaining specifically to critical infrastructure or critical information infrastructure. However, establishing such policies are complicated by several factors, including that nations often define these concepts differently according to technological innovations combined with known or suspected Internet threats and online capabilities of **cybercriminals** versus those of information security professionals.

Suggested Readings: Coleman, K. (2008, April 25). *Cyber-attacks and cyber-disasters: Are you prepared?* Retrieved from TechNewsWorld Web site: http://www.technewsworld.com/story/62725.html?welcome=1209755132; Cordesman, A. H. (2001). *Cyberthreats, information warfare, and critical infrastructure protection: Defending the U.S. homeland (CSIS).* Westport, CT: Praeger; Hyslop, M. (2007). *Critical information* *infrastructures: Resilience and protection.* New York: Springer; Committee on Critical Information Infrastructure Protection and the Law, National Research Council. (2004). In S.D. Personick & C.A. Patterson (Eds), *Critical information infrastructure protection and the law: An overview of key issues.* Washington, DC: National Academy Press.

Samuel C. McQuade, III

CRYPTOGRAPHY AND ENCRYPTION

Since mankind developed a written language, there has always been a need to keep messages and information secret. Cryptography is the practice of protecting messages from unwanted viewing. Throughout history there have been many methods of concealing text messages or the meaning of them. Early Egyptians substituted unknown pictographs for known symbols to obscure the message. Later, Spartans used a device called a "skytale." It was a device that consisted of a leather belt wrapped around a wooden cylinder. Text was then written lengthwise along the cylinder. After the belt was removed, the message was obscured until the belt was wrapped around a cylinder with the same diameter. As electronic communication became the dominant method for passing messages, a new form of cryptography called encryption became prevalent.

Encryption is the process by which a message, also known as plaintext, is transformed into an unintelligible set of characters, also known as ciphertext. Encryption usually involves some mathematical function that can be applied to the text of the original message. By World War II, mechanical and electromechanical cipher machines were in wide use. The primary type of cryptography machine of the period though was a manually driven device. The Germans made heavy use of an electromechanical rotor machine known as Enigma. Enigma was deconstructed originally in 1932 by a Polish mathematician, Marian Rejewski, who was able to decipher a pattern and method of encryption allowing the evolution of Enigma to be tracked. At the outbreak of war in 1939, the Polish government shared their findings with British and French intelligence agencies. British cryptologists at Bletchley Park began working on a method to decode Enigma and eventually became successful in deciphering military messages that were transmitted by the Germans. Aside from the atomic bomb developed by the Americans, this was regarded as the most well-kept secret of World War II.

There are various methods of encrypting messages depending on the type of communication that is being protected. In general, the more valuable or sensitive the data, the greater or "stronger" the encryption needs to be. All encrypted data require a "key" to decipher. The key is like a key to a car or building, because it enables people to unlock the meaning of what otherwise is gibberish or a message that does not really mean what it purports to mean. During World War II, the British Secret Intelligence Service and French Resistance regularly broadcast clearly understandable radio messages in either English or French that actually meant something very different from the audible information transmitted. But only those people who knew the key to the coded message could discern what military actions were needed or were about to occur. In many forms of computer-generated encryption a key is created during the encrypting process. Computerized keys normally consist of a string of values that are mathematically incorporated into an algorithm to generate ciphertext (i.e., indiscernible code of some kind). This key is then required to decrypt the ciphertext into "plaintext"—a written language like English, French, German, Russian, and so forth.

For many years the U.S. federal government restricted the creation and use of so-called "strong encryption," which until approximately 2002 was legally classified as a type of munitions. Until that time the U.S. government limited the exportation of cryptographic techniques and technology to foreign nations, but due to the **Internet** was never completely successful in controlling importation of encryption software. The most famous example of conflict surrounding the creation and export/import controls of the federal government over encryption involved the *Pretty Good Privacy (PGP)* computer program developed by Philip Zimmermann in 1991. He became the formal target of a criminal investigation by the U.S. government for munitions export without a license. In the 1990s cryptosystems that used keys larger than 40 bits were considered munitions within the U.S. export regulations; PGP has never used keys smaller than 128 bits. After several years the investigation of Zimmermann was closed without any filing of criminal charges against him or anyone else.

PGP software provides reasonably strong encryption, cryptographic privacy, and authentication for users. PGP is often used for signing, encrypting, and decrypting emails to increase the security of digital communications. Shortly after this program was released, it was found outside the United States. One form of key-based data encryption is symmetric encryption or *private key encryption*. In private key encryption, a message is encrypted using a single key known to both senders and receivers of an encrypted message. A huge disadvantage of this is that all recipients of the message who want to decrypt it must share a single key. While this form of encryption can be strong, practical use of it requires a different approach that allows recipients to decipher a message but not constantly worry about the need for different keys utilized by individuals or groups of people who need to send or receive coded messages. After all, once a key is known by any unauthorized party, all future messages that rely on a specific key for deciphering message contents will be regarded as possibly being compromised. For this reason private key encryption is usually used to encrypt data that are not going to be transmitted.

To resolve the problem of key distribution, *public key encryption* was conceived of in the mid-1980s. In this method public key algorithms use a pair of keys to encrypt messages. One key is private, known only to its owner. The other key is published by a trusted source, which indexes and distributes public keys to users. To send an encrypted message using public key encryption, say to a person named John Doe, a person would encrypt the message with Doe's public key that he acquired from a trusted source. Once the message is received by John Doe, only he will be able to decrypt it by using his own private key. In this way not only can digital messages be sent securely, they can also be signed to authenticate who the sender of the message was. A *digital signature* consists of a message sender using his or her private key to encrypt the message. Public key encryption is usually employed in email and other forms of transmitted communications.

A third type of widely used encryption is called *one-way hash*. One-way hashes are algorithms that calculate a numerical sequence from a given set of data. There is no key involved in hashes. Hashes are used to confirm that a set of data has not changed between the time it was saved and reopened, or sent and received via the Internet. Any change to the data set will change the value of the hash value calculated from and for that unique data set. The most common hash function is the "MD5 sum." This hash is used to verify that files posted to the network remain unchanged after they have been downloaded.

Suggested Readings: Kruse, W.G., & Heiser, J.G. (2002). *Computer forensics: Incident response essentials.* Boston: Addison-Wesley; Schneier, B. (2000). *Secrets and lies: Digital security in a networked world.* New York: John Wiley & Sons, Inc.; Wang, W. (2001). *Steal this computer book 2.* San Francisco: No Starch Press; Menezes, A., van Oorschot, P., & Vanstone, S. (1996). *Handbook of applied cryptography.* Boca Raton, FL: CRC Press.

Gary Scarborough

CYBER BULLYING, THREATS, HARASSMENT, AND STALKING

Each year thousands of adolescents and adults are bullied, threatened, harassed, and/or stalked online. The sensation is attributable to more and more people using computers and other types of information technology (IT) devices such as PDAs and cellular phones to access and use the **Internet**; to voluntarily or unintentionally post personal information about themselves to social computing forums, Web sites, blogs, and chat rooms; and unscrupulous and/or illegal behaviors of cyber offenders who intentionally use the same technology and Internet resources to harm people in these ways. When youth are involved, this problem is often considered "cyber bullying," although adults such as teachers and school administrators have also reported being victims of cyber bullying by youth. In reality anyone can be bullied, threatened, or harassed online, and some people are also stalked online as well as in person or both.

In the United States the federal government and many states have passed laws banning these types of illicit behaviors, although legal definitions and common understanding of what actually constitutes violations of criminal laws and even social norms online vary considerably. For example, currently, there is no universally accepted definition of online harassment. The term can be difficult to define because it is open to interpretation. Online harassment may best be thought of as a set of abusive behaviors that involve using the Internet to send or post harmful messages to or about a person or persons. Online harassment can also be thought of as one aspect of cyber bullying involving the use of technologies such as email, instant messaging, pager and cell-phone text messaging, or Web sites to support deliberate, repeated, and hostile behavior by individuals or groups against another person or persons. In most cases, the illicit behaviors are intentional, repeated, and aggressive.

Some experts distinguish between different types of online harassment. For example, it may involve offensive or insulting messages repeatedly sent electronically to a victim. Alternatively, it can involve sending or posting denigrating or inaccurate information about a victim to others with the intent to disrupt friendships or damage their reputation. It may also involve impersonation such as when an offender poses to be a victim online and posts information incurring disrespect or revenge from their friends or associates. Lastly, "outing" involves electronically spreading very personal information about a victim to others, while "exclusion" involves deliberately ignoring or refusing to communicate online with a victim (Willard, 2006). This last category can be a form of abuse when a person is repeatedly excluded and made to feel as though he is not fitting in with a popular group. And oftentimes what begins online transcends into classrooms, employment settings, or social functions and leads to property damage and/or physical harm to victims. Conversely, harassment that is initiated offline can also transcend into the cyber world.

Although online harassment may be considered by some people to be of minor consequence, it should be taken seriously even if intimidation, threats, or stalking are not involved. Simply ignoring cyber bullying or online harassment in any form disrespects the victim(s) involved and can lead to complications. In general, when adults are involved, official reporting to authorities or other legal actions may be appropriate. When juveniles are involved, parental and professional judgment is required, because while confronting bullies can sometimes be useful in preventing further harm, this is usually predicated on a systems approach that may require intervention by parents, school officials, police, or other appropriate stakeholders such as Internet service providers. Unfortunately, many juveniles fail to report online harassment to adults, often because they fear that their technology use will be restricted or because they believe adults will overreact.

When harassment occurs on a more serious level, particularly when it involves threatening behavior, it can become online stalking involving the repeated sending of highly threatening, intimidating, or offensive messages. Although the difference between harassment and stalking may not always be clear, the level of fear and distress experienced by victims varies considerably depending on their age, gender, personal circumstances, and the nature of the online messages causing harm. For example, online stalking can involve direct threats to hurt someone or encouragement to commit suicide. Online stalking is often associated with an intimate offline or online sexual relationship, and may involve a predator seducing younger victims online in order to carry out sex-related crimes in person.

As previously noted, online harassment and stalking that involves threatening behavior are considered criminal offenses in most jurisdictions. Federal law 18 U.S.C. Chapter 110A addresses stalking and domestic violence, and federal law 18 U.S.C. 875 makes it illegal to transmit any communication in interstate or foreign commerce containing threats to injure another. In addition, federal law 47 U.S.C. 223 prohibits online harassment that involves a direct communication between a stalker and a victim. However, depending on future case law rulings, this may not cover situations in which messages are posted to Web sites, blogs, or chat rooms.

Harm from any level of cyber bullying or online harassment can be significant, particularly as information can be posted or forwarded to a large number of people in a short amount of time. In an especially tragic case, 13-year-old Megan Meier committed suicide in 2006, at least partially because of online harassment. Meier was befriended by a boy named Josh Evans on the popular social networking site MySpace. After a period of time, Evans turned on Meier and began insulting her online. Other teens on MySpace joined in with insults of their own, and a short time later Megan hanged herself with a belt in her bedroom. In a surprising twist it was later discovered that Josh Evans did not actually exist. His profile was allegedly created by a teenage neighbor of Meier and/or the neighbor's mother to find out what Meier was saying about them.

The Internet itself does not cause online harassment or stalking. However, it may make it easier to do. For example, communicating online can be affected by the lack of inhibition, or what Willard (2006) describes as "disinhibition," facilitated online because technology may create an illusion of invisibility. Perhaps feelings of being anonymous or unknown when using computers online can lead to a belief that identities cannot be discovered. And to the extent that computer users may not know for certain with whom they are communicating online, people who harass or stalk online may feel less empathy for the victim and not understand that they are hurting him.

Suggested Readings: Belsey, B. (2004). Web site available at www.cyberbullying.ca; Conn, K. (2004). *Bullying and harassment: A legal guide for educators.* Alexandria, VA: ACSD; Espelage, D., Bosworth, K., & Simon, T. (2000). Examining the social context of bullying behaviors in early adolescence. *Journal of Counseling and Development, 78*(3), 323–333; Glover, S., & Huffstutter, P.J. (2008, January 9). L.A. grand jury issues subpoenas in web suicide case. *The Los Angeles Times.* See http://www.latimes.com/news/printedition/california/la-me-myspace9jan09,0,993796.story?coll=la-headlines-pe-california; Li, Q. (2006). Cyber-bullying in schools: A research of gender differences. *School Psychology International, 27*(2), 157–170; Patchin, J., & Hinduja, S. (2006). Bullies move beyond the schoolyard: A preliminary look at cyberbullying. *Youth Violence and Juvenile Justice, 4*(2), 148–169; Willard, N. (2006). *Cyberbullying and cyberthreats: Responding to the challenge of online social cruelty, threats, and distress.* Eugene, OR: Center for Safe and Responsible Internet Use; Ybarra, M., & Mitchell, K. (2004). Online aggressors and targets: a comparison of associated youth characteristics. *Journal of Child Psychology and Psychiatry, 45*(7), 1308–1316; Ybarra, M., Mitchell, K., Wolak, J., & Finkelhor, D. (2006). Examining characteristics and associated distress related to internet harassment: Findings from the second youth Internet survey. *Pediatrics, 118*(4), 1169–1177.

James P. Colt

CYBERCRIME

Proliferation of computing and networked devices throughout the world, including computers, PDAs, and cellular phones is among the most profound technological changes in human history. Increasing capacity of information technologies (IT) to transform ways we work and function as a society is unprecedented. However, any technological advancement provides potential avenues for abuse and harm. Behaving in ways that are uncommon or unacceptable within a particular cultural setting may be considered deviant. When deviant acts rise to a level of causing harm, they are considered to be against the law (i.e., criminalized). "Cybercrime" is a broad term covering all the ways in which computers and other types of portable electronic devices such as cell phones and PDAs capable of connecting to the **Internet** are used to break laws and cause harm. A slightly more technical definition would be "use of computers or other electronic devices via information systems such as organizational networks or the Internet to facilitate illegal behaviors" (McQuade, 2006, p. 16).

Cybercrime has come about and evolved with the Internet and other advances in IT that have afforded people new ways to cause harm in society. It can be traced to the onsets of important, but technologically different, crime concepts, including (McQuade, 2006, pp. 10–16): (a) *computer-related crime*—"illegal behaviors in which one or more computers were helpful but not necessary to commit a criminal act"; (b) **computer crime**—"behaviors for which one or more computers were required to commit a consummate criminal act (i.e., the overall criminal activity could not have been accomplished without using a computer)"; (c) *computer abuse*—"use of computers in ways that cause harm to individuals, groups, or organizations, that may also violate established policies or procedures, but do not rise to the level of violating existing crime laws"; and (d) *IT-enabled deviancy*—"behaviors involving use of computerized or telecommunications devices in ways that violate social norms." Cybercrime can also be traced to technological developments in *organized crime* and *white collar crime*.

The term "cybercrime" is sometimes used synonymously with *technological crime, high technology crime, high tech crime, economic crime, Internet crime, digital crime,* or *electronic crime,* among other labels used by people to describe crime committed with computers or other IT devices. This can be confusing for students and other people trying to learn about cybercrime and ways to prevent it. This is especially true given that so many types of cybercrime and abuse of information systems, including (McQuade, 2006, p. 132): (1) *negligent use of information systems* while violating security policies or engaging in unsound information security practices and thereby exposing systems and data to cyber attacks; (2) *conventional crimes involving use of computers or other types of electronic IT devices* for communications and/or record keeping in support of their illegal activities; (3) *online fraud* such as **phishing**, spoofing, spimming, or otherwise deceiving people online for financial gain as in cases of credit card fraud and **identity theft**; (4) **hacking**, *computer trespassing, and password cracking* in order to break into computer account passwords and/or unlawfully enter information systems to commit online and/or offline crimes; (5) *malicious writing and distribution of computer code* that involves creating, copying, and/or releasing **malware** (i.e., disruptive or destructive viruses, Trojans, worms, or adware/spyware programs); (6) *digital piracy* of music, movie, and/or software especially via peer-to-peer networks; (7) cyber harassments, threat, intentional embarrassment, or coercion, including **cyber bullying**; (8) online stalking and other cyber-sex offending, including sending unwanted pictures or text of a sexual nature, promoting sex tourism, or using the Internet to facilitate *human trafficking* for sexual or other purposes; (9) *academic cheating* and *scientific misconduct* by students, teachers, or professors to plagiarize (i.e., take written credit for the writing or ideas of others), cheat on assignments or exams, or fake research methods or findings; (10) *organized crime* that involves use of the Internet by ethnic-based gangs to facilitate combinations of illegal and legal activities such as smuggling and selling of people, weapons, and drugs; (11) *government and free-lance spying* including **corporate espionage** that involves illicit use of spyware and key logger software to discover data that can be stolen or used to commit additional crimes; and (12) **cyberterrorism** by people trying to advance "social, religious or political goals by instilling widespread fear or by damaging or disrupting **critical information infrastructure**."

Suggested Readings: Albanese, J. (1984). Corporate criminology: Explaining deviance of business and political organizations. *Journal of Criminal Justice, 12,* 11–19.

Samuel C. McQuade, III

CYBERCRIME ATTACKS

Major cybercrime attacks are those that involve numerous offenders, massive numbers of victims, or very large amounts and values of digital assets, or that otherwise jeopardize national **critical information infrastructure**. Examples include widespread **malware** programs released onto the **Internet**, network takedowns as the result of distributed **denial of service attacks**, and theft of personal information and credit card information of thousands of consumers in the course of computer hacking to carry out **identify theft** on a grand scale. The potential for major cybercrime attacks was first glorified in the 1983 movie titled *WarGames*. In this fictional story a computer savvy teenager named David Lightman (played by Matthew Broderick) and his friend Jennifer Mack (actress Ally Sheedy) hacked into the U.S. military's missile defense system and accidentally nearly started World War III. A typical large-scale cyber attack can include one or more of the following types of activities: volume identity theft, organizational extortion, personal blackmail, major **privacy** violations, denial of services, email spamming, and multiple network disruptions.

The first major cybercrime attack was accomplished by Robert T. Morris Jr. on November 2, 1988, when he released the first Internet worm program and unintentionally caused the slowdown of thousands of computers. Since that time, coordinated cybercrime attacks against businesses, government entities, and the Internet itself have become a mainstream event in daily computing. Large commercial cyber defense companies such as Symantec, Trend Micro, McAfee, and others today maintain cyber threat centers staffed with teams of computer security experts that monitor for major cybercrime attacks on an hourly basis. Such organizational efforts complement information security services provided by **Computer Emergency Response Teams (CERTS)**.

Today hundreds of millions of computers are simultaneously connected to the Internet. This along with weak (although improving) information security practices by organizations and computer users throughout the world make major cybercrime attacks involving sophisticated malware relatively common. Consider, for instance, that in 2007 alone, the People's Republic of China stands accused by the U.S. Department of Defense of engaging in numerous computer network intrusions of both commercial and government institutions. Other countries such as Great Britain, Germany, and France have made the same allegations. On June 20, 2007, the Department of Defense was forced to take over 1,500 of its workstations offline due to a coordinated cybercrime attack that appeared to have culminated from numerous smaller attacks over a two-year period. There are countless other such examples and their numbers are growing every day.

Information security experts now recognize ways in which malicious software, such as the Nugache and Storm Trojans that began appearing in 2006–2007, can be used to distribute massive amounts of targeted **spam** for profit and even be rented for illicit purposes. What once was science fiction and the consequences of lone computer hackers may now be accomplished by determined criminal groups, terrorist organizations, or hostile governments able to retain technical services of highly skilled computer users. The threat of major cybercrime attacks has become so serious that information security and digital assets protection are among top priorities of large financial organizations and other types of organizations running complex information technology networks. In addition, several governments throughout the world, including agencies of the U.S. military, are now taking aggressive steps to protect critical information infrastructure and prepare for the possibility of defending against major cybercrime attacks within the context of **network central warfare**.

Suggested Readings: Brewin, B. (2008, March 3). *Pentagon: Cyberattacks appear to come from China.* Government Executive.Com; Fox Newswire. (2007, June 22). Pentagon cyber attack forces 1500 PCs offline; Frantz, D. (2007, January). Spy vs. spy: Corporate espionage's ugly new twist. *Conde Nast Portfolio,* 98-103; Krebs, B. (2006, December 22). Cyber crime hits the big time. *Washington Post* Web site: http://www .washingtonpost.com/wp-dyn/content/article/2006/12/22/AR2006122200367.html; MacNeal, K., & Etges, R. (2007, September). Cyber warfare and defense strategies. *ISSA Journal,* 6–10.

Michael J. Kozak

CYBERCRIMINALS

An important aspect of understanding **cybercrime** is that forms of it come about and evolve with technologies that make possible certain types of abusive, harmful, or unethical behaviors. Quite frequently such behaviors are not initially prohibited by state and federal crime laws, but eventually become illegal. Examples in the evolution of computing and telecommunications technologies include wire fraud, computer hacking, **identify theft**, **corporate espionage**, and spamming among other types of crime now committed via the **Internet** with computers and other types of electronic devices. Since cybercrimes emerge and evolve with technologies over time, and since most people in modern societies are users of information technologies (IT) and the Internet, we are forced to wonder about cybercriminals: Who are they really?

Cybercriminals can be classified into the following 12 distinctive forms of information systems abuse and crime:

1. *Negligent users* who violate security policies or do not practice sound information security practices and thereby expose their data or that residing on a network to harm;
2. *Traditional criminals* of conventional crimes who use computers or other types of electronic devices for communications and/or record keeping in support of their illegal activities;
3. *Fraudsters and thieves* including those who phish, spoof, spim, or otherwise deceive people for financial gain;
4. *Hackers, computer trespassers, and password crackers* (also known as white or gray hat hackers) who, in the tradition of the original hacker ethic, use computers to illegally explore, learn about, and take control of systems in order to pull mischievous pranks, and who may also find, exploit, or expose security vulnerabilities;
5. *Malicious code writers and distributors* who create, copy, or release disruptive or destructive viruses, Trojans, worms, or adware/spyware programs;
6. *Music, movie, and software pirates* who use IT to violate copyright laws by illegally copying, distributing, downloading, selling, or possessing software applications, data files, or code;
7. *Harassers and extortionists* who use technologies to threaten, annoy, or coerce;
8. *Stalkers, pedophiles, and other cyber sex offenders* who use online and/or in-person methods when needed to acquire illegal sexual pleasure from or power over people;
9. *Academic cheats* who use a variety of tools and techniques to plagiarize or cheat on assignments or exams, or who fake research methods or findings for profit or fame;
10. *Organized criminals* including ethnic-based gangs who use computers or electronic devices in the course of their legal and illegal business enterprises;
11. *Corporate, government, and free-lance spies* who use simple-to-complex tools and methods of espionage including spyware and key logger applications to snoop for personal or professional purposes; and
12. *Cyber terrorists* who seek to advance their social, religious, or political goals by instilling widespread fear or by damaging either critical infrastructure or **critical information infrastructure**.

Society continues to redefine what is illegal through creation of new statutory laws and through case law decision making, which occurs when judges take into consideration how activities in a case being tried relate to existing laws and legal precedents governing how laws have previously been interpreted. It is not uncommon for attorneys to make arguments about why certain behaviors should or should not be considered illegal under existing laws. Recent examples include cases like: (1) *United States v. Robert Morris Jr.,* which first applied the federal *Computer Fraud and Abuse Act of 1986* to the creation and release of a worm software program onto the Internet; (2) *United States v. Michael Williams,* in which the U.S. Supreme Court in 2007 struck down the so-called "pandering" aspects of the *PROTECT Act of 2003,* making it still legal in the United States to distribute fake images of **child pornography** as a form of freedom of expression under the First Amendment of the U.S. Constitution (see encyclopedia entry on **Laws, Children Online**); and (3) *United States v. Lori Drew,* who allegedly helped create a MySpace account in the name of Josh Evans, a 16-year-old boy who did not exist, in order to chat with teenager Megan Meier who subsequently committed suicide. The case is the first time the *Computer Fraud and Abuse Act of 1986* was used to prosecute a case involving social networking.

Researchers who specialize in advancing knowledge and understanding abut crime and crime **victimization**, many of whom are considered "criminologists," periodically create and study categories of offenders. Their efforts complement changes and new understanding brought about through evolutions in law and technology. Notable researchers who have studied types of high tech crime offenders include: (a) Donn Parker who first studied computer abusers in the 1970s; (b) M. J. Lee who in 1991 differentiated between hackers, crackers, phreakers, and pirates; and (c) David Wall who in 2001 described offenders who engage in cyber trespassing, deception and theft, pornography and obscenity, or violence via the Internet. In 2004 Sam McQuade and Tom Castellano used a statistical method to distinguish between five types of system abusers among a random survey sample of 873 college students they called hackers, harassers, pirates, academic cheats, and data snoops (i.e., people "who guess passwords or illegally gain access to information systems solely to look at data and files" [McQuade, 2006, p. 127]). Some criminologists have argued that it is pointless to try to categorize cybercriminals because cyber offending is so widespread that profiling them is not practical or useful. Indeed, it is now well understood among researchers that cyber offending within society is not limited to insider employees of an organization, nor to young males who are savvy and curious about IT as was once true of computer hackers, nor limited by gender, age, socioeconomic status, or political points of view.

So who are cybercriminals really? The answer to this question is complicated not only by reality that it can be anyone who abuses information systems like the Internet along with computers or other IT devices such as cell phones, but also by evolving societal norms and cultural standards for ethical behavior. What one person regards as immoral, socially inappropriate, or illegal may not be regarded in the same way by someone else. This is why there are legal disputes regarding controversial uses of computers, and the creation, distribution, or possession of certain kinds of data such as pornographic materials, **malware**, and **intellectual property** like music, movies, and software that are frequently shared via peer-to-peer networks. The answer to the question also depends on who is considered a "criminal." In the United States someone merely suspected or accused of committing a crime is not officially a criminal until he has been tried and convicted of one or more activities prohibited by law.

However, the label of being a criminal may stick with someone long after he has served time in jail or prison, paid any fine imposed by a court of law, provided restitution to crime victims, and served out time in community service or on probation or parole. Therefore who "cybercriminals" are really depends on a combination of legal, technological, and social factors along with how the term is defined. Conceivably anyone can become an abuser or misuse IT.

Suggested Readings: McQuade, S.C. (2006). Computer abusers and cybercriminals. In *Understanding and managing cybercrime* (Chap. 4). Boston: Allyn and Bacon; National White Collar Crime Center & West Virginia University. (1996). *Proceedings of the Academic Workshop,* Bureau of Justice Assistance Grant No. 96-WC-CX-001; Wall, D. (2001). *Crime and the Internet.* London: Routledge.

Samuel C. McQuade, III

CYBERCRIMINALS, FAMOUS

As any new technology gains mainstream acceptance, it is invariably used to commit crimes. Often, law enforcement lags behind technology, requiring new laws to be written to regulate these new crimes. While still in its infancy, the **Internet** has already spawned a number of well-known criminals. The most famous of these **cybercriminals** include Robert Morris Jr., Kevin Poulsen, and Kevin Mitnick. What is distinctive among these former criminals is that they have all gone on to become respected professionals who provide information security advice to organizations.

One of the earliest examples of crime involving the Internet revealed just how vulnerable the Internet could be to malicious acts. In 1988 Robert Morris Jr. was a doctoral (Ph.D.) candidate at Cornell University. During his time there as a graduate student, Morris released the first Internet worm. The self-replicating program swept through thousands of computers, infecting approximately 10 percent of the estimated 60,000 computers then on the Internet. Although Morris may not have intended to cause any damage, the consequences were grave. His worm coding effectively disabled the Internet until system administrators could remove the program from infected systems and patch the vulnerabilities it had exploited. Morris was later convicted under the *Computer Abuse and Fraud Act* and sentenced to three years probation, 400 hours of community service, and a $10,000 fine. Robert Morris Jr. went on to become a Professor of Computer Science at Massachusetts Institute of Technology (MIT).

Kevin Poulsen, a skilled computer and telephone network hacker, began his criminal career early in life. Caught breaking into private and government information systems, Poulsen was recruited as a security expert by a government contractor. During the day he would work his legitimate job, but at night Poulsen would break into phone company offices to steal equipment and manuals. Tipped off that the authorities were looking for him, Poulsen fled arrest. During his time on the run, in 1990, Poulsen and two accomplices manipulated a telephone network to win a "call in" radio contest hosted by KIIS-FM in Los Angeles, California. Poulsen won a Porsche automobile, money, and a trip to Hawaii. Eventually, however, Poulsen was captured and convicted for this crime. He was sentenced to four years in prison, three years probation during which he could not use a computer, and fined $58,000. After prison, Poulsen worked for information technology (IT) publications, eventually becoming senior editor at *Wired Magazine.*

The most notorious hacker ever sought by law enforcement is Kevin Mitnick. During his criminal career, Mitnick hacked into computer systems owned by Pacific Bell, Digital Equipment Co., Santa Cruz Operation, the University of Southern California, Sprint, and the California Department of Motor Vehicles, among other organizations. In 1989, while already on probation for another violation, Mitnick fled from authorities. For two years Mitnick remained a fugitive, using his hacking skills to stay one step ahead of authorities. Mitnick was finally apprehended in Raleigh, North Carolina, in 1995. By that time he had become known as "America's Most Wanted Computer Outlaw" (Mohay et al., 2003, p. 121). Kevin Mitnick would spend the next four years in prison awaiting trial. After four years, he accepted a plea agreement of five years imprisonment with credit for the four years he had already served. Following his release, Mitnick was restricted from using computers for an additional three years. Since his release from prison in September, 2000, Mitnick has authored two books on computer security and started a consulting firm. One book, *The Art of Deception,* focuses on **social engineering**, which Mitnick used for so many years as a hacker.

Since the active cyber offending years of Morris, Poulsen, and Mitnik, numerous other individuals have committed and been prosecuted for high-profile **cybercrimes**. Several of these people have illegally created and distributed **malware** onto the Internet, causing millions of dollars in damage to information systems, computers, and other types of IT devices. These offenders and other perpetrators of major cybercrimes now number several dozen—too many to describe in this short article. However, it is interesting to note that relatively early cybercrime offenders may have been identified as such because when they committed their offenses the activities were considered by law enforcement authorities, the media, and the public to be fairly unusual or sensational by standards used to gauge the seriousness of crimes at that point in history. Arguably, contemporary cybercrimes, and especially those affecting thousands of organizations and potentially millions of users in short periods of time, are far more serious. Given this reality, society can be assured of always experiencing relatively notorious cybercriminals.

Suggested Readings: Borzillo, C. (1993, May 8). From contest stars to prison stripes; Three frequent L.A. winners indicated for fraud. *Billboard,* 64; Rogers, R., & Beale, J. (2004). *Stealing the network: How to own a continent.* Rockland, MA: Syngress Publishing; Filiol, E. (2005). *Computer viruses: From theory to applications.* Paris: Springer; Mohay, G., Anderson, A., Collie, B., De Vel, O., & McKemmish, R. (2003). *Computer and intrusion forensics.* Norwood, MA: Artech House Inc.; Weber, M.J. (2004). *Invasion of privacy: Big brother and the company hackers.* Boston: Premier Press.

Gary Scarborough

CYBER/INTERNET CULTURE

"Cyber culture" emerged as a natural outgrowth of **computerization**, which began with commercialization of the **Internet** in 1988 and initiation of the World Wide Web in the early and mid-1990s. The boundaries of cyber culture are not well defined and the term is used interchangeably with "Internet culture." In general, these concepts have to do with the customary ways in which people behave and interact with each other in virtual communities. However, the cyber/Internet culture includes a wide range of computer and information technology (IT)–related issues such as the following: (1) Internet-enabled democratization, which implies that everyone in the connected world can more easily participate in and contribute to political processes; (2) cybernetics, which is the perceived or predicted "cyborgization" of the human body and human society (as inspired by Manfred Clynes and Nathan Kline who used it in an article about the advantages of self-regulating human-machine systems in outer space); and (3) a variety or combination of subcultures like the **hacker subculture**, *open source movement, digital pirating scene,* **digital youth culture**, and now mainly defunct *cyberpunk* enclave. Like all human cultures in the history of humankind, cyber culture continues to evolve pushed forward by technological forces that enable people to develop new ways of interacting. The emergence and increasing use of **Leetspeak** is a prime example of clever and interesting ways in which humans learn to communicate using the Internet. This too is an aspect of cyber culture.

The *Oxford English Dictionary* is known to have listed the earliest reference of "cyber culture" in 1963 when A.M. Hilton predicted that technology would support social conditions to bring about automation and computerization of society. The *American Heritage Dictionary* expanded upon the definition by Oxford, defining cyber culture as a culture stemming from the use of computer networks, as for communications, entertainment work, and business enterprises. It is important to note that "cyber culture" is a reference to online interactions only. Rather, cyber culture transcends the online and offline attitudes people have about the Internet as well as their computing activities in realms of physical places and **cyberspace**. Cyber culture is endemic to on-line computers, and increasingly the use of portable IT devices such as cellular phones that allow for uploading and downloading of digital files to and from the Web, taking and sending of digital photos, instant messaging, and so forth. In other words, cyber culture occurs because of and is mediated by computers and other types of IT devices.

Cyber culture is associated with social and cultural movements for the advancing of computer and information sciences. It was influenced in the beginning by early Internet users, frequently the inventors and creators of the computer networking technologies. Cyber culture is manifested in many ways including blogs, *social networks,* online games (especially MMORPGs), chat and messaging programs, bulletin board systems, peer-to-peer networks and virtual worlds in which people may create and assume the identity of avatars (i.e., fictional digital characters). Youth who now use the Internet to engage in such activities exemplify and, whether they know it or not, are helping to define, perpetuate growth, and shape cyber cultural norms. Indeed, the so-called digital youth culture is a subset of cyber culture in that it relies heavily on social networks and other forms of communications by and among youth via IT devices. The "old guard" who invented the Internet and related technologies, along with people who may still ascribe to the original "Hacker Ethic," are steadily being outnumbered by newer generations of Internet users who may not know about or even care about such things. For people who have never known a world without computers, the Internet, and the World Wide Web, such things may be of historical interest, but they are not amazed—they simply adapt new IT as it becomes increasingly available, interoperable, and affordable. For many people, their lives now revolve around using the Internet. To the extent this is true for individuals and groups of people, they are likely influenced by cyber culture.

Suggested Readings: Clynes, M., & Kline, N. S. (1960, September). Cyborgs and space. *Astronautics, 26–27* and 74–75; Kitchin, R. (1998). Theoretical perspective: Approaching cyberspace. In *Cyberspace: The world in the wires.* New York: Wiley; Lessig, L. (2006). *Code 2.0: Code and other laws of cyberspace.* New York: Basic Books;

Macek, J. (2005). *Defining cyber culture (v. 2)*. Retrieved from http://macek .czechian.net/defining_cyberculture.htm; Rheingold, H. (1993). Daily life in cyberspace. In *The virtual community: Homesteading on the electronic frontier*. New York: HarperCollins.

Neel Sampat

CYBER SAFETY AND ETHICS INITIATIVES

With the emergence of the World Wide Web in the mid-1990s millions of people began using the **Internet**. This was about the same time in history that worldwide **computerization** really took off with the following: (1) personal computers becoming more powerful, (2) other types of information technology (IT) devices becoming more interoperable, (3) software applications being created to support people in virtually any type of computer-related task, (4) memory media including CDs and eventually flash drives becoming very affordable with very large data storage capacities, (5) high speed broadband connectivity being extended into smaller and rural communities, and (6) Web pages and Web content expanding exponentially. Among new Internet users were youth who were increasingly learning to use computers at school and in their homes. As opportunities to access the Internet along with the variety and affordability of portable IT devices increased, the modern **digital youth culture** took shape. Seemingly overnight very young children were accessing the Net and visiting Web sites specially designed with content to promote their learning about a wide range of topics. Online video gaming also became popular as a complement to offline gaming already long provided by video gaming machines, computers, and console game devices.

Amidst this flurry of technological innovation and accompanying societal transformations, **cybercrime** also took on newer and more complex forms. As youth were learning to use the Internet and IT devices, sometimes in risky, harmful, or criminal ways, concern developed about how young people could become safer and more responsible when they went online. As a result, beginning in the late 1990s, numerous cyber safety and ethics education initiatives were developed by government, private, and nonprofit organizations. Many but not all of these organizations offered Internet safety and cyber ethics content for children and/or awareness and instructional information that educators and parents can use to influence, supervise, or positively role model appropriate online activities and behaviors for youth (see encyclopedia entry on **Prevention Education**). Several agencies of the U.S. government have helped to fund and support public awareness about the need for Internet safety, information security, and cyber ethics. In 2005, the Office of Juvenile Justice and Delinquency Prevention (OJJDP) initiated an Internet safety campaign aimed at parents and children. The campaign featured "Safe at Home" advertisements, conveying the need for parents to pay attention to Internet activities of their children. Ads were included in 2005 Little League Regional Championships and World Series program materials. Also in 2005, the U.S. Department of Homeland Security in partnership with numerous private sector and educational organizations launched an Internet safety, information security, and cyber ethics campaign tied to National Cyber Security Month (October). The **National Center for Missing and Exploited Children** (NCMEC) and Wired Kids, Inc. have also provided online resources to aid students, educators, parents, and law enforcement officers about ways to prevent cybercrimes against youthful victims.

Beginning in 2006, The Cyber Safety and Ethics Initiative was initiated in the Greater Rochester and upstate New York region. This was significantly influenced by research conducted by the Rochester Institute of Technology (RIT) (see encyclopedia entry on **Research on Cybercrime**). The Initiative is a nonprofit partnership between the Rochester Institute of Technology (RIT), numerous area school districts, the Diocese of Rochester Department of Catholic Schools, other higher education institutions and private schools, and regional offices of three national organizations, including: (1) The National Center for Missing and Exploited Children (NCMEC), (2) the **Information Systems Security Association (ISSA)**, and (3) InfraGard, a program of the Federal Bureau of Investigation dedicated to information sharing between public and private sectors about critical infrastructure protection. Also among the founding organizations is Time Warner, Inc., which is one of several private sector corporations and individuals who have contributed financially to the Initiative. The mission of the Initiative is to advance K–12 education along with parent and workforce training in topics inclusive of Internet safety, information security, and cyber ethics. The Cyber Safety and Ethics Initiative is distinguished from similar efforts because of its focus on cybercrime prevention for youth and adults and its reliance on scientific research to drive development of education and training programs for national capacity building to better protect **critical information infrastructure**.

Suggested Readings: U.S. Department of Justice. (2008). Office of Justice Programs. Office of Juvenile Justice and Delinquency Prevention. Available at http://ojjdp .ncjrs.org/; The Cyber Safety and Ethics Initiative. (2008). CSEI Homepage: http:// www.bcybersafe.org/; The National Center for Missing and Exploited Children. (2008). NMEC Homepage: http://www.ncmec.org/.

Samuel C. McQuade, III

CYBERSPACE

The word "cyberspace" was first seen in print in 1982, but author William Gibson popularized the word and concept of cyberspace with his 1984 science fiction classic, *Neuromancer.* Gibson's description of cyberspace consisted of a fully immersive virtual reality through which users of computer networks from all over the world could communicate and interact with each other. That is essentially what has come about through invention of the **Internet** and World Wide Web, although these technological platforms differ and are also different from cyberspace, being more two dimensional and containing less of the popular science fictional aspects of virtual reality. Soon after the Internet became commercialized in 1988, online games and subscription-supported social networks, such as America Online and Compuserve, became forums for people to communicate and collaborate together online, or what is commonly referred to as "in cyberspace." As the Internet of the early 1990s effectively became what is now known as the World Wide Web, or simply "the Web" or "the Net," new capabilities and complexities came into being. These electronic realities combine technology with cognitive perceptions of places where people can interact. Just as phone conversations prior to the Internet took place "somewhere" or "nowhere" between people located in different locations, cyber activities that include text and/or audible and visual conversations or interactions between people, along with a myriad of other real-time or delayed interactions, occur through use of telephone phones, cell phones,

PDAs, and computers. Of course, cyberspace, just like the place where phone calls happen, is not really a place at all. Rather, it is an amorphous realm in and through which people interact using computers and other IT devices that are connected to the Net.

Many applications that are available for free, for sale online, or in physical stores now offer people the ability to socially and professionally network with people whom they have never actually seen much less met in person. Millions of people form purely online relationships as well as online personal or business relationships that begin online and become physically interactive over time. The opposite is also true: some people who initially establish in-person relationships in the physical realm in which people actually live may eventually part company but retain association online through the wonders of cyberspace. In the process of living offline and online, many people even create and/or assume the identities of avatars, which enable them to live fantasy lives in electronic gaming and other cyberspace environments.

For most people living in computerized societies, cyberspace has become an important if not vital aspect of their culture and everyday lives. Prominent aspects of cyberspace continue to be seen and felt in science fiction, such as Gibson's novel mentioned above, as well as in *social networking forums,* military life, and the growing *online gaming* community. Cyberspace is also becoming financially and personally significant via the online gaming and other entertainment industries inclusive of gambling, music, and movies—all multibillion-dollar industries that allow people to participate in increasingly interactive ways resembling real-life experiences.

Today approximately 13 percent of the global population (i.e., approximately 838 million people) have access to the Internet, and cyberspace continues to expand in terms of its users, content, capabilities, and technological complexities. Some people falsely believe cyberspace, or at least access to the Web, can or should be controlled. For example, some nations legally ban certain types of political or sexual-related content being created, posted, or accessed from within its borders. Some parents throughout the computerized world also attempt to restrict certain types of Internet content from being accessed by their children by installing Web site filtering software. However, given expanding wireless Internet connections and an increasing number of affordable mobile devices, controlling access to the Net or any Web content is difficult, especially if users are determined. New technology is also emerging that is focused on bringing more of current science fiction (holograph and three-dimensional virtual reality) to future science fact. It will not be long until people are living even larger portions of their lives online in the richly diverse worlds of cyberspace.

Suggested Readings: *CIA World Fact Book* via http://www.internetretailer.com/internet/marketing-conference/29522-worldwide-internet-access-inches-up.html; Gibson, W. (1984). *Neuromancer.* New York: Berkley Publishing Group/Ace; Graham, A.C. (1981). *Chuang-tzu: The Inner Chapters.* London: Unwin Paperbacks; Internet Retailer. (2003, June 2). Worldwide Internet access inches up. *Internet Retailer.*

Andrew Perry

CYBERSQUATTING

Cybersquatting is the act of registering an *Internet domain name* that incorporates a trademark, such as the name of a well-established company, with the intent to extort money from the trademark holder. The term "squatting" is derived from early settlers who established residence on unclaimed land or other unoccupied property. Cybersquatting extends this concept to **cyberspace** and Internet domain names that are controlled by an international organization called the Internet Corporation for Assigned Names and Numbers (ICANN). This organization works through domain registrars, usually companies such as Network Solutions, to delegate ownership and control of specific domain names to individuals and firms. For example, the domain name "microsoft.com" is owned by the Microsoft Corporation. Similarly, the world famous chain of restaurants known simply as "McDonalds" actually belongs to McDonalds Corporation, which has a registered Internet domain name of mcdonalds.com.

Any individual is allowed to purchase the registration rights of a particular domain name through any one of several existing ICANN registrars. Normally, this is an uneventful process, but can be complicated when companies already share all or part of the same name or slogan, or when *copyright* and *trademark* issues are involved. In the United States, cybersquatting is illegal under the *Anticybersquatting Consumer Protection Act (ACPA)*. This federal law was passed in 1999 to assist copyright and trademark holders in disputes regarding the registration of domain names but also applies "to people who: (1) have a bad faith intent to profit from a domain name; and (2) register, use or traffic in a domain name; (3) that is identical, confusingly similar, or dilutive of certain trademarks" (chillingeffects.org). In cases where two trademark holders stake a claim to the same domain, the legal issues can be very complex. Courts have generally interpreted the ACPA as applying to cases where one party has clearly intended to infringe on the trademark of another entity and based rulings on whether or not a malicious intent is proven (*Virtual Works, Inc. v. Volkswagen of America, Inc.,* U.S. Ct. of Appeals, 4th Circuit, 2001).

One notable cybersquatting case was *People for the Ethical Treatment of Animals v. Michael T. Doughney*. In this case, Mr. Doughney registered the domain name "peta.org" and created a Web site named "People Eating Tasty Animals." People for the Ethical Treatment of Animals (PETA) sued Mr. Doughney for trademark infringement. Lawyers representing the firm argued that PETA's trademark was being infringed upon. PETA won the case and was able to gain control of the peta.org domain name for its own use.

Resolving disputes can be difficult because the **Internet** is an international network, and although ICANN is an international corporation many countries do not have laws forbidding cybersquatting. In 2000, the family of the musician Jimi Hendrix pursued legal action against Denny Hammerton, the registrant of the domain name "jimihendrix.com." The case went to arbitration at the World Intellectual Property Organization (WIPO), a part of the United Nations that deals with **intellectual property** disputes at the international level. In this case, the family of Jimi Hendrix won control over the domain name that Mr. Hammerton had registered (*Experience Hendrix, L.L.C. v. Denny Hammerton and The Jimi Hendrix Fan Club,* 2000). By 2007 WIPO had received "a record 2,156 complaints alleging the abusive registration of trademarks on the Internet...representing an 18% increase over 2006 in the number of generic and country code Top Level Domain disputes" processed its Arbitration and Mediation Center (WIPO, 2008).

Suggested Readings: American Bar Association. (2008). *U.S. Patent and Trademark Office: Basic facts about registering a trademark.* Available at http://www.abanet.org/ intelprop/comm106/106trade.html#etr; Electronic Freedom Foundation et al. (2008). *Chilling Effects Clearinghouse: Frequently Asked Questions (and Answers) about*

ACPA. Available at http://www.chillingeffects.org/domain/faq.cgi#QID682; *Experience Hendrix, L.L.C. v. Denny Hammerton and The Jimi Hendrix Fan Club.* (2000). Available at http://www.wipo.int/amc/en/domains/decisions/html/2000/ d2000-0364.html; *PETA v. Doughney.* (2000). Available at http://cyber.law .harvard.edu/stjohns/PETA_v_Doughney.html; United Nationals World Intellectual Property Organization (WIPO). (2008). Available at http://www.wipo.int/portal/ index.html.en; *Virtual Works, Inc. v. Volkswagen of America, Inc.* (2001). U.S. Ct. of Appeals, 4th Circuit. Available at http://www.4lawschool.com/property/virtual.shtml.

Shaun M. Jamison

CYBERTERRORISM

Even before the infamous terrorist attacks involving hijacked airlines that occurred on September 11, 2001, against the U.S. Pentagon and other American targets, the notion of cyber terrorist attacks against the **critical information infrastructure** of the United States was being seriously considered by military planners. In 1997 Mark Pollitt combined a definition of **cyberspace** with the U.S. Department of State's definition of "terrorism" to offer the following definition of cyberterrorism: "Premeditated, politically motivated attack against information, computer systems, computer programs, and data which result in violence against noncombatant targets by sub national groups or clandestine agents." A similar definition was offered in a 2003 Congressional report that referred to cyberterrorism as "the politically motivated use of computers as weapons or as targets, by sub-national groups or clandestine agents intent on violence, to influence an audience or cause a government to change its policies." Thus the goal of so-called "cyberterrorism" is to attack information systems to instill fear in those who have the capability to make political changes deemed necessary by the attackers.

In today's world in which entire regions and even countries are dependent on *information systems* for their basic needs, disruption for even a short time of critical services such as banking and commerce, communications, manufacturing, national security, and transportation could be devastating. Fortunately, there has never been an officially confirmed act of cyberterrorism anywhere in the world, although the theoretical possibility of such an event is real. Imagine what would happen if computer systems controlling telecommunications switches and electrical power grids could be hacked into and shut down: what do you think would happen? This is what many information security experts are desperately worried about and working to prevent against.

In October 2002, a **denial of service (DOS) attack** targeted the 13 primary domain name servers (DNS) that control **Internet** functioning. Called the "largest and most complex" attack in Internet history, it caused seven of the servers to completely shut down and two others to suffer "severe degradation." This left only four Internet DNS to support ongoing Net data exchanges. Without these servers in operation, it becomes impossible to match a domain name with its corresponding Internet Protocol (IP) address; unless a user knows the actual IP address, he would be unable to access a Web page. This would likely cripple the Internet for the vast majority of users worldwide. A similar attack was launched against the 13 servers in February 2007; however, new safeguards halted it before it took any of the servers down. To date, the perpetrators of the two attacks and their reasons for launching them remain unknown.

Also, in April 2007, numerous news organizations affiliated with Associated Press reported that computer servers located in Russia had been used to launch cyber attacks against the critical information infrastructure of Estonia. The attacks shut down many government, media, and financial organization Web sites and led to diplomatic talks that explored possibilities for creating a North Atlantic Treaty Organization (NATO) supported research center capable of identifying the sources of cyber attacks. And in January 2008 an analyst with the U.S. Central Intelligence Agency (CIA) publicly revealed that *hackers* had successfully disrupted electrical power grids in several U.S. cities, but officially the United States has never experienced overt acts of cyberterrorism. Previous major cyber attacks affecting critical information infrastructure provides clues about what the effects could be. In February 2000, a hacker launched Denial of Service (DOS) attacks against Yahoo, CNN.com, Amazon, Buy.com, and eBay, which severely limited their access to the Web sites of these companies. The cyber attacks were followed by further attacks on ZDNet.com, a news portal, and the online trading sites E*Trade and Datek Online. An investigation into the attacks led to the arrest of a 15-year-old Canadian teenager with the online nickname "Mafiaboy." One year later it was discovered that the initial vulnerabilities that allowed Mafiaboy to take these Web sites down still existed and that the companies hosting the Web sites remained potential targets for future attacks.

Suggested Readings: CNN.com. (2000, February 9). *FBI vows action as Internet attacks continue: Strikes hit E*Trade, ZDNet, eBay, Amazon, others.* CNN.com Web site: http://archives.cnn.com/2000/TECH/computing/02/09/cyber.attacks.03/index.html; ComputerWire. (2002, October 23). *Feds investigating "largest ever" Internet attack. The Register* Web site: http://www.theregister.co.uk/2002/10/23/feds_investigating _largest_ever_internet; Gaudin, S. (2007, March 13). *ICANN: Anycast and communication foiled February's root server attack. InformationWeek* Web site: http:// www.informationweek.com/news/showArticle.jhtml?articleID=198000575; Harrison, A. (2000, February 9). *Cyberassaults hit Buy.com, eBay, CNN and Amazon.* ComputerWorld Web site: http://www.computerworld.com/news/2000/story/ 0,11280,43010,00.html; Marsan, C.D. (2002, October 28). *DDoS attack highlights 'Net problems: Episode called crude, ineffective. . . but concerns mount about future problems.* NetworkWorld Web site: http://www.networkworld.com/news/2002/1028 DDoS.html; McMillan, R. (2008, January 19). *CIA says hackers have cut power grid. PC World* Web site: http://www.pcworld.com/article/id,141564-c,hackers/ article.html; Messmer, E., & Pappalardo, D. (2001, February 8). *One year after DoS attacks, vulnerabilities remain.* CNN.com Web site: http://archives.cnn.com/2001/ TECH/internet/02/08/DDoS.anniversary.idg/; Pollitt, M.M. (1997). *Cyberterrorism: Fact or fancy?* Dorothy Denning's Web site: http://www.cs.georgetown.edu/~denning/ infosec/pollitt.html; Wilson, C. (2003, October 17). *Computer attack and cyber terrorism: Vulnerabilities and policy issues for Congress.* Congressional Research Service: Report for Congress (RL32114).

Sara E. Berg

CYBER WHIMSY

In the context of cybercrime definition one might not think of the theft of computer resources and/or personal productivity of employees as illegal, yet the use of corporate or governmental systems in furtherance of personal gain adds to their financial burden in the same manner that would apply to taking home a ream of paper each week. "Cyber whimsy" represents an attempt to illuminate economically harmful processes that may be taken for granted. There is always a risk in coining a new term or expanding the use of a word to include new meanings, but the construct of "cyber whimsy" is not based in its creation; rather it is reflected in its utility to identify rising **Internet** communication phenomena. The World Wide Web has created a medium in which all participants are on an equal footing at initial access. Given that equality and ease of access, we can reach out to people across the globe on nothing more than impulse and with the use of appropriate search tools. As a result, we often have the experience of receiving email and forwarded email from well-meaning individuals or those who are only superficially related to us by an unseen thread. This type of email is not to be confused with **spam**, which by definition is problematic and may be economically harmful.

An Abuse of Time and System Resources

These types of email usually contain a sentimental story or a description of activities that is meant to pique our interests and perhaps encourage us at a deep personal level. The fundamental way in which this email (cyber whimsy) is differentiated from spam is the intentionality of its sender. While the recipient may fail to meaningfully distinguish its hoped-for utility, the sender was motivated by well-meaning concern and used the Internet as a vehicle to reach out to others. In many ways this bears a resemblance to common use of the telephone, but there is one important difference in this process. With the telephone we do not normally call other people we do not know for emotional reasons. Rather we might seek to meet someone personally or drop them a note via snail mail. This approach would seem to be less abrasive than calling someone directly and risking the possibility of offending them. Consider that with today's technology it is possible to send an ecard to someone within the corporate environment. Your intention is to let your co-worker know that you wish him a speedy recovery. The actual impact on the sponsor's IT network is likely to go unrecognized, given that a simple gesture like this may require the commitment of significant computing resources, and given the advanced integration of audiovisual technology with email capabilities. Yet we would be reluctant to use an employer's postage capabilities for private matters given the obvious nature of the implied costs.

Given the anonymity provided by Internet contact, it is not a surprise that a cyber whimsy approach to contact with unknown others has matured and blossomed. Individuals using the Web have developed a protective mask that sets a psychological distance between themselves and others. We can approach this media and bridge that distance without incurring great risk of personal harm or identification. Therefore we find ourselves much more likely to reach out into the void of **cyberspace** and make the inquiry, "Is anybody out there...can anybody hear me?" We often do so by offering a piece of Web wisdom as a token peace offering, hoping that others will not be offended by our actions. Perhaps there is an existential meaning to this drive toward connectedness. For our purposes we will restrict our exploration to the question of what causes an individual to take the initial step to reach out to others known or unknown in such a personal manner.

There are two elements to which we may attribute this behavior. Both of these elements are intrapersonal in nature, but are used in an interpersonal manner. Perhaps this internal struggle is just the re-creation of man trying to find life's meaning by interacting with others.

At the most basic level this type of behavior can best be identified as *psychogenic,* that is, a behavior that emerges from the individual's mind and constitutes an attempt to forge a link with someone else. What makes this behavior unique is that it represents the individual's attempt to meet some perceived internal need. Once identified, the individual will reduce this drive by taking action that is consistent with his perceived need and therefore reduces any anxiety that he may have experienced. In this context the individual is operating out of a set of beliefs that speak of his individual needs and therefore is unique to his character.

The second element to which we may attribute this type of behavior is identified as *sociogenic,* given that the individual is operating out of a sense of what is in the best interest of society and its members. Therefore the sender of cyber whimsy is likely to be motivated by concerns for each individual who receives his forwarded email. He is likely to want it to be a force for good in another person's life, but not at the risk of seeming to be overly intrusive. Therefore the Web offers the perfect mechanism to reach out to others while at the same time reducing risk of being viewed as socially inappropriate. These internal motivations are what significantly differentiate cyber whimsy from spam. They are all centered upon the intentionality of the sending part.

Consider the following application of this theory. An individual receives a forwarded message that appears to distort the meaning of an upcoming religious holiday. The person sending the forward is a family member who is well aware of the receiver's beliefs, but is so removed from this type of thinking that it is likely he did not consider its effect upon the receiver. The recipient is one of about 25 persons to whom this forward has been sent. The names and email addresses of all of the email's receivers are listed on the email. At a deep psychological level our recipient feels that this type of email is insulting to his underlying belief system and feels that he is obligated to respond to the author-forwarder. This type of internal dialogue is *psychogenic* by definition since the dialogue is emerging out of the individual's own thoughts and emotions. The result is a drive to rectify what is construed as a situation that reflects poor tastes at a minimum. The response to the original sender would be the manner in which the receiver processes his psychological discomfort.

In addition to feeling an obligation to remediate the situation with the author-forwarder, this individual also feels an obligation to reach out to all of the other recipients and in a mild manner find a way to offset his association by receipt of this communication, which may been perceived as derogatory. In other words, he does not want to have his name associated with a document that may imply his endorsement of these views. Merely staying quiet in this situation is not an option. The individual feels not only a need to address the author-forwarder but also a responsibility to correct the misperception of endorsement by silence that could emerge if no further actions were taken. So the individual drafts a mild response and sends the email to all of those listed on the original email, thereby in effect notifying the others that this is not personally acceptable. The motivation for this type of response is clearly sociogenic given that the intention is to reach out to others and attempt to correct any misperception of endorsement that the original material was acceptable. The focus of this action is rooted in the attempt to disassociate from the original sender of the materials and it is founded in concern for the thoughts of others.

All of the efforts imply the utilization of personal or corporate resources that contributes to the bottom line of operating expenses. In addition, the receiver is likely to feel stressed and frustrated when receiving such email from family, friends, customers, or colleagues. While we can readily understand the underlying intentions of the sender, we are likely to be faced with the choice of enduring these experiences or addressing the sender in a personal setting and explaining why we do not wish to receive these forwards. We undertake this action at the risk of offending the other, who sees his behavior as well meaning and contributing to or perhaps enhancing some aspect of our life with his message. Enter these grounds at great personal risk of incurring someone's wrath. Of course, the other option is to explore one's software tools and screening resources and attempt to route this type of communication to an unmonitored disposal site. Either way we handle these attempts, it is likely to produce a sense of frustration and anxiety in addition to the largely unrecognized economic costs associated with these well-intentioned gestures.

To say that we are cognitively complex individuals is an understatement. To say that our internal and external communications are multidimensional distorts the challenges inherent in effectively reaching out to others. We are already tasked with a problem that often exceeds our best abilities to be clear and concise. The result is a breakdown in dialogue and often a misinterpretation of the meaning of others. Adaptation of the term "cyber whimsy" is encouraged to help classify the actions of ourselves and others, providing a neutral environment to understand the true nature of communication. It is not meant to further burden the system of thought that underlies our attempts to connect with each other. But in truth may also help us to identify the way in which we operate as individuals and the manner in which we derive our emotional responses. This approach to self-knowledge is consistent with cognitive theory, which describes the internal mechanism of actions through which we understand ourselves and our fellows.

Suggested Readings: Cobb, S. (2002). *Privacy for business: Web sites and email.* Saint Augustine, FL: Dreva Hill LLC; Mayo-Smith, D. (2005). *Conquer Your Email Overload.* New York: Penguin Global; Song, M., Halsey, V., Burress, T., & Blanchard, K. (2007). *The hamster revolution: How to manage your email before it manages you* (Foreword). San Francisco, CA: Berrett-Koehler Publishers.

Kevin J. McCarthy

D

DEDICATED CYBERCRIME INVESTIGATION AND PROSECUTION UNITS

As the reality of computer crimes became widely recognized beginning in the late 1980s, the federal government and states within the United States began passing *computer crime laws* that prohibited certain types of online activities such as hacking. The first computer crime law in America was the federal *Computer Crime Fraud and Abuse Act of 1986.* Along with passage of federal and state computer crime laws was a realization that law enforcement and prosecution agencies needed to establish designated high tech crime units consisting of professionals trained in certain technical aspects of computer software engineering and information systems network administration. In 1989 the National Institute of Justice, serving as the research and development (R&D) arm of the U.S. Department of Justice, commissioned a research report that focused on issues pertaining to "dedicated computer crime units" (McEwen, Fester, & Nugent, 1989). Today, many organizational units specializing in the investigation and prosecution of **cybercrimes** exist within federal, state, and large metropolitan law enforcement agencies.

Establishing a special cybercrime unit is challenging for several reasons, including the "relatively few of America's 18,000+ police agencies (over eighty percent of which consist of twenty-five or fewer officers) possess the financial, personnel and techno-logical resources" that are necessary (McQuade, 2006, p. 337). In addition to financial constraints often faced by government law enforcement and prosecution agencies, public officials have historically been reluctant to have agency personnel focus on crimes that occur online rather than "on the street." Traditional property crimes and crimes of violence, especially those brought to public attention by the media and as the result of systematic crime reporting methods such as the National Crime Report (NCR) system administered by the Federal Bureau of Investigation (FBI) and the Bureau of Justice Statistics (BJS), usually take on priority status within the minds of public officials responsible for preventing and controlling crime. There are good reasons for this: who would argue that protecting people is not more important than protecting data stored on information systems? The problem, of course, is that many forms of traditional crime including those that result in property damage and violence are increasingly being committed with the aid of computers, portable electronic devices, and the **Internet**.

Cybercrime and the need for specialized cybercrime investigation and prosecution units is becoming more important as reflected in the number of state, federal, and international laws prohibiting many types of harmful Internet-based activities. The importance of cybercrime, and therefore the need for more dedicated cybercrime investigation and prosecution units, can also be seen in increasing governmental regulations requiring compliance with information security standards set out for certain employment sectors. For example, in the United States, the financial services sector, health care administration organizations, and agencies of the federal government are required to meet information systems security requirements pertaining to the protection of data, installation and maintenance of firewalls, **malware** detection and prevention, **privacy** policies, and training of personnel, among other issues. Television, radio, and Internet-based media organizations are also raising awareness about various kinds of cybercrimes, such as **identity theft**, **phishing** scams, and threats posed by *bot networks*. Each of these forms of cybercrime and many others underscore the need for specialized cybercrime enforcement and prosecution units.

Where specialized units do exist they typically consist of a few to large numbers of personnel who have received training in matters relating to cybercrime, information systems security, and/or so-called computer crime laws. Some federal, state police, and large metropolitan law enforcement agencies are supported with **computer forensics** laboratories capable of recovering and analyzing digital data from a wide variety of computerized devices. Field officers engaged in routine responses to crime are also increasingly aware of cybercrime activities and what to look for with respect to tangible physical evidence at crime scenes (e.g., photographs depicting youth without their clothes on, hard copies of financial records in many different names, and various storage media such as CDs, DVDs, and flash drives). "Computer-related documentation such as software user manuals may also provide clues needed to help profile cybercriminals and solve cases" (McQuade, 2006, p. 368). As awareness about cybercrime and professional training for law enforcement officers and prosecutors increases, cybercrime task forces involving multiple levels of government agencies are beginning to form. Frequently these task forces work closely with particular prosecutors assigned to cybercrime cases with local district attorney, state-level Offices of Attorneys General, or U.S. Attorney offices. Since the mid-1990s the U.S. Department of Justice has maintained a special prosecution unit called the **Computer Crime and Intellectual Property Section (CCIPS)**. The unit now employs numerous attorneys and investigators who participate in the prosecution of federal and international cybercrime cases of importance.

Suggested Readings: Computer and Intellectual Property Section–Criminal Division. (2002). *Searching and seizing computers and obtaining electronic evidence in criminal investigations.* Washington, DC: Department of Justice; Casey, E. (2001). *Handbook of computer crime investigation: Forensic tools & technology.* Burlington, MA: Academic Press; McEwen, J. T., Fester, D., and Nugent, H. (1989). *Dedicated computer crime units.* Washington, DC: National Institute of Justice; Prosise, C. (2001) *Incident response: Investigating computer crime.* New York: McGraw-Hill Companies.

Samuel C. McQuade, III

DENIAL OF SERVICE ATTACKS

Denial of service (DOS) attacks are **cybercrimes** in which the primary goal is to deny users of computers or other types of electronic devices access to an information system or its resources. DOS attacks often involve flooding a computer network with massive amounts of data in a short period of time so that servers cannot keep up with the amount of data being transmitted. The effect is prevention, disruption, and/or minimization of legitimate network traffic. DOS attacks may also inhibit users from accessing network-related applications or services needed. While some attacks simply bombard networks with large amounts of traffic from thousands of compromised or virus-infected systems on the **Internet**, other attacks may trigger a "SYN Flood" in which a high number of connection attempts consume entire network connection capabilities. Thus, most DOS attacks are aimed at compromising network efficiency or connectivity.

Other forms of DOS attacks include attacking a CPU, its memory, process table, or disk capacities. For example, DOS can involve the sending of thousands of emails with attachments to information systems, thereby saturating connection capabilities or available disk space. Other attacks may try to force a targeted system into generating large amounts of errors, thereby consuming additional processing capabilities as the result of keeping error logs. An attacker may also attempt to lock out system or user accounts by constantly trying various password combinations. If the system is configured to lock out an account after several failed attempts to access it, legitimate users will subsequently be denied using the network for a period of time until the account access controls are restored. Additionally some systems may be vulnerable to errors or will stop responding if a certain network packet is received.

Distributed denial of service (DDOS) attacks are even more threatening to information systems. In these types of attacks infected systems called *botnets* that have previously attacked and effectively been taken over are capable of being remotely controlled. This situation allows DOS attacks such as those previously described to be launched through many networks and geographic areas simultaneously. DDOS attacks may employ thousands of botnets with a combined power to bring down all but the largest computer networks. Imagine if your country were attacked from every country in the world and from all of the nation's borders at the same time. This is what DDOS attacks are like. Such massive amounts of traffic derived from many sources of attack make DDOS among the most threatening forms of cybercrime.

DOS and DDOS attacks are a form of malicious programming created by rogue computer programmers, by criminal elements that may be highly organized, or by military organizations of countries that employ offensive **network centric warfare** tactics. In late April 2007, the small European country of Estonia became victim to a large-scale DDOS attack. The attack crippled Web sites of the government, banks, and schools. The sources of these attacks were difficult to identify due to their distributed nature; however, many sources believe that elements within Russia were responsible for the attack.

Networks of compromised systems (i.e., botnets) can also be rented on the Internet and used to launch large-scale DDOS attacks against particular organizations as a means to intimidate, to extort from, or to incapacitate a competitor. These attacks may cause significant financial loss and compromised reputations of organizations victimized due to their perceived inability to prevent DOS or DDOS attacks in the first place. In truth, however, DOS and DDOS are very difficult to completely prevent. Information security best practices, such as removing or disabling unneeded services, updating operating system and application security patches, enabling system quotas (e.g., disk, process, and CPU) on information systems, monitoring usage statistics and log files for unusual activity, deploying firewalls and routers with built-in DOS protections, and deploying fault tolerant designs, often are the best methods of prevention. Many network service providers now provide a DOS monitoring and prevention service. With many countries, such as the United Kingdom, now outlawing DOS/DDOS attacks, organizations victimized in these manners are encouraged to report these cybercrimes to law enforcement agencies.

Suggested Readings: CERT Coordination Center. (1997, October 2). *Denial of service attacks.* Pittsburgh, PA: Carnegie Mellon University. Retrieved October 7, 2007, from http://www.cert.org/tech_tips/denial_of_service.html; Kirk, Jeremy. (2007, May 17). Estonia Recovers from massive denial-of-service attack. *Network World.* Retrieved October 7, 2007, from http://www.networkworld.com/news/2007/051707-estonia-recovers-from-massive-denial-of-service.html; Article by Outlaw.com. (2006, November 12). *UK bans denial of service attacks.* Published by *The Register* on Web site http://www.theregister.co.uk/2006/11/12/uk_bans_denial_of_service_attacks/.

Paul Lepkowski

DIGITAL YOUTH CULTURE AND SOCIAL NETWORKING

Digital youth culture refers to young people who regularly use computing technology to interact with each other online. This concept was first described in terms of "digital natives" and "digital immigrants" by Marc Prensky in 2001 to distinguish between young people who grew up using computer technology versus older people who did not. Unlike previous generations of Americans who grew up watching television shows such as *Captain Kangaroo* (1955–1984), *Mr. Rogers' Neighborhood* (1968–2001), and *Sesame Street* (1969–present), today's youth are growing up using computers, mobile phones, and MP3 players along with televisions increasingly connected to the **Internet** to access all sorts of Web content. Much of this content is specifically intended for children and adolescents, but other content is designed for adults only. Youth who have grown up accessing the Net for their information may not always know what is appropriate, factual, or legal for them to view or use.

The emergence of digital mediums has resulted in the creation of Web forums intended for teenagers that adults would not normally be involved in. These take the form of instant messaging clients, chat rooms, community message boards or forums, and blog style social networking sites. Often participating youth are able to exclude or include people of their choosing in these forums. **Privacy** controls are an essential part of identifying who can and cannot visit a personal Web page or contact youth via a messenger service. Privacy controls often allow users to minimize or layer information they reveal about themselves online (i.e., their "appearance" or "digital footprint"). However, these controls are only as effective as the settings that the user knows about and chooses to enable, along with the type and amount of information that is shared with others online. Given potential flaws in computer coding, discovery of exploits have also been found in the privacy settings of software, such as those used by social networking firms like MySpace and Facebook. When this happens, personal information posted by millions of youth participants can become known despite their efforts to keep certain information from becoming publicly known.

For millions of young people, cyber spaces are becoming more important than physical places that society has traditionally established to accommodate youth entertainment and recreational needs. Youth with access to the Internet may prefer to meet privately or publicly but online rather than in person. For many years classic teen "hangouts" such as rollerblade or ice skating rinks, movie theaters, and burger joints have become less popular in favor of online gaming and other computing activities. Increasing fuel prices are also impacting the ability of teenagers to "go out" and hang out in public settings, as are bans on unsupervised youth under the age of 18 from occupying certain places like shopping malls. Hanging out after school in public, in lieu of participating in extracurricular activities (e.g., sports teams, theater, or student clubs,), is increasingly being displaced in some communities by youth visiting each others' homes with or without parents or guardians present. However, mobile IT devices such as cell phones that enable email, instant messaging, and up/downloading of digital files are also changing youth social dynamics and culture.

In utilizing IT devices, youth can express themselves in creative ways with varying amounts of anonymity and privacy just depending on content they post and technological ways in which they do this. Since 2005 online social networking forums have facilitated worldwide communications among youth as never before. Having a personal Web page on MySpace, Facebook, Friendster, or a similar social networking forum is part of what many young people consider "cool" if not necessary in order to be accepted by their online and/or in-person friends. For many participants of such forums, having a Web page dedicated to and revealing of their personal life enables outreaching to an "invisible audience" of peers who may wish to interact. In short, social networking provides a technological means through which to meet new people and make friends online.

As a result, digital youth culture can be considered an important aspect of growing up in computerized societies as well as an extension of complex real-world (i.e., non-cyber) social interactions. In other words, for millions of youth there is a distinction between being online or offline because they live simultaneously within the realms of cyberspaces and physical places. This has complicated traditional social dynamics and challenged notions of what may be considered normal versus deviant behaviors, moral or ethical versus immoral or unethical behaviors, and legal versus criminal behaviors. In other words, youth who have grown up with computers, other IT devices, and the Internet may be developing different standards for behaving online as opposed to when they are not using the Internet, because they are interacting more and more via **cyberspace** where social sanctions are not clearly defined or as consistently sanctioned as they are in the real world. Being out of line or "misbehaving" in an online social networking or gaming environment will not likely bring about the same kind or level of complaint or punishment that doing this at home, in school, or in a workplace setting would.

Abusive and criminal behaviors in social networks have resulted in negative public reactions in the media and concern among parents, educators, and legislators.

The October 17, 2006, suicide of Megan Meier allegedly stemming from a cruel hoax on MySpace was particularly sad and brought cyber bullying under closer scrutiny by social networking firms and society in general. Concerns about youth creating fake profiles in order to carry out harmful activities online or, conversely, to protect their real identities are also increasing along with social networking popularity.

Technology controls for signifying real profiles are typically quite limited when it comes to verifying age or an email address for admission by a social networking Web site host, both of which are easily defeated by the creation of alternate email accounts and/or simply lying about one's age.

In conclusion, the digital world has impacted how youth behave and interact. It has created new methods for forming social groups and establishing interconnections between their members. Social interactions, beginning with physical contact, are no longer a necessary defining point of friendship. In the digital world, people need merely search for a common interest on a social network and request to be added as a friend. The dynamic of social interactions between and among youth continues to change as online computing becomes more complex and arguably less manageable. Today's youth are using more types of IT devices to access the Net for more purposes at younger and younger ages. For better and worse they are engulfing themselves in online activities that may involve little or no adult supervision. As the Internet and IT continues to evolve and be used in new ways, social interactions and digital youth culture will too.

Suggested Readings: Boyd, D. (2007). *Why youth (heart) social network sites: The role of networked publics in teenage social life.* MacArthur Foundation Series on Digital Learning—Youth, Identity, and Digital Media Volume, edited by David Buckingham. Cambridge, MA: MIT Press; Hine, T. (2000). *The rise and fall of the American teenager.* Reprint edition. New York: Harper Perennial; Kirkpatrick, M. (2008, March 24). *Facebook security lapse leaves private photos exposed, even Paris and Zuck's.* Retrieved from ReadWriteWeb Web site: http://www.readwriteweb.com/archives/facebook_security_lapse_private_photos.php; Michels, S. (2007, December 3). *No charges in MySpace suicide.* Retrieved from ABC News Web site: http://abcnews.go.com/TheLaw/story?id=3946124; Prensky, M. (2001). Digital natives, digital immigrants. *On the Horizon, 9*(5). MCB University Press; Stern, A. (2007, November 8). *MySpace hacked using simple HTML exploit—Alicia Keys and others targeted.* Retrieved from Center Networks Web site: http://www.centernetworks.com/myspace-hacked.

Neel Sampat and Samuel C. McQuade, III

E

ELECTION AND VOTING FRAUD

As with numerous other aspects of modern life, digital technology is increasingly being used to facilitate federal, state, and local elections in the United States. *Electronic voting* (or *e-voting*) has become a blanket term for this phenomenon, and it encompasses several different methods of casting and/or counting votes via electronic means. While the intent of e-voting is to make the election process more efficient and secure, some experts maintain that at least some of the resulting technologies and products have significant security flaws, making voting machines vulnerable to vote tampering or accidental miscounts.

E-voting entered into wide public consciousness in the wake of the extremely close and controversial results of the 2000 presidential election between Al Gore and George Bush—an election that highlighted problems associated with mechanical voting machines. These devices are designed to literally punch holes in paper ballots in order to record and enable machine reading of votes. However, unlike programming punch card devices that were new and integral to second generation computer data input during the late 1960s and early 1970s, aging voting machines that use this same basic technology often leave "hanging chads" on ballots that cause counting inaccuracy, disqualification of legally cast votes, and claims of election fraud, especially in instances of other types of irregularities.

To prevent such problems, election officials in the State of Nevada installed and successfully tested touch screen voting machines between 2001 and 2005 for county and state races, thus paving the way for other states and political jurisdictions to adopt similar computerized voting devices. However, concerns about assuring the confidentiality, integrity, and authenticity of votes cast electronically remain in many polling jurisdictions. Some officials, as well as political science and computer experts, worry that hackers or others may be able to break into insufficiently protected information systems to manipulate or destroy electronically cast votes, even to the point of changing who wins or loses a given race.

In 2007, California Secretary of State Debra Bowen commissioned computer security experts to evaluate several types of e-voting machines. The experts found that three different models of the systems (sold by Diebold Election Systems, Hart Inter-Civic, and Sequoia Voting Systems) fell short of federal security requirements. As a result, Bowen had these systems decertified for use in California, along with a fourth system, which was submitted by company officials too late to be tested. Bowen later recertified the three systems provided their use is limited to one per polling place and a number of other stringent conditions are met.

It should be noted that there are various types of e-voting systems, ranging from paper-based systems, such as optical scan systems, which use computers to tabulate votes, to completely digital, touch screen–style digital recording electronic (DRE) machines. DRE machines have become a particular target for some computer experts for a number of reasons, among these are the fact that they often do not include hard copy records of each vote, which can make verification of vote counts less reliable. In 2006, the Diebold AccuVote-TSx, a popular DRE system, was examined by computer scientists from Princeton University in 2006. The scientists found that malicious software capable of undetectably altering votes, as well as associated records logs and counters, could be easily installed in under a minute. The scientists also found that it was also possible to install malicious software that would automatically spread to other voting machines during standard election activities, altering the other machines in the same way it was. A number of other researchers have performed similar analyses on Diebold and similar DRE systems with similar results.

Punch card–style voting machines are still used in a majority of polling jurisdictions within the United States, and it will be expensive and time consuming to completely change the voting technology throughout the nation. Some people debate whether the technological changeover is worth the cost and effort. Since vote counting in America and other nations throughout the world is still successfully conducted with paper ballots, and since paper receipts must still be capable of being produced in instances requiring computerized vote recounts, some contend that paper-punch voting machines should be properly maintained, repaired when necessary, or remade using the same basic technology rather than relying on newer electronic e-voting methods. Others, however, feel that the problematic aspects of e-voting are solvable, and that paper-punch systems are too outdated, unreliable, and obsolete. The debate is likely to continue for quite some time.

Suggested Readings: Bellis, Mary. (1997). *The history of voting machines.* Retrieved from *About.com.* http://inventors.about.com/library/weekly/aa111300b.htm; Feldman, A., J. Halderman, and E. Felten. (2006). *Security analysis of the Diebold AccuVote-TS voting machine.* Princeton, NJ: Center for Information Technology Policy and Department of Computer Science, Princeton University. Retrieved from http://itpolicy .princeton.edu/voting/ts-paper.pdf; McQuade, S. (2006). *Understanding and managing cybercrime,* 150–152. Boston, MA: Pearson/Allyn and Bacon; Simons, B. (2007, August 13). California: The top to bottom review. *The Voter.* Retrieved March 10, 2008, from http://www.votetrustusa.org/index.php?option=com_content&task =view&id=2554&Itemid=113.

Eric Walter

ELECTRONIC FRONTIER FOUNDATION

The Electronic Frontier Foundation (EFF) is a nonprofit legal and advocacy organization dedicated to protecting **privacy**, free speech, and consumer rights. Much of the organization's work has focused on cyber legal issues. During the 1990s, for example, EFF helped U.S. courts to establish through the *Bernstein v. U.S. Department of Justice* case that computer code is a form of protected speech as indicated by the First Amendment to the U.S. Constitution. In 2005, the EFF sued record label Sony BMG for including antipiracy spyware on CDs, which secretly installed itself on user's computers. The case was eventually settled and Sony BMG agreed to recall the tainted CDs. And in the so-called "Apple v. (John and Jane) Does" case decision of 2006, the EFF defended the rights of online journalists to protect the identities of their confidential sources of information. The EFF has also lobbied and/or filed suit against the *Uniting and Strengthening America by Providing Appropriate Tools Required to Intercept and Obstruct Terrorism (USA PATRIOT) Act.* Enactment of this law questioned the U.S. National Security Agency's domestic surveillance program, which was instituted following the terrorist attacks against the World Trade Center and Pentagon on September 11, 2001. These and many other legal activities have helped to establish the EFF as a premier organization internationally recognized for protecting online privacy, free speech, and other rights of computer users.

EFF was founded in 1990 by Mitch Kapor, John Perry Barlow, and John Gilmore, who were inspired by the U.S. government's clumsy handling of Operation Sundevil. In this federal law enforcement operation Robert J. Riggs, Craig Neidorf, and others were investigated by agents of the U.S. Secret Service and subsequently charged by federal prosecutors for allegedly using the online publication *Phrack Magazine* to distribute a sensitive E911 emergency telephone system document belonging to the BellSouth Company. Controversy swirled around the actual value of the document and the fact that officials of BellSouth had actually made even more technical documents public before the contents of the E911 manual acquired by defendants in the case discovered it through a hacking incident. In a related action, federal agents also raided Steve Jackson Games, Inc., located in Austin, Texas, "on the mistaken belief that a manual for the computer game Cyberpunk was actually a cryptic instruction book on how to commit computer crimes" (McQuade, 2006, p. 257). Jackson Games suffered grievous financial damage as a result and nearly went out of business. The case caused enormous outrage among early **Internet** user community members. A lawsuit against the government by Steve Jackson Games forced the government to pay $300,000 in damages and attorneys' fees and established the necessity for law enforcement agencies to obtain a warrant to access and read electronic mail.

Now headquartered in San Francisco, California, the EFF also has offices in Toronto, Canada, Brussels, Belgium, and Washington, D.C. Drawing on the skills of public policy experts, attorneys, computer and technology experts, as well as others, the Foundation works through the courts and also provides outreach to policy makers, the press, and the general public on related technology issues.

Suggested Readings: Eggen, D. (2007, August 14). Lawsuits may illuminate methods of spy program. *Washington Post* Web page: http://www.washingtonpost.com/wp-dyn/content/article/2007/08/13/AR2007081301113.html; Electronic Frontier Foundation. (2007). Web site: http://www.eff.org/; Davidson, P. (2006, May 12). "Climate has changed" for data privacy. *USA Today* Web site: http://www.usatoday.com/money/companies/2006-05-11-biz-privacy-usat_x.htm; *Steve Jackson Games, Inc. v. United States Secret Service,* 36 F.3d 457 (1994); Sterling, B. (1992). *The Hacker Crackdown: Law and Disorder on the Electronic Frontier.* New York: Bantam.

Eric Walter

ETHICAL USE OF COMPUTERS

The ethical use of computers and other types of electronic information technology (IT) devices is known as "computer ethics" or "cyber ethics." These concepts informally emerged beginning in the 1950s with the invention of mainframe computers initially used by U.S. government agencies, followed by colleges and universities. However, the term "computer ethics" was not articulated until Walter Maner did so in the mid-1970s. The ideas behind computer ethics involve complex considerations about how to behave properly—i.e., according to the laws, social customs, and moral standards of society—when using IT devices and information systems including the **Internet**. All forms of technology, including IT, used by people that allow people to access and use public and privately owned networks along with information should involve responsible use of computers, cell phones, PDAs, and other devices. For example, if a person uses a computer to access and share information over the Internet, he should do so in ways that comply with applicable civil and criminal laws and/or in ways that do not violate the rights of or harm other people. This, the essence of cyber ethics, can be difficult to achieve in certain instances. Today the ability to access information quickly online has created an "on-demand society" consisting of many people who frequently do not consider the possible harm they may be causing to other people.

The first users of computers faced many unprecedented challenges having to do with network access along with the use and exchange of data. As computer use and complexity increased, opportunities arose that allowed even more and comparatively unrestricted access to information via the Internet. Over time users were empowered with newer technologies and also were conditioned to access and respond to information in a variety of ways, according to their own interests, often with little adult or managerial oversight. Consider the modern practice of "flaming" that occurs when people disrespectfully interact with each other online. Frequently this happens when a person comments or posts something in a defamatory, insulting, or hostile manner about another person or organization only to have it negatively reacted to. Such online "shouting" can disrupt chat forums, blogs, and other online community exchanges, causing emotional harm or worse to people or organizations involved or named.

Computer/cyber ethics is a critical issue in modern societies in which millions of people now use many types of IT devices in their everyday lives. Cybercrime statistics along with an increasing number of research studies indicate that young people as well as adults do not behave ethically online, and that, beginning with a person's earliest exposure to computers, he can easily become a victim and victimizer of other people. Academic misconduct, **piracy**, cyber bullying, and other forms of online abuse and **cybercrime** cause harm in various ways, but what is considered responsible use of IT devices and information systems varies among people and situations. Not everyone, for example, believes that pirating music is wrong, even though it is illegal: while many young people would never think of stealing a music CD from a store in a shopping mall, they will use peer-to-peer networks to illegally download songs without paying to do so. What do you think about this issue? Can you think of other cyber-crime issues or online behaviors that are controversial?

Today society debates cyber ethics in areas pertaining to copyright and other **intellectual property** rights issues, the creation and enforcement of laws, formulation of public policies, professional codes of conduct, information security practices, software license agreements, and hardware reseller's mandates, among other issues. Technology use struggles against regulation, with consumers, businesses, and governments all seeking to predominate over what constitutes the ethical use of computers. With no uniform standards on computer use, a few employment sectors and professional membership associations are creating their own codes of conduct. At the organizational level these frequently take the form of "acceptable computer/network use policies" and may be complemented with cyber ethics training. Unfortunately, the results amount to a "wild west approach" to cyber ethics, with conflicting interests among different populations and groups of computer users. In cyber ethics, there is no such thing as "model traffic laws" as exist throughout the United States when it comes to operating motor vehicles. All too often IT users make up their own "rules" when using the Internet, which is the social equivalent of everyone driving any way they desire with little or no regard for other motorists.

The results of this lack of uniformity is that overall guidance on good behavior and best practices tends to be absent from users' initial computer experiences and in their continued decision-making processes. Thus children, when first taught how to use computers or portable gaming devices, are seldom provided with age-appropriate instruction in cyber ethics. The same is true for millions of youth and young adults who may go through their entire educational preparation in middle school, high school, and college without receiving any cyber ethics training. Since most users of computer technology lack any formalized ethical instruction, it is no surprise that the **social and economic impacts** and levels of harm caused by cybercrimes are increasing.

As users age, their exposure, experience, and technical capabilities to engage in cybercrime activities increase. Lacking cyber ethics education along with instruction in information security and Internet safety contributes to online **victimization** and offenses. In recognizing this, many institutions and organizations are providing guidance, information, and model practices and policies related to sound use of IT devices. I-SAFE, Inc. and the **National Center for Missing and Exploited Children (NCMEC)** are two nonprofit organizations that develop online instructional resources for teachers, parents, and youth that relate to using computers responsibly. Adults need to review the current information on technology and educate themselves on impact in areas of concern. For example, businesspeople and business owners need to understand their firm's policies on the use of technology, or, if a person owns a business, he needs to ensure that he has a policy aligned with his corporate goals. Educators and government officials need to create ways to enable parents and members of the community to learn basic computer etiquette, and then provide uniform instruction options for students and others. To stay current on the issue, a person need only search the Internet on the term "ethical computer use," "computer ethics," and "cyber ethics," or, where available, take a course having to do with the philosophy of ethics that emphasizes controversial online behaviors.

Suggested Readings: Bynum, Terrell Ward, and Simon Rogerson. (2003). *Computer Ethics and Professional Responsibility.* New York: Wiley-Blackwell Publishing;

Computer and Technology Ethics Case Studies at Vanderbilt University Center for Ethics Web site: http://www.vanderbilt.edu/CenterforEthics/cases.html; Computer Usage Policy of the University of Virginia Web page: http://itc.virginia.edu/policy/ethics.html; Computer Professionals for Social Responsibility Web site: http://www.cpsr.org/issues/ethics/cei; Editorial Board of the Stanford University Encyclopedia of Philosophy (2001 onward), at http://plato.stanford.edu/board.html; Johnson, Deborah G. State of New Jersey Department of Education Web site: http://www.nj.gov/education/techno/htcrime/info.htm.

Andrew Perry

F

FRAUDULENT SCHEMES AND THEFT ONLINE

Using the **Internet** means continually experiencing all sorts of tricks and schemes designed to defraud people out of their money or other valued assets including confidential data. Fraudulent schemes and theft online is now so common that they rival, if not surpass, the number of traffic violations seen everyday on streets or highways. A main difference, of course, is that **cybercrimes** involving fraud and theft often occur unseen on the Internet's superhighways and can negatively affect hundreds, thousands, or even millions of people all over the world in very short periods of time and even simultaneously. Further, **cybercriminals** can launch their schemes from anyplace in the world that offers Internet connectivity. Consequently, and unlike traditional frauds and theft, they will nearly always remain unknown, hiding within the seemingly limitless bounds of **cyberspace**, until long after their crimes have taken place.

Today's high tech fraud schemes and online theft generally employ the same principles that fraudsters and thieves have always used: motivation, imagination, criminal intent, knowledge, access to suitable targets, lulling them into a false sense of security, and technological skills. Thus, fraudulent schemes involve acquiring valued items by deceit. "Fraud committed using stand alone or networked computers or other types of electronic devices can be accomplished in several different ways that are particularly deceptive because techniques involved often require technical understanding of how IT and computers can be abused" (McQuade, 2006, 68). Let us consider several ways in which online fraud and theft can occur.

Credit card fraud typically occurs online after cybercriminals establish or otherwise gain access to a financial account. Then, while using false identification or pretending to be someone else, they will make purchases for goods and services in the name of this other person who may or may not actually exist. On October 18, 2005, a federal grand jury in Cleveland, Ohio, indicted Kenneth J. Flury, age 41, with bank fraud in connection with his scheme to defraud CitiBank. In this case Flury allegedly stole CitiBank debit card account numbers, personal identification numbers (PINs), and confidential account information of real account holders. Flury then fraudulently encoded this information onto blank ATM cards and used the cards to make cash advances at ATMs in the Cleveland area exceeding $384,000. Flury wire transferred about $167,000 of the stolen money via Western Union to other cybercriminals who provided the stolen financial account information from CitiBank branch offices located in Europe and Asia. Mr. Flury was among 19 co-defendants indicted by the U.S. government, a result of the so-called "Shadowcrew" investigation conducted by the U.S. Secret Service. He subsequently pled guilty to conspiracy in connection with his activities. As a moderator and administrator of the group's Shadowcrew Web site, Flury pled guilty to conspiracy. He was sentenced to 32 months in federal prison and fined a total of $300,000. The *United States v. Flurry* case demonstrated a technique known as "carding," which involves making fraudulent debit or credit cards. Once fake bank cards are made, fraudsters will use them along with financial account numbers to purchase things in person or online, although online purchases are preferred so that they cannot later be physically identified by witnesses in the event of a police investigation. Sometimes fraudsters will have merchandise delivered to locations they know are safe.

> Larger reputable online merchandising firms prevent this form of fraud by building in database purchasing rules that match credit card numbers being used to purchase goods with other account information such as the cardholder's name, address and account password. This information is often used along with the card's three or four digit security code to help assure that a credit card being used for an online purchase is actually in the possession of a person authorized to make the charge. To overcome fraud prevention checks, attackers often seek and acquire additional information about accounts and authorized card holders. Fraudsters usually also take care not to place an order by telephone or online in a way that can be traced to them. (McQuade, 2006, p. 69)

Another method of credit card fraud involves offering popular items for sale on online auction sites at very low prices, allowing bidders to run up the price, receiving payment for the merchandise, and then never shipping the items. However, as winning bidders provide personal and credit card account numbers, this information will be used to commit additional frauds by purchasing items online or via a telephone. Information about how to commit online fraud is abundant on the Net, as are Web sites that specialize in illegally selling credit card account information for fraudulent purposes.

Identity theft typically involves acquiring and then unlawfully using someone's financial account information to acquire goods and services in someone else's name. Many instances of this type of cybercrime involve numerous victims who are defrauded over a period of time until their available credit and money is exhausted. "It is a form of cybercrime that encompasses frauds involving any type of monetary or credit instrument along with personal identification documents" (McQuade, 2006, p. 69). Consequently, each time a person makes a financial transaction that reveals his name, address, phone number, date of birth, driver's license number, and/or Social Security number (SSN) he risks using such confidential information to carry out identity theft. "This is true of online, phone and traditional in-person purchases that produce records of transactions listing sales information that any unscrupulous employee of a restaurant, retail firm, government agency or other type of firm can simply copy down and use for fraudulent purposes" (McQuade, 2006, p. 70).

What really distinguishes identity theft from ordinary credit card and other forms of fraud, however, is criminal assumption of someone else's identity (or more likely, multiple identities simultaneously). Fraudsters commonly impersonate real people or pretend to be someone who does not really exist or has already died. Online hacking and data mining chat room text or social networking sites, stealing postal mail or unshredded hard copy documents, "dumpster diving" for paper records or undestroyed hard drives of old computers that have not been properly recycled, along with online checking of public records or obituary notices, and even strolling through a cemetery and comparing the information on gravestones with public records of deceased persons are all means of assuming or creating false identities. Once a person's identify and corresponding financial account information has been acquired, online fraud may be only a few keystrokes away from becoming a reality. (For more information, see the encyclopedia entry about **identity theft** by Sara Berg.)

Web and email spoofing occurs when cybercriminals create Web sites, Web-based traffic, email, or instant messages that appear to be legitimate in every way but are actually fraudulent communications designed to socially engineer people into giving up confidential information that can then be used to commit crimes. Web and email spoofing typically occur together "as when an attacker sends an e-mail with a link to a spoofed web site" (McQuade, 2006, p. 71). Oftentimes these messages purport to be from a bank, a retail firm, a utility company, or other legitimate organization such as a government agency. **Phishing** emails, for example, often appear to have been sent by technical service representatives or managers who inform people receiving the message of the urgent need to update financial accounts or other types of transactional records. Messages frequently entice people to click on a Web link within the email to confirm or update account information. If they fall for this gag, they will find themselves on a very official Web site and then be prompted to confirm or update account data. While this is occurring, cybercriminals will be monitoring the data input and potentially will use it for identity theft or other fraudulent purposes.

Several variations of this fraudulent scheme now occur on the Internet, which is why reputable organizations conducting business online advise their customers that they will never send online messages that request anything about transactional accounts.

> However, fraudsters who employ web and email spoofing are getting more sophisticated all the time and many people who do not heed such warnings are conned and victimized again and again as their name and other confidential information...[get] distributed all over the Net...MessageLabs, a leading provider of managed email security services to businesses worldwide, reportedly detects 80-100 new phishing websites each day. (McQuade, 2006, p. 71)

In addition to conning people out of their confidential information, phishers are now involved with organized networks of criminals and collaborating with money launderers by sending email "**spam**" and instant messaging "spim." This is increasingly occurring with *bot networks* that allow cybercriminals to remotely access and control computers widely dispersed throughout the world but closely interconnected on the Web. Cybercriminals are thus able to send massive amounts of email and instant messages that sometimes take the form of advertisements. These serve as clever and very deceptive ways of enticing users of information technology (IT) devices to click on Web links that take them to Web sites embedded with semiautomated data mining operations manned by cybercriminals.

Not all phishing is criminal, although it may be regarded as socially abusive because its purpose is to deceive people into believing things that are not true or doing things based on false information. During the fall of 2004, Alek Komarnitsky of Lafayette, Colorado, decorated his home with more than 17,000 lights to celebrate Halloween, Thanksgiving, and then Christmas. He also created a Web site that featured photos and a webcam video of his house. His home lighting system drew the attention of the Denver-based TV station KMGH, which flew a helicopter over the house in order to broadcast footage of the sensation to area viewers. Komarnitsky himself was aboard the flight claiming how visitors to his Web site could remotely control his home's computerized light show online. However, unbeknownst to TV viewers, and over 4 million visitors to his Web page, his wife was actually inside the house manually turning sets of lights on and off. When asked later about the deceit, Komarnitsky claimed the hoax was just his way of promoting holiday cheer. Fortunately, Komarnitsky's hoax apparently did not result in any specific or substantial indirect harm. No one, for example, is known to have done something on the basis of the prank that resulted in negative consequences for themselves or anyone else, although TV station personnel wasted time and money was spent to fuel the chopper flight. The incident does reveal, however, how gullible people can be, especially when trusted media sources, which have also been duped, widely report fraudulent facts and contrived circumstances as being true. Avoiding fraudulent schemes, such as those involving Web site and email spoofing, require "users of IT devices including computers and cell phones [to] remain wary of the people and technology they interact with online because you cannot always be sure of who or what you are actually communicating with" (McQuade, 2006, p. 72). It is hoped that trusted computing system technologies including encryption and digital signature methods will evolve to reduce these concerns. Until that happens, users beware!

Fraudulent schemes and online theft also occur as the result of natural disasters and other life circumstances that people periodically encounter. Following major tragedies caused by people and natural disasters, financial aid is often sought by nonprofit organizations

> to provide food, clothing, temporary shelter, medical supplies, infrastructure clean up and sanitation for disease control. Relief agencies such as the American Red Cross usually request monetary donations because it offers flexibility for purchasing needed goods and services while minimizing shipping costs and delays in providing assistance to victims. Following the infamous aircraft terrorist events of September 11, 2001 and the earthquake and tsunamis disaster that suddenly struck several pacific island nations on December 26, 2004 people from around the world provided monetary donations and volunteered to help victims of these disasters. Governments from around the world pledged and provided financial assistance plus other types of support in each of these instances, as they have following many other disasters. Unfortunately tragedies present opportunities for disaster fraud in which people are duped into providing charity that lines the pockets of fraudsters rather than helping victims in need! (McQuade, 2006, p. 73)

In June 2006 the federal Government Accountability Office (GAO) reported that the Federal Emergency Management Agency (FEMA) had been duped into erroneously paying out over $1 billion in disaster relief to alleged victims of the Katrina and Rita hurricanes that struck the Gulf Coast in 2005. Hundreds of people received a total of approximately $5.3 million simply on the basis of providing the agency with a post office box number that correlated to places like cemeteries or UPS stores rather than a valid residential address. One person received 26 separate payments from FEMA totaling $139,000 after using 13 different Social Security numbers and addresses, of which eight addresses did not even exist. Many people received payments for rent while simultaneously being reimbursed for hotel charges. In another instance FEMA paid $8,000 for someone to stay for five months in a California hotel and provided him with $6,700 in rent money for the same period of time.

High tech disaster schemes can involve several different forms of fraud, including:

(1) *telemarketing fraud* methods that play on donor sympathies to fraudulently solicit funds for fictitious human service agencies; (2) *false advertising schemes* as when for example, a portion of funds spent on trinkets or products are pocketed instead of being forwarded to disaster victims as promised; (3) *service provider fraud* as when repair or cleanup contractors make off with funds without performing work promised; (4) submitting *false damage claims* to insurance firms of government agencies such as the Federal Emergency Management Agency (FEMA) of the U.S. Department of Homeland Security; (5) *insider trading* such as "pump-n-dump" schemes in which stock market brokers spread false rumors that a company's stock is about to take a sharp price increase thereby inducing people to buy, and then suddenly pull out their own stock investments after the increased purchases do indeed falsely inflate the price; (6) *cybersmear campaigns* (the opposite of pump'n dump schemes) in which individuals or firms are defamed for allegedly doing things or maintaining relationships, etc., that are not true and end up costing them money; and (6) *ad hoc frauds* that adopt one or more of these or other methods of conning people out of their money, possessions or information. (McQuade, 2006, p. 73)

Online frauds involving these and other methods are common. In one instance following the terrorism of September 11, 2001, a man received an email requesting financial support for a group of computer experts attempting to locate Osama bin Laden who reportedly had masterminded the aircraft hijacking crashes into the World Trade Center in New York City and Pentagon located in Washington, D.C. In another instance the popular beverage firm Snapple, owned by Cadbury-Schweppes, was falsely accused on Web sites of having maintained an association with Osama bin Laden. The activity allegedly compromised business sales until the Web-based information was removed. And in a telemarketing scheme, voice mail messages communicated the need for emergency 911 systems to better assist victims of the attacks reportedly carried out by Osama bin Laden's terrorist organization Al Qaeda (McQuade, 2006, p. 73).

Online fraud can also involve hoaxes delivered by email or instant messaging. Typically these describe software applications known to have security vulnerabilities. Hoax messages then go on to describe what should be done to fix these technical programming problem(s). Messages usually appear to originate from a source and are designed to be passed along online to people who the recipient of the message knows and cares about. Instructions detail particular files suspected of containing **malware** programs, but which are actually necessary for smooth computer system operation. Unfortunately, unsuspecting victims often locate and delete these files on their systems only to discover their IT devices will no longer operate properly.

Fraud as the result of people using computers and the Internet has become so prevalent that some users have begun to fight back. For example, at 419eater.com, you can read dozens of stories of people who responded to fraudulent e-mails by pretending to be willing participants and then reverse engineer the scam artists into performing bizarre acts. Some of these vigilante fraud-fighters have even been known to send packages COD to the scammers with the intention of sticking them with substantial shipping and international importation fees! However, merely by opening spam sent as part of a fraudulent scheme may result in an individual being technologically marked and tracked as a potential victim who is worth sending more scam offers to. (McQuade, 2006, p. 74)

A more conventional way to fight back is by practicing sound information security strategies as a matter of lifestyle, and by reporting suspected cybercrimes to proper authorities, many of which are described in this book.

Suggested Readings: McQuade, S. (2006). *Understanding and managing cybercrime,* 67–74. Boston: Allyn and Bacon; The Silver Lake Editors. (2006). *Scams & swindles: Phishing, spoofing, ID theft, Nigerian advance schemes investment frauds: How to Recognize and avoid rip-offs in the Internet age.* Lansdowne, PA: Silver Lake Publishing; Thomes, J. T. (2000). *Dotcons: Con games, fraud & deceit on the Internet.* Bloomington, IN: Writers Club Press; Wall, D. S. (2007). *Crime and the Internet.* London, England: Taylor & Francis; Wells, J., & Association of Certified Fraud Examiners. (2004). *The computer and Internet fraud manual.* Austin, TX: Association of Certified Fraud Examiners, Inc. Willcox, B. (2005). *Diary of an eBay fraud case.* Pittsburgh, PA: Red Lead Press.

Samuel C. McQuade, III

G

GAMING ONLINE

Millions of people today utilize computers to play video games and other simulations, both offline and online. Online gaming has been defined as a technology that enables players to connect with each other for purposes of online competition, adventure, or learning. Online games are played over some form of computer network, now typically on the **Internet**. One advantage of online games is the ability for individuals to connect to relatively small, older multiplayer games (with perhaps 8 to 60 players) or *massively multiplayer online role-playing games (MMORPGs)* that may have as many as several thousand simultaneous players. Everquest, World of Warcraft, and Final Fantasy XI are examples of MMORPGs. With the 2007 release of the sci-fi action-adventure first-person shooter game Halo 3, the electronic gaming industry passed a financial earnings milestone by its creator Bungie Studios of Microsoft Corporation, making over $175 million dollars in a single day! This tops the largest box office earnings for a movie shown in a conventional theater (e.g., *Spider-Man 3* also released in 2007, which earned $148 million in ticket sales within its opening weekend). This serves as a stark illustration of the commercial value of electronic gaming, an industry currently valued at approximately $20 billion.

The first multiplayer computer game was Spacewar, developed in 1962 by Steve Russell, Martin Graetz, and Wayne Wiitanen, who were students attending the Massachusetts Institute of Technology (MIT). Spacewar allowed two players to simulate spaceship-to-spaceship combat on a mainframe computer network. PLATO, developed at the University of Illinois also in the 1960s, is considered be the first location of an online community for education and gaming. During the 1970s online gaming evolved from relatively simple computer simulation games to fantasy role-playing games and first-person adventure games. ATARI's consumer release of Pong in 1972 is generally regarded as the true beginning of modern video games. As it was prior to the creation of the personal computer, computer systems of this period were essentially giant community networks that allowed many users to access resources simultaneously. This was the beginning of what eventually would become the Internet and basis for MMORPGs.

At about the same time, in 1975, the prototypical role-playing fantasy and miniatures game Dungeons and Dragons, created by Gary Gygax and Dave Arneson, was released initially as a tabletop fantasy role-playing game. Fantasy gaming and then science fiction gaming quickly evolved throughout the 1980s into shared online first-person adventures.

With the advent of personal computers single player games grew in popularity, but by the early 1990s the ability to collaborate and compete online became widespread. Online gaming can be divided into two main categories. One consists of digitized versions of traditional board, playing card, and other games of chance. The second category includes the more recent addition of arcade style combat, adventure, fantasy, and science fiction role-playing "dungeon crawl" games. The early 1990s saw the release of the largest multiplayer software-based game DOOM, in which players could then (and still can) connect to each other via computer modems or server-based networks and play either cooperatively or competitively online.

As the online gaming community has increased in numbers, so too have the types of games and **cybercrimes** that can also occur in gaming environments. In the 1990s the makers of the major computer operating systems bundled simple games of chance such as poker onto personal computers. Since that period in time online gambling technologies have also grown via lottery tickets, offtrack betting, fantasy football, and so forth. In the process modern criminals have demonstrated abilities to compromise information systems that provide this form of entertainment. Also during this time period the advent of the multi-user dungeons (MUD) enabled players to interact in a social setting, using text-based messages in a process known as "mudding." Some observers believe mudding created the foundation for MMORPGs, for what is now known as social networking, and for the **social engineering** that frequently occurs within these environments and is fundamental to the commission of cybercrimes. For example, Everquest and World of Warcraft MMORPGs are both frequently targeted by **cybercriminals** who attack players' character profiles and then sell the information to other players for money or in-game items. For example, suppose Player A downloads a macro that allows him to control the powers of his online game character in more fluid ways. In actuality the macro tool is most likely a form of **malware** that keylogs usernames and passwords, which is then automatically sent to another person's computer, say that of Player B. Player B could then log into the game as Player A, pretend to be Player A, and sell or transfer Player A's game items. Note that selling game items can be within the gaming environment (i.e., involving virtual money), or even online through an auction or non-auction Web site that lists the game item as being for sale. Industry experts call any form of stealing character login information as "spear-phishing," which relates to selecting targets to attack online (see entry on **Attack Vectors**). Firms that host online games regard spear-phishing as a violation of their End User License Agreement (EULA).

Other forms of online game abuse include what is commonly referred to as "farming for items" or "grinding for experience." Farming in multiplayer games, more specifically in MMORPGs, typically involves organizing a group of players to collect currency or items in the game world by performing a series of in-game tasks repeatedly. Organized farming and grinding groups known as farming parties or grinding parties, respectively, have sprung up in recent years with the advent of online markets within gaming worlds. One prime example of farming often occurs in World of Warcraft, wherein groups of people collect gold or rare items such as special weapons or armor only to sell these virtual goods for real world money via online auction sites or personal Web sites as described above. Because many computer users currently spend countless hours and real money online creating characters and special characteristics for them, people who violate a EULA are effectively committing an online abuse of information systems.

It is quite possible that a significant amount of the buying and selling of virtual gaming items involves defrauding real people or lead to other crimes.

> In March 2005, Qui Chengwei (41) stabbed to death fellow online gamer Zhu Caoyuan in Shanghai, China for selling a virtual cybersword for 7,200 yuan that the men had previously jointly won in an online auction. Reportedly Chengwei had leant the dragon sabre to Caoyuan, but reported it to police as being stolen after learning Chengwei resold it for the equivalent of $870. At the time of the murder Chinese intellectual property laws had no provisions for determining rightful ownership of the virtual sword or its value, because although players must invest time and money to acquire such virtual property, such assets constitute data for which there exists no legally admissible proof of ownership or legally recognized estimates of market value. (McQuade, 2006, p. 240)

The legal basis for establishing ownership of *virtual property* in various places is likely to remain unresolved for a long time, and this is an emerging challenge for civil and criminal justice systems throughout the world.

Suggested Readings: Adams, E., & Rollings, A. (2006). *Fundamentals of game design.* Game Design and Development Series. Upper Saddle River, NJ: Prentice-Hall; Bellis, M. (2008). *Computer and video game history.* About.com Web site: http://inventors.about.com/library/inventors/blcomputer_videogames.htm; Castronova, Edward. (2006). *Synthetic worlds: The business and culture of online games,* new ed. Chicago, IL: University Of Chicago Press; Furfie, B. (2008). *Trojans penetrate online gaming. PC Retail Magazine* Web site: http://www.pcretailmag.com/news/28704/Trojans-penetrate-online-gaming; Woolley, D. (1994). *PLATO: The emergence of an online community.* Electronic Frontier Foundation Web site. Retrieved from http://w2.eff.org//Net_culture/Virtual_community/plato_history.article; Interactive Gaming Council. (2007, August 29). *Time to regulate Internet gambling.* Reprinted from *Newsday.* Interactive Gaming Council Web site: http://www.igcouncil.org/index.php?option=com_content&task=view&id=186&Itemid=47; *The evolution of games.* (1998). Emulators Unlimited Web site: (http://www.emuunlim.com/doteaters/play1sta1.htm).

Andrew Perry

GOVERNMENT INTELLIGENCE GATHERING

Increasingly, transnational criminals, terrorists, and hostile governments use the **Internet** and digital technology. In the process threats to societal well-being and relative peace have increasingly swayed toward the unpredictable for law enforcement organizations, intelligence agencies, and military personnel, which, although having access to the same technologies, must radically change their outlook and continually adopt new tools and methods to keep up with threats posed to **critical information**

infrastructure by **cybercrime**. (See encyclopedia entry on **Theory of Technology-Enabled Crime, Policing, and Security**.) Faced with such threats, government officials charged with the responsibility to detect and intervene when necessary to prevent crime, including acts of terrorism or threats to national security, must take aggressive steps to monitor communications signals and the activities of hostile individuals and groups. In a more perfect world, for example, government officials would have detected and worked to prevent the 2001 aircraft hijacking attacks on the Twin Towers in New York and the Pentagon in Washington, D.C., before they happened.

Democratically elected governments in free societies, along with their policing, intelligence, and military resources, are subject to many laws designed to safeguard the rights of citizens or residents. Since its founding as an independent nation, America has set out certain legal principles guaranteeing several important rights deemed necessary to preserve long-term survival of our way of life. The United States Constitution and its Amendments, along with a substantial body of criminal and civil statutory laws, and thousands of case law rulings that establish legal precedents frame what is expected and allowed by the people and by local, state, and federal government agencies. When violations of these laws are determined to occur, sanctions including fines, imprisonment, and penalties may and should be imposed to punish and deter offenders and to make society safer and functioning as intended by legislative branches who represent the will of the voters.

Americans are traditionally suspicious of government, particularly when it comes to their **privacy**. This distrust is not without merit; along with the many beneficial, legitimate, and justified actions the federal government has taken through the years, there have also been periodic violations of privacy and heavy-handed law enforcement tactics. This has been especially true during periods of war or long-standing fears about threats to national security, as during the Cold War (1950–1990), rising concerns about transnational organized crime (1960–present), and the "war on terrorism" (2001–present). Consequently, targets of government surveillance, infiltration, and disruption have included organized crime organizations dating from the end of World War II when hostile governments like the former Union of Soviet Socialist Republics (USSR) posed threats to the United States and allied nations.

Threats to national security are traditionally viewed as coming from either outside or inside of national borders, or a combination of these. Laws governing which agencies should be involved to gather and analyze intelligence information about national security threats have been established on this basis, taking into account also whether persons suspected are U.S. citizens. The *Federal Intelligence Surveillance Act of 1978* among several other provisions for processing national security threat information generally established that the Federal Bureau of Investigation has a lead role investigating domestic (within border) threats and that the Central Intelligence Agency (CIA) leads international (outside of border) threat investigations. In other words and in general, the CIA does not have authority to "spy" on Americans who are living and working on American soil, and the FBI does not have authority to investigate Americans who travel abroad. This is an oversimplification of how things work in practice, and periodically federal law enforcement agencies (e.g., FBI) and those of the intelligence community (e.g., CIA) exchange information and collaborate depending on the nature of the investigation.

Innovations in communications and transportation technologies have fundamentally changed the ways in which criminal organizations now operate. The result is that law enforcement and intelligence agencies are challenged as never before.

They continually struggle to gather and analyze data having to do with financial accounts, telephone records, international travel, criminal histories and associations, Internet communications, and so forth in order to detect crime and threats to national security. And they struggle continually to do so by legally using superior technological methods. Historically, however, certain government officials and agencies have inappropriately targeted individuals and groups. During the Civil Rights Movement of the 1960s, for example, Dr. Martin Luther King Jr. and other political activists were unfairly and illegally placed under government surveillance on beliefs that public demonstrations seeking equality of civil rights for African Americans constituted a threat to national security.

During this tense period in American history numerous individuals and groups who protested against the Vietnam War or appeared to be sympathetic to socialist or communist ways of governance were also illegally spied on by agencies of the federal government. In the wake of the Watergate scandal of the early 1970s that drove President Richard Nixon from office, the U.S. Senate formed a special commission to look into allegations of illegal intelligence gathering conducted by the Federal Government. Known officially as the Congressional Committee to Study Governmental Operations with Respect to Intelligence Activities, and more commonly known as the "Church Committee" (named after its chairman, Senator Frank Church [D-ID]), it determined the following (McQuade, 2006, pp. 255–256):

- From 1953 to 1973 nearly a quarter of a million first class letters were opened and photographed in the United States by the Central Intelligence Agency (CIA) producing a CIA computerized index of nearly 1.5 million names of people and who they corresponded with.
- From 1940 to 1966 at least 130,000 first class letters were opened and photographed by the FBI in eight U.S. cities also to record what people were corresponding with each other about.
- From 1967 to 1973 over 300,000 people were indexed in a CIA computer system, separate files were created on approximately 7,200 Americans, and records were kept on over 100 domestic groups in connection with Operation Chaos.
- From 1947 to 1975 millions of private telegrams sent from, to, or through the United States were obtained by the National Security Agency under a secret arrangement with three U.S. telegraph companies.
- From the mid-1960s to 1971 an estimated 100,000 Americans were the subjects of U.S. Army intelligence files.
- From 1969 to 1973 intelligence files on more than 11,000 individuals and groups were created by the Internal Revenue Service, which initiated tax investigations on the basis of political rather than tax criteria.
- At least 26,000 individuals were at one point during this period of history catalogued on an FBI list of persons to be rounded up in the event of a national emergency.

The Church Committee concluded that governmental officials and agencies involved in gathering and analyzing data pertaining to perceived national security threats often did so illegally. In some instances authorities were determined to have ignored laws designed to protect privacy, and to have done so over long periods of time. This is what lead to Congress and then President Gerald Ford enacting the *Foreign Surveillance Intelligence ("FISA") Act of 1978*. The law established the United

States Foreign Surveillance Court to oversee requests for surveillance of suspected spies or their agents within U.S. borders.

The terrorist attacks on the World Trade Center and the Pentagon changed much for Americans and millions of other people living throughout the world. Following the attacks the federal government enacted the *USA PATRIOT Act of 2001* to provide government intelligence and law enforcement agencies with unprecedented surveillance, search, and seizure authority. It also updated the FISA Act to include surveillance of suspected terrorists as well as spies. In the months that followed, it was revealed that the Department of Defense and its contractors were developing powerful counterterrorism data mining and analysis capabilities.

> The *Total Information Awareness* program, as it was originally referred to (and re-dubbed *Terrorism Information Awareness* program apparently to help appease Congressional and public concern over government snooping), used facial recognition and data integration analysis technology to identify individuals as well as behavioral and other patterns, trends, relationships and anomalies indicative of terrorism. Personal information about millions of people, such as their driver's license record, telephone calls, financial transactions, recorded contacts with police, visas and work permits, etc. could all be tracked via a super networked database. (McQuade, 2006, p. 258)

Privacy advocates, and especially the American Civil Liberties Union (ACLU) along with others organized against it, cited the potential for government misuse. Congress agreed and voted to shut down the program in 2003. The component technologies behind it survived, however, as legislators subsequently added a classified annex to a defense appropriations bill that maintained funding for the project and moved its component technologies to other government agencies. The legislators included a requirement that the technologies could only be used for military or intelligence purposes against foreigners.

Another controversial post-9/11 government activity is the so-called "domestic spying program" that in part involves wireless wiretapping of American citizens by the National Security Agency (NSA). Secretly authorized by the administration of President George Bush and officially referred to as the Terrorist Surveillance Program, the program allows the NSA to monitor, without warrants or oversight from the Foreign Surveillance Court or any other judicial body, phone calls, emails, Internet activity, or other communication that involves any person or persons outside the United States, even if the person or people they are talking to are within the United States. This controversial program is deemed necessary by its advocates because of ways in which terrorists are now using information systems such as the Internet, along with computers and mobile electronic devices like cell phones, to exchange messages and alter their communication methods faster than FISA provisions and the Foreign Surveillance Court can process. In other words, terrorists are reportedly able to scramble about the world coordinating their efforts via wired and wireless communications faster than authorities can track them if they are required to acquire approval from the Foreign Surveillance Court every time they need to.

As of this writing the true scope of the Terrorist Surveillance Program is unknown and under classified review by the U.S. Congress. Details of the program remain out of public view for fear of compromising secret methods of government intelligence data gathering and analysis. Several members of Congress have been highly critical of the program, insisting that it is a clear violation of the FISA Act. Administration officials have countered that the FISA requirement was superseded by powers inherent in the "Authorization for Use of Military Force against Terrorists" that Congress granted President George W. Bush shortly after 9/11. In the summer of 2008, this remained an unresolved legal and political issue.

Regardless of how the ongoing controversy about the Terrorist Surveillance Program turns out, it is important that current and future law enforcement officers, intelligence agents, prosecutors, and information security professionals understand that abuses of the past can recur, especially in times when government officials and others in power perceive national security to be at stake. It is imperative that Americans vigilantly maintain a balance between security needs of the nation and Constitutional rights of the people. To be sure, this is not easy and the stakes for miscalculating are very high. It is upon this balance of security and privacy along with other civil rights that American society is based. To these extraordinary ends, it is useful for criminal justice and information security professionals, along with other clear-thinking members of society, to periodically ask a series of questions originally suggested by the Church Committee in the course of investigating unethical and illegal spying by agencies of the federal government (U.S. Congress, 1976):

1. Which governmental agencies actually engage in domestic spying?
2. How many citizens are targets of governmental intelligence activities?
3. What standards govern the opening of intelligence investigations and how can it be known when intelligence investigations have been terminated?
4. Where do current targets fit on the spectrum between those who commit violent criminal acts and those who seek only to dissent peacefully from government policy?
5. To what extent does information being collected include intimate details of the targets' personal lives or their political views, and has such information been disseminated and used to injure individuals in their personal, social, or professional affairs?
6. What actions beyond surveillance are intelligence agencies taking, such as attempting to disrupt, discredit, or destroy persons or groups who have been the targets of surveillance?
7. Are intelligence agencies being used to serve the political aims of presidents, other high officials, or the agencies themselves?
8. How are agencies responding either to proper orders or to excessive pressures from their superiors? To what extent are intelligence agencies disclosing or concealing information to them or from outside bodies charged with overseeing agency policies and actions?
9. Are intelligence or law enforcement agencies acting outside the law? What currently is the attitude of such agencies toward the rule of law?
10. To what extent is the executive branch and the Congress controlling intelligence and law enforcement agencies and holding them accountable for their surveillance activities?
11. Generally, how well is the federal system of checks and balances between the branches of government working to control intelligence activity?

Suggested Readings: McCue, C. (2007). *Data mining and predictive analysis: Intelligence gathering and crime analysis.* Boston, MA: Butterworth-Heinemann; McQuade, S.C. (2006). *Understanding and managing cybercrime,* 255–259. Boston: Allyn & Bacon; Popp, R.L., and J. Yen, eds. (2006). *Emergent information technologies and enabling* *policies for counter-terrorism.* IEEE Press Series on Computational Intelligence. New York: Wiley–IEEE Press; Shulsky, A. N., and G. J. Schmitt. (2002). *Silent warfare: Understanding the world of intelligence,* 3rd ed. Dulles, VA: Potomac Books Inc.; U.S. Congress. (1976, April 26). *Final report of the committee to study governmental operations with respect to intelligence activities.* Washington, DC: Government Printing Office.

Samuel C. McQuade, III and Eric Walter

H

HACKING AND THE HACKER SUBCULTURE

Definitions for the term "hacking" have varied through the decades. Essentially, terms used for this concept have pertained to people gaining unauthorized access into information systems including computer networks. Breaking into a computer system or exceeding network permissions are considered forms of *computer trespassing*. As defined in federal and many state computer crime laws, computer trespassing now extends to individuals who exceed their authorized permissions within a given computer network. Originally, however, beginning in the late 1950s, a "hack" was a slang word first used by students of the Massachusetts Institute of Technology (MIT) when referring to "a clever, benign, and ethical prank or practical joke, which is both challenging for the perpetrators and amusing to the MIT community" (MIT IHFTP Hack Gallery, 1997). As computer technologies began to be incorporated as part of research programs at MIT and other universities across the United States, hacking began to include clever and innovative programming.

The environment at MIT—a combination of available technology, ambitious students, and general disdain for security measures—produced what became and is still known as the "Hacker Ethic." This philosophy was embraced among students who studied and used early computer systems and was eventually explained by Steven Levy in his 1984 book titled, *Hackers: Heroes of the Computer Revolution.* As explained by Levy (1984, p. 40), the Hacker Ethic consisted of the following six major principles:

(1) Access to computers, and anything which might teach you something about the way technology in the world works, should be unlimited and total. Always yield to the Hands-on Imperative! (2) All information should be open and free; (3) Mistrust authority, promote decentralization; (4) Hackers should be judged by their hacking, not bogus criteria such as degrees, age, race, or position; (5) You can create art and beauty on a computer; and (6) Computers can change your life for the better.

Hacking has always been a social activity, bringing together communities of computer experts to discuss and share information about the machines they hack on. People who originally considered themselves hackers had creative and prankster-like attitudes towards computing. But as computer and networking technologies became more advanced and more accessible, many new computer users assumed the hacker label and began to use the Hacker Ethic to justify criminal activities. The news media in turn reported on new forms of computer crime committed by these individuals, and this resulted in a general belief by the public that all activities labeled as hacking were illegal. Unfortunately, this was not true historically and remains a common source of confusion even today. As the legend of the criminal hacker was spread by news media, the common meaning of the word began to change. Movies such as *Wargames, The Net,* and *Hackers* further solidified the image of the criminal hacker in the public view. While the news media and popular entertainment pushed the hacker label farther away from the original Hacker Ethic, the community aspect of hacking remained. Criminal hackers banded together to form "hacking groups" online through bulletin board and Internet relay chat (IRC) systems. These groups would brag about their latest exploits, which allowed law enforcement officers to access these online forums in order to gather evidence against criminal hackers.

However, a recent surge in the number of people engaged in various forms of hardware modifications has began to shift the popular definition of the word "hacker" back towards that of the original, noncriminal definition. Similar to the original MIT computer hackers, these groups push various forms of equipment and consumer electronics to their limits, legally performing modifications and voiding warranties. Publications such as *Make* magazine are targeted at these new hardware hackers, providing articles on the newest how-to and do-it-yourself projects. Hardware hacking may occasionally violate the *Digital Millennium Copyright Act* in the process of circumventing copyright protection schemes built into devices, but is largely unintentional. Currently, many activities labeled as hacking are highly malicious, with many modern "hackers" accessing information systems for financial gain or destructive purposes. Hackers who engage in illegal activities are commonly known as "black hat hackers," whereas those who use their skills for what they believe are ethical and appropriate purposes are known as "white hat hackers." However, this distinction is often somewhat badly defined, and the use of the term "grey hat hackers" has grown increasingly common to reflect the often blurry ethical and legal lines crossed in the process of hacking.

Today, people who describe themselves as hackers are a diverse group, including both those who subscribe to the original hacker ethic and those who engage in criminal activities. As a whole, this group of people represents a hacker subculture that today includes Web sites, publications, and conferences attended by thousands of people throughout the world. One of the most famous events attended by real and aspiring computer hackers, as well as people generally interested in the hacker subculture, is DEFCON, which is held annually in Las Vegas, Nevada. DEFCON and similar conference, workshop, and social gatherings regularly convened in locations throughout the United States and other countries tend to blend criminal and noncriminal hacking beliefs and practices. Discussions range from **social engineering** fundamentals to the feasibility of criminal laws applying to **cyberspace**. Topics such as these may draw a diverse audience depending on the type of event, including self-identified hackers, academics, law enforcement, and criminal organizations, all of whom have ties to the broader hacker subculture.

Suggested Readings: IHTFP Hack Gallery. (1997). See MIT IHTFP Hack Gallery Web site: http://hacks.mit.edu/; Levy, S., (1984), *Hackers: heroes of the computer revolution*, Harmondsworth,UK: Pengun; Stallman, R. (2004). *The hacker's ethics.* Retrieved June 18, 2007, from The Cyberpunk Project Web site: http://project.cyberpunk.ru/idb/hacker_ethics.html; Sterling, B. (1992). *The hacker crackdown.* New York: Bantam.

Nathan Fisk

I

IDENTITY THEFT

Identity theft, also referred to as *identity fraud,* is a criminal act where one individual misrepresents himself by pretending to be someone else. This is typically done by illegally using the victim's personal information to open new financial accounts, use existing financial accounts, or do some combination of the two. Identity theft may be committed during the course of a single incident, or it may occur over a long period of time. Although the act of pretending to be someone else is certainly not new, the terms "identity theft" and "identity fraud" are not believed to have been used in print until 1991. Similarly, identity theft was not made a federal crime until 1998, when the *Identity Theft and Assumption Deterrence Act* (U.S. Public Law 105-318) was passed. Given increasing worldwide **computerization** and a public by and large still learning how to protect themselves, their computer equipment, and their data, identity theft is a major and increasingly problematic crime. In 2003 a research report by the Federal Trade Commission revealed that 27.3 million Americans had been victimized by identity theft in the preceding five years, with nearly 10 million people suffering financial losses, ruined credit, and other problems within just 12 months preceding the study. It was further reported that identify theft crimes cost businesses and financial institutions $48 billion and consumer victims over $5 billion in direct out-of-pocket costs (McQuade, 2006, p. 201).

In order to commit identity theft, offenders generally need to do two things. First, they must obtain a victim's unique personal information, such as name, address, date of birth, phone number, credit card number, or Social Security number. Second, they must illegally use that information for fraudulent purposes. "Fraud" refers to an illegal act being done with trickery or deceit. In some states, the offender does not actually have to use the victim's information to be prosecuted for fraud; merely possessing a person's information after it is obtained illegally is enough to be recognized as a crime.

There are many ways in which the offender can obtain personal information about a person in order to commit identity theft. Some of these are "offline" through physical means, such as when an offender goes through the victim's trash to find discarded documents such as credit card applications and pay stubs. Other methods are "online" via a computer or the **Internet**, such as when victims respond to **phishing** ploys and enter personal information on dummy Web sites set up to look like legitimate ones, or when they volunteer personal information to blogs, chat rooms, or social networking Web sites.

Identity theft may involve any number of different fraud-related crimes that are committed through the misuse of a victim's personal information. According to the Federal Trade Commission (2007), identity theft most commonly takes the form of the following: (a) *credit card fraud,* as when an offender illegally uses existing credit or debit cards in someone else's name; (b) *telephone or utilities fraud,* involving illegal setup and/or use of a telephone, cellular phone, water supply, electricity, garbage collection, or other utilities account; or (c) *bank fraud,* which refers to offenders using existing checking or savings accounts, or illegally opening a new financial account, or engaging in fraudulent electronic funds transfers to conduct transactions in someone else's name.

Identify theft may also involve employment-related fraud in circumstances of an individual obtaining a job in the victim's name. Government benefits and insurance fraud can also be related to identity theft as when offenders make false claims for money, products, or services to which they are not legally entitled. For example, identity thieves often try to obtain or create false government documents such as a driver's license, passport, birth certificate, or Social Security card in order to pretend to be someone else or acquire certain benefits (e.g., Medicare, Medicaid, or veterans' benefits). Loan fraud is another type of financial crime often related to identity theft. This may occur when an offender obtains a new loan such as a business, personal, student, car, real estate, boat, or other type of consumer loan.

It is important to understand that a victim of identity theft can be affected by any or all of these types of fraud over time and from anyplace in the world where one or even multiple perpetrators access the Internet. Similarly, an offender may misuse a single type of account, or he might open a number of different accounts and simultaneously victimize several people living or working anyplace in the world. Victims of identity theft are encouraged to report unauthorized use of their financial or other transactional accounts to proper authorities, including their local police or sheriff's department, the U.S. Federal Commerce Commission, and the **National White Collar Crime Center**.

Suggested Readings: Berg, S.E. (2008). Identity theft causes, correlates, and factors: A content analysis. In F. Schmallager and M. Pittaro (Eds.), *Crimes of the Internet.* Upper Saddle River, NJ: Prentice-Hall; Federal Trade Commission. (2007). *Identity theft victim complaint data: January 1, 2006–December 31, 2006.* Retrieved May 21, 2007, from the Federal Trade Commission Web site: http://www.ftc.gov/bcp/edu/microsites/idtheft/downloads/clearinghouse_2006.pdf; McQuade, S.C. (2006). *Understanding and managing cybercrime.* Boston: Pearson Education, Inc.; Neuffer, E. (1991, May 27). One name's double life: David Lombardi lost his ID cards, acquired coworker's debts and crimes. *Boston Globe.* Retrieved March 26, 2005, from National Newspapers via ProQuest; Neuffer, E. (1991, July 9). Victims urge crackdown on identity theft: Say officials often fail to act on complaints. *Boston Globe.* Retrieved March 26, 2005, from National Newspapers via ProQuest; Sharp, T.,

Shreve-Neiger, A., Fremouw, W., Kane, J., & Hutton, S. (2004, January). Exploring the psychological and somatic impact of identity theft. *Journal of Forensic Sciences, 49*(1), 131–136.

Sara E. Berg

INFORMATION ASSURANCE

Information assurance is a broad concept that pertains to the need to ensure the *confidentiality, integrity, and availability (CIA)* of data contained on information systems. This includes systems that make up **critical information infrastructure** that society relies on for many basic functions. For many years prior to widespread utilization of the **Internet** and the World Wide Web, information professionals responsible for the security of organizational computer/information systems tended to think in terms of "protecting the C.I.A. of data." This began to change in 1997 with publication of the U.S. President's Commission on Critical Information Infrastructure Protection (PCCIP) report titled, *Critical Foundations: Protecting America's Infrastructures.* This influential U.S. government report described the reality that many nations, including the United States, increasingly depend on the security of *critical infrastructures* like airports, sea ports, dams, bridges, and other physical assets, along with cyber security of information systems (e.g., for communications, banking and commerce, manufacturing, transportation, defense, education, and so forth.) Thereafter, and in recognition that computer systems maintained by organizations were almost invariably connected to the Internet and part of national critical information infrastructures, security professionals throughout the computerized world increasingly thought and communicated with references to "information assurance" rather than in specific terms of "C.I.A." Today "information assurance" is a term universally used by information security professionals along with CIA goals, which are applicable to personal, organizational, state, regional, and national computer systems.

The important points here are that there are many different types of data requiring differing levels of assurance and accessibility, and providing information assurance is a responsibility as distributed as information itself. Institutions and professionals who manage information on behalf of people need to be cognizant of information assurance in terms of the CIA of data. Banking officials, for example, must be able to access financial accounts in order to effect and log transactions involving money. Similarly, doctors must be able to monitor the health of people and prescribe new treatments based on their medical history records while keeping all such information confidential. And professors access student records in order to adequately provide academic advising and other assistance that students periodically need. Information assurance is like a two-way street: professionals who access and use personal data share responsibility with all users for assuring its protection.

Protecting critical information infrastructure (CII) has occurred since at least World War II, during which the United States relied on wired and wireless communications systems. Some writers have even observed that CII began with telegraph and then telephone systems in the nineteenth century. However, prior to this period in history nations did not rely on electronic systems for commerce, provision of utility services, transportation, education, and a myriad of government and private sector services to the extent that modern societies now do. Given the extent to which societies now depend on electricity to operate telecommunications and computing systems, protecting CII is vitally important. Research is revealing that organized crime, terrorist organizations, or other nations are now launching **malware attacks** against organizations throughout much of the computerized world. These attacks may well constitute threats to the national or economic security of any country that relies on CII for its basic societal functions.

Even though governments throughout the world are more likely to be the targets of foreign nations or terrorist organizations, motives for organized crime groups for launching these types of attacks against a nation's CII are not as clear, or may even appear to be illogical in nature. Organized crime thrives on the government protected economies to sustain the legal branch of their enterprises, and more legal goods and services can be provided for profit during times of peace. This is true also when the population has better disposable income during a thriving economy; they tend to be more willing to spend it when security measures are more relaxed. The other end of the spectrum is that organized crime profits from black markets, which are potentially more lucrative and are poorly regulated geographically, politically, and economically.

Adolescent hackers with no specific foreign backing or agenda have already demonstrated their ability to compromise secure systems of the U.S. government.

> In 1998, authorities detected intrusions into Department of Defense computer systems that appeared to be coming from the Middle East. Due to the timing and the ongoing Iraqi weapons inspections at the time, it was assumed that these attacks were originating from Iraq. A subsequent investigation called *Solar Sunrise,* however, found the perpetrators to be two teenagers from California and another from Israel. The teens were later prosecuted but not found guilty of any international conspiracy, nor any connection to organized crime or terrorist groups. (McQuade, 2006, p. 58)

There have been many additional cybercrimes since that time that have disabled portions of the Internet and affected critical information infrastructure assets in the United States and in other countries.

In the United States the U.S. Department of Homeland Security (DHS) has the primary responsibility for ensuring protection of national critical infrastructure that includes computing and telecommunications systems vital to information infrastructure. The Department carries out this aspect of its mission with several programs that are intended to promote public awareness about the need for information security and to prevent **cybercrime**. DHS coordinates with numerous other federal departments and agencies, as well as with many key entities such as the National Cyber Security Alliance that participates in protecting the nation's critical infrastructure assets that are privately owned or controlled. The Department also has a lead role in updating the National Response Plan that addresses all forms of disaster, major cybercrimes affecting critical infrastructure, and acts of terrorism. The National Infrastructure Coordinating Center (NICC) (formerly known as the National Infrastructure Protection Center) now serves as an extension of the Homeland Security Operations Center (HSOC). The HSOC serves as the primary national level multiagency hub for domestic situational awareness and operational coordination. The HSOC also includes DHS components, such as the National Response Coordination Center (NRCC), the Regional Response Coordination Center (RRCC), and the Interagency Incident Management Group (IIMG).

Suggested Readings: Best, R.A.J. (2001). *Intelligence and law enforcement: Countering transnational threats to the U.S.* Washington, DC: Congressional Research Service;

Best, R.A.J. (2001). *The National Security Agency: Issues for Congress.* Washington, DC: Congressional Research Service; Brake, J.D. (2001). *Terrorism and the military's role in domestic crises management: Background issues for Congress.* Washington, DC: Congressional Research Service; Clinton, W.J. (1996, July 15). *Executive Order 13010—Critical Infrastructure Protection.* Washington, DC: Government Printing Office; Cordesman, A.H., and Cordesman, J.G. (2002). *Cyber-threats, information warfare, and critical infrastructure protection.* Westport, CT: Praeger; Dunn, M., & Wigert, I. (2004). In A. Wenger & J. Metzger (Eds.), *International CIIP handbook: An inventory and analysis of protection policies in fourteen countries,* 2nd ed. Zurich, Switzerland: Swiss Federal Institute of Technology; Ellis, J., Fisher, D., Longstaff, T., Pesante, L., & Pethia, R. (1997, January). *Report to the President's Commission on Critical Infrastructure Protection.* Pittsburgh, PA: CERT Coordination Center, Carnegie Mellon University; Greenemeier, L. (2005). *New cybersecurity center to warn law enforcement of critical infrastructure attacks.* Information Week Web site: http://informationweek.com/story/showArticle.jhtml?articleID=170000319; McLoughlin, G.J. (1996). *The national information infrastructure: The federal role.* Washington, DC: Congressional Research Service; Moteff, J., Copeland, C., & Fischer, J. (2003, January 29). *Critical infrastructures: What makes an infrastructure critical?* Washington DC: Congressional Research Service; National Academy of Engineering. (2003). *Critical information infrastructure protection and the law.* Washington, DC: The National Academies Press; National Commission on Terrorism. (2000). *Countering the threat of international terrorism.* Washington, DC: Government Printing Office; President's Commission on Critical Infrastructure Protection. (1997). Critical foundations: Protecting America's infrastructures. Washington, DC: Government Printing Office.

Samuel C. McQuade, III

INFORMATION SYSTEMS SECURITY ASSOCIATION

The Information Systems Security Association (ISSA)® is a not-for-profit, international organization of information security professionals and practitioners. It provides educational forums, publications, and peer interaction opportunities that enhance the knowledge, skill, and professional growth of its members. With active participation from individuals and chapters all over the world, the ISSA is the largest international, not-for-profit association specifically for security professionals. Over 10,000 members living and working throughout the world include practitioners at all levels of the security field in a broad range of industries, such as communications, education, health care, manufacturing, financial services, and government. The ISSA international board includes experts, many of whom are considered to be among the most influential private security professionals in the United States and elsewhere. These board members represent Dell Computer Corporation, EDS, Forrester Research Inc., Symantec, and Washington Mutual, among several other firms. With an international communications network developed throughout several industrial sectors and levels of government, the ISSA is able to promote prevention of **cybercrime** through enhancement and administration of information technology systems. Indeed, the primary goal of the ISSA is to promote management practices to help ensure the confidentiality, integrity, and availability of data and information systems resources.

The ISSA also facilitates interaction and education to create successful environments for global information systems security and for the professionals involved. Accordingly, ISSA works as follows to: (1) Organize international conferences, local chapter meetings, and seminars that offer educational programs, training, and valuable networking opportunities; (2) provide access to information through the ISSA Web site and an online newsletter and monthly journal; (3) offer support for professional certification and development opportunities for security practitioners, including the **Certified Information Systems Security Professional (CISSP)** credential; (4) create opportunities for members to join committees and boards, which provide significant leadership for the security industry; (5) facilitate discussion among security professionals on key issues, such as the National Strategy to Secure Cyberspace, in order to create a unified voice for security professionals around the world that can influence public opinion, government regulations, the media, and other important audiences.

One example of a local ISSA chapter is based in Rochester, New York. Its members are employed in numerous firms and large corporations, as well as in government and nonprofit organizations. Consultant members of the chapter actively service organizations and communities throughout upstate New York, including Canandaigua, Newark, Batavia, Corning, Elmira, and Ithaca. On behalf of ISSA chapters in the United States and beyond, the Rochester chapter became a founding organizational member of the Cyber Safety and Ethics Initiative, which in 2008 completed the largest computer crime and **victimization** survey inclusive of over 40,000 kindergarten–twelfth grade students, along with hundreds of teachers and parents of 14 separate school districts. The chapter hosts quarterly meetings featuring presentations on security topics given by area professionals and an annual two-day "Security Summit," which attracts participants from throughout the upstate New York region.

Suggested Readings: Booz, A. H. (2005, November 8). *Convergence of enterprise security organizations.* Report commissioned by the American Society of Industrial Security International (ASIS), the Information Systems Security Association (ISSA), and the Information Systems Audit and Control Association (ISACA); Information Systems Security Association Web site: http://www.issa.org/; McMillan, T. (2007) *Change your career: Computer network security as your new profession (Change your career).* New York: Kaplan Publishing; High Technology Crime Investigators Association. (2008). International High Technology Crime Investigators Association (HTCIA) Home Page. Retrieved from http://www.htcia.org/; Stamp, M. (2005), *Information security: Principles and practice.* New York: Wiley-Interscience.

Allen Scalise

INTELLECTUAL PROPERTY

Intellectual property (also known as "IP") consists of documented original *ideas* or legitimate rights to use these for specific purposes as when a book publisher buys the rights to print a novel written by someone or a manufacturing company buys the right to employ one or more patents to make a new product line. There are four basic types of intellectual property including: (1) works of *copyright,* which include original works of authorship such as music, movies, photographs, along with written materials such as books, articles, and Web pages; (2) *trademarks,* composed of "any name, symbol, color, sound, product shape, device or combination of them" (McQuade, 2006,

p. 301) used to distinguish things of value from those of potential competitors (e.g., a company logo such as the familiar McDonald's restaurant "golden arches" symbol); (3) *patents* of inventive or innovative designs for such things as technology devices, drugs, and even plants as well as methods used to create these; and (4) *trade secrets,* which consist of plans and R&D efforts to invent something new.

It has been estimated that worldwide value of intellectual property actually exceeds that of tangible things that have already been produced. This theory is based on the assumption that nearly all things past, present, and future are based on documented or otherwise protected ideas and that similar or new things of the future invariably builds on past knowledge in certain if not significant ways. Because intellectual property is potentially exceedingly valuable and increasingly created and archived in digital form, it is a high priority target for cyber offenders such as some computer *hackers* and individuals hired to carry out **corporate espionage**. Nations as well as individual firms are also concerned about protecting intellectual property because their economic wealth depends on preserving legal rights to profit from new ideas along with inventive products and services. In the United States, intellectual property rights are afforded by *intellectual property laws* and certain state and federal government agencies such as the U.S. Copyright Office and U.S. Patent and Trademark Office.

Suggested Readings: McQuade, S.C. (2006). Cyber laws and regulations (and specifically Intellectual property law, pp. 295–301), in *Understanding and managing cybercrime*. Boston: Pearson Education, Inc.; U.S. Copyright Office Web site: http://www.copyright.gov/; U.S. Patent and Trademark Office Web site: http://www.uspto.gov/.

Samuel C. McQuade, III

INTERNATIONAL CYBERCRIME LAWS AND AGREEMENTS

The essential challenge confronting law enforcement authorities and other regulatory agencies is the transnational aspect of **cybercrime** and its societal, economic, and personal impacts. This challenge is at the heart of efforts to define new enforceable agreements about what constitutes an acceptable and working understanding of jurisdiction. Without agreement on the revision of jurisdictional competence, the process of administering justice in transborder cybercrime (McQuade, 2006) is stymied from the beginning. In what environment will we be able to identify, charge, arrest, and prosecute those defendants who commit cybercrime? Even more challenging is the process of availing ourselves of the legal tools provided through the civil court process. Today if a state authority is able to identify an illegal or fraudulent corporate activity that causes public harm, it can take a proactive stance and use civil process to deter or limit the scope of harm as the underlying lawsuit makes its way through the court system. No such legal parallel exists at this time to combat the harmful effects of international cybercrime. Authorized enforcement services are challenged by loopholes, unclear or ambiguous definitions, and cultural variations on the acceptability of predatory business (legal and illegal) activities.

An additional regulatory challenge is the emergent cyberpsychopathology of those who design and release viruses or other destructive mechanisms against the global family of computer users. These cyberpsychopaths cause significant harm to unseen and unaware users by infecting computers and attempting to manipulate or destroy data stored in various global information systems. They may be motivated by political, economic, corporate, or personal attempts to gain a perceived advantage at the cost of others. What legal tools are currently available to adjudicate these matters? Would the defendant be tried in the country of origination or in the jurisdiction suffering the most harm? How is "nature of harm" defined, given the potential for significant damage in multiple functional dimensions? If an individual cybercriminal has the capacity to impact households, institutions, businesses, corporations, and governments, what would be the impact of an organized and coordinated effort to undermine the cyber sphere? This is a potential catastrophe and will require practical legal remedies and effective vigilance in an informed and alert global cyber sphere.

Given these challenges, how can national interests be safeguarded in the face of differing international interests and priorities? How can individual defendants be identified, arrested, and prosecuted in the current climate of jurisdictional conflict and competition? How can judicial competence be determined in the distribution or redistribution of **malware**? What measure of **victimization** can be utilized to meet the legal requirements of substantial proof across a global environment? Will affected nations delegate legal authority to the home countries of the cyber offenders? Would more than one nation seek to prosecute these activities under terms of collaborative agreements?

We have entered a new level of understanding of how to communicate our ideas, concerns, and interests in an atmosphere largely dominated by self-interest. Clearly, "cyberspace extends beyond the geopolitical boundaries that traditionally define legal jurisdiction" (McQuade, 2006). What are the responsibilities and obligations of governments that extend global protections to its citizenry who operate in multiple levels of cyber transient transactions?

The above questions describe the gaps in our legal methodologies and their practical limitations.

The lack of regulatory and responsive institutions within cyber society starts with the concept of geostatus. The existing definition of geostatus is found in the framework enacted in the Convention on Rights and Duties of States (inter-American), December 26, 1933 (Montevideo Convention), which defines a geopolitical entity as a bona fide country having a permanent population, a defined territory, and a government with the capacity to establish and maintain relations with other national states (Montevideo Convention, Article 1). Because cyber society challenges this definition of geostatus, the first step in its protection is to bring into existence a cogent, coherent, and enforceable international agreement that governs human activities—individual and corporate—in diverse physical locations. To make such an agreement effective, nations will have to endorse the notion of cyber harm and its effects across cultural, political, and economic interests. Recognition of this functional element of international jurisprudence will serve as the transcendent feature that bridges "traditional geopolitical nation-state boundaries" (McQuade, 2006). Effective jurisdiction in the environment of **cyberspace** will work through a combination of national laws and international agreements.

The term *international agreement* includes articles of agreement, pacts, conventions, protocols, and treaties. International agreements define the nature of specific understandings between the endorsing nations within the international community. The context of these agreements have often focused upon issues of commerce, sea and air navigation, human rights, and mutual assistance, including the control of international criminal activities. The effect of these types of agreements is to produce a coherent international legal regime and to implement effective strategies that address international concerns with a strong potential for conflict. This type of interaction by agreement is utilized by nations that recognize that it is in their own best interests to cooperate with other nations. In addition to national interests, there are a variety of international organizations that regulate and enforce international agreements while at the same time representing the interests of its member nation states. One of the first concrete steps in this area can be seen in the form of the Council of Europe's Convention on Cybercrime, which addresses international cooperation concretely in terms of extradition, and more generally by laying out the basic principles and procedures of cybercrime law among the countries that participate in it. These principles and procedures are collectively called Mutual Legal Assistance (MLAT). This elegant tool stands in stark contrast to the lack of understanding regarding international cybercrime and its potentially immense consequences.

One entity committed to the design and enforcement of international agreements is the United Nations, which has facilitated the implementation of approximately 25,000 treaties since its inception in 1945. The United Nations and its subordinate bodies and committees provide the foundation and dialog essential for drafting cooperative international agreements. In this context a treaty is generally approved via ratification of the signatory countries in separate legal and political processes. What emerges from this forum is a methodology for addressing complex issues as they arise between member states. Each nation will subsequently approve or disapprove a treaty, either in part or in whole according to its own national interests (see the UN *Treaty Handbook,* 2006, for a detailed description of the treaty-making process).

For example, in the United States, Article 2 of the Constitution establishes the protocol for initiating and approving treaties with other nations. The president is obligated to send signed treaties to the U.S. Senate, which "advises and consents" whether or not to ratify treaties by a two-thirds consenting vote from its members. Thus, all treaties are regulated through the process of direct representation, not just presidential initiative. Given that legal limitation, the president is still empowered to mandate matters of foreign policy through the use of executive orders. This approach to matters of international agreements can be implemented with or without the approval of the Senate.

Focusing upon the issue of international crime control becomes exponentially more complex as we undertake the task of generating agreements in the face of varying definitions of crime and punishment within the context of an acceptable understanding of what constitutes justice (McQuade, 2006). These structural variations may impede the effective administration of legal processes in the framework of current international cybercrime agreements. Though unintended, these policy and procedural obstacles have the capacity to complicate attempts at effective justice administration and may even erect barriers that obscure international prosecutorial endeavors.

These are the challenges inherent in formulating international agreements on matters involving cybercrime. These challenges will require an adaptive approach to transnational cybercrime activities. Beyond the issues of jurisdiction and enforceability lies an invitation to analyze "what" has already been implemented and understanding "what" works and "what" does not work in today's cyber society. Beyond the "what" question lies a more tantalizing search in the question of "why" strategies do or do not work. And this fractional approach to understanding is closely followed by the most decisive question regarding the "how to" approach for management of international cybercrime.

While each of these aspects may seem so elementary as to lead the reader to wonder why they even deserve mention, their appearance in this article points to the elemental nature of organized international efforts to prevent and control crime in cyber society. Further, they underscore the opportunities available to astute individuals seeking a productive career in an area of scientific inquiry, incorporating individual initiative and a capacity to delimit the known boundaries of soft and hard technology (McQuade, 2006). There will always be individuals and entities seeking illicit gain at the expense of others. Cyber society permits them to do so in an anonymous setting at this time. Future cyber detectives will strip away the mask of anonymity regarding identity and a geographic location and will function in a global enforcement network providing national responsiveness in a climate of international agreement.

Suggested Readings: *Convention on rights and duties of states (inter-American).* (1933, December 26). Available through the Avalon Project, Yale University Law School (http://www.yale.edu/lawweb/avalon/intdip/interam/intam03.htm); United Nations. (2006). *Treaty handbook (revised edition).* New York, USA: United Nations Organization. Office of Legal Affairs. Available at http://untreaty.un.org/English/TreatyHandbook/hbframeset.htm; Murphy, S. (2006). *Principles of international law.* Concise Hornbook Series. St. Paul, MN: Thomson West; Eagan, M.N., & Richards, J.R. (1998). *Transnational criminal organizations, cybercrime, and money laundering: A handbook for law enforcement officers, auditors, and financial investigators,* Kindle ed. Boca Raton, FL: CRC Press; Goodman, S.E., & Soefaer, A.D. (2000). *The transnational dimension of cyber crime and terrorism.* Retrieved from http://www-hoover.stanford.edu ; Blanpain, R. (ed.). (2004). *International encyclopaedia of laws: Cyber law.* International Encyclopaedia of Laws, Lslf ed. Dordrecht: Kluwer Law International; Schwarenegger, C., & Summers, S. (2008). *The emergence of EU criminal law: Cyber crime and the regulation of the information society.* Studies in International & Comparative Criminal Law. Oxford, London, England: Hart Publishing.

Samuel C. McQuade, III and Thomas Schiller

INTERNET

The Internet is a collection of many interconnected information systems that transmit data over wired and wireless telecommunications networks all over the world. Commonly referred to as "computer networks," these information systems may link a wide range and variety of computers and other types of information technology (IT) devices. The Internet allows computer networks to communicate with each other and creates a computer-based global information system. The Internet allows people who use IT devices to have information literally at their fingertips. It has revolutionized communication, government services, education, commerce, manufacturing, transportation, and many forms of recreation.

The basis for routing data over computer networks linked to the Internet is the Generic Top Level *Domain Name System (DNS)*. This system provides for universal resource locator (URL) addresses, for example, Web sites ending with familiar .com, .org, .gov, and .edu addresses, and maps numerical machine identifiers to geographic locations.

This system was developed in 1998 by the U.S. Department of Commerce's National Telecommunication and Information Administration (NTIA) with support from a

California-based corporation, the Internet Corporation for Assigned Names and Numbers (ICANN), and in cooperation with foreign governments and entities including the World Intellectual Property Organization (WIPO). The Generic Top Level Domain Memorandum of Understanding is the formal document that provides an international framework for ongoing administration and enhancement of the DNS. Policies contained in this document were developed in cooperation with the Internet Assigned Numbers Authority (IANA), which manages the DNS to promote Internet stability and robustness for all types of communications purposes. IANA works with advice and oversight of the Internet Policy Oversight Committee whose members represent an international body of key government, industry, academic and not-for-profit organizations. (McQuade, 2006, pp. 54–55)

A common misunderstanding about the Internet is that it is synonymous with the World Wide Web (www). The two are not the same, though they are closely linked. While the Internet, also known simply as the "Net," provides an electrical backbone consisting of wired and satellite telecommunications systems, the World Wide Web uses the Internet to send and retrieve data via a Web browser software application such as Mozilla Firefox or Microsoft Internet Explorer. Early use of the Internet utilized only above-and-below-ground (i.e., buried) telephone lines for the transmission of data. When a telephone line was open, a computer could connect to the Internet via a modem and then begin sending and receiving data. Much of today's Internet still uses telephone lines, but many portions of the Net utilize technologies such as fiber optic cable lines and cellular telephone satellite connections. The use of these technologies has greatly increased the speed and flexibility of sending and receiving via the Internet.

The capability to send a certain amount of data in a specified period of time is known as bandwidth. For example, if a computer connects to the Internet at 54 Mbps, this means that 54 Megabits of data can be sent and/or received every second. A connection speed of 11 Mbps would potentially be relatively slow, especially when downloading pictures, videos, and other data intensive media. The same is true regardless of whether a person is using a desktop or laptop computer, or a portable device such as a PDA or cell phone. It is also important to realize that without adequate security measures in place, wireless devices can broadcast Internet signal connections and data that other computer/device users can access.

The birth of the Internet dates to creation of **ARPANET** in 1969 with the original packet switching network technology invented with the guidance of J.C.R. Licklider and other researchers, scientists, and engineers throughout the United States. This project was funded by the U.S. Department of Defense during the Cold War (1947–1991). In the beginning, ARPANET was primarily designed to transmit data and facilitate communication between government agencies, colleges, and universities. Originally the network connected only the University of California (Los Angeles), University of California (Santa Barbara), Stanford University, and the University of Utah. By 1974 computers from about 50 different organizations were interconnected through ARPANET, and by 1981 there were approximately 213. The Internet as we now think of it emerged around 1983 when the military computer network known as "MILNET" was created to support U.S. government agencies and branches of the armed services. By 1988 there were approximately 20,000 users of the Internet. By the late 1980s commercial firms were using the Internet, and in 1993 the World Wide Web began. By 1995 there were 16 million users of the Internet, and in 2007 there were one billion, three hundred and nineteen million (1,319,000,000) users.

Use of the Internet and World Wide Web continues to increase exponentially. One group aiming to foster this growth with further innovations in online computing and communications is Internet2. This is a nonprofit U.S. consortium founded in 1996 as a nonprofit organization. The purpose of Internet2 is to discover the full potential of Internet technology and further promote collaboration and innovation. It is headed by government officials along with members of the research, development, and education communities. Internet2 (also known as Internet II or simply "I.2.") is designed to help strengthen network infrastructure by sharing the resources and capabilities of its members, and to help develop technologies and next generation production services. The Internet2 network provides the necessary bandwidth required by many campuses involved in experiments, applications, and networking. Internet2 membership consists of 70 corporations, 45 government agencies, and 200 universities. But beginning in 2005 college students in the United States also began using Internet II to pirate music, movies, and software because it afforded a faster and less cluttered network than the Internet, and because evidence of pirating is less likely to be discovered on Internet II.

Suggested Readings: Internet2 Web site: http://internet2.edu/; Bridis, T. (2005). Students face suits over use of "Internet2." *San Diego Union Tribune* Web page: http://www.signonsandiego.com/uniontrib/20050413/news_1b13music.html; Internet History: From ARPANET to Broadband. (2007). *Congressional Digest* [serial online] *86*(2), 35–64. Retrieved March 28, 2007, from Academic Search Elite; Internet; Internet World Stats Web site: http://www.internetworldstats.com/stats.htm; Leiner, B.M., Cerf, V.G., Clark, D.D., Kahn, R.E., Kleinrock, L., Lynch, D., Wolff, S., et al. (n.d.). A brief history of the Internet and related networks. In *Histories of the Internet*. Retrieved November 24, 2007, from Internet Society (ISOC) Web site: http://www.isoc.org/Internet/history/.

Paul R. Soto

INTERPOL

The International Criminal Police Organization, commonly called "Interpol," is headquartered in Lyon, France. Its mission in part is to quickly facilitate investigations of an international nature including cases of **cybercrime**, terrorism, organized crime, international drug smuggling, and trafficking in human beings (e.g., for sex slavery). Interpol was created in 1923 and in 2008 consisted of 186 member countries organized into four administrative regions: Europe, Asia, Africa, and the Americas. Regional branches assist criminal justice and security organizations of nations within regions and throughout the world in the investigation of cybercrime cases that cross national boundaries. Particular forms of cybercrime of interest include **phishing**, money laundering, currency counterfeiting, financial crimes involving electronic payment systems, and **intellectual property** crimes. Interpol maintains a core group of investigators with expertise related to information systems security and who have professional experience with dedicated cybercrime investigation units from throughout the world. These experts periodically communicate with pharmaceutical makers, Internet service providers, software companies, central banks, and other types of organizations to prevent crimes committed over the **Internet** and help protect consumers from various types of cyber fraud. Given the increasing amount of Internet-based crimes, Interpol is becoming increasingly important in worldwide efforts to combat cybercrime.

Suggested Readings: Fooner, M. (1989). *Interpol: Issues in world crime and international justice.* Criminal Justice and Public Safety. New York: Springer; Anderson, M. (1989). *Policing the world: Interpol and the politics of international police co-operation.* New York: Oxford University Press; Interpol. (2008). Interpol Home Page. Retrieved from Interpol Web site: http://www.interpol.int/.

Samuel C. McQuade, III

L

LAWS, CHILDREN ONLINE

We often find ourselves experiencing controversy that frames individual rights against the need to establish and enforce some method of policing the **Internet**. What is all of the fuss about? Should people not be able to decide for themselves what is appropriate to consume online? Where should society draw the line of censorship, either with laws derived over time through the establishment of social norms, as the result of what is considered morale and decent, or today via the ability of parents and schools to install Internet blocking and filtering software on computers? At what point should adolescents, who naturally begin to explore and experience human sexuality and are often formally taught about such things in school, be allowed to experience online content of a sexual nature? In the United States, viewing of pornographic Web sites by persons less than 18 years of age is culturally discouraged and illegal in many states. Creating, distributing, or storing **child pornography** is strictly illegal even for adults. Legal issues having to do with pornography are nothing new and in the United States date back to at least the Victorian era (1837–1901).

In the late nineteenth century U.S. Postmaster General Anthony Comstock was successful in having the federal government criminalize sending obscene materials through the U.S. Postal Service. Until America amended its tariff laws in 1930, several classical literature readings like *Ulysses* authored by James Joyce were banned because they contained content that was considered indecent in that period of American history. Prohibitions against the creation, distribution, or possession of pornography were relaxed throughout America in the years amidst considerable social and political controversy. During the 1960s publishers of sexually liberal magazines such as *Playboy, Hustler,* and *Eros* were indicted for violating federal or state-level indecency laws after publishing what was then considered obscene content. "In 1973 and again in 1987 the U.S. Supreme Court ruled that state and local courts could restrict materials that were patently offensive, appealed to prurient interests, and were without serious literary, artistic, political or scientific value as determined by local community standards" (McQuade, 2006, p. 320). By 1988 with commercialization of the Internet, sexually explicit content became readily available online.

Legal issues pertaining to the need to protect children and youth online are now being considered in the context of a world in which young people are so familiar with the use of information technologies that they may often see their own ability to defeat technological limitations and/or controls as a way to show up their parents and teachers, or a badge of honor and subject to brag about among their friends both offline and online. Indeed, research completed by Rochester Institute of Technology (RIT) investigators in 2008 revealed that among 10,028 middle school students surveyed (in grades 7–9 attending 14 different school districts), 7 percent reported having defeated *Internet filtering/blocking programs* installed by their parents within the previous year. A child who successfully out-wizards such technological restraints can become an online folk hero in the **digital youth culture**. Many youth derive recognition and self-esteem by developing technological skills, perhaps especially when challenged to do so or told they cannot do something online. For example, learning to communicate in **leetspeak** is highly respected by many youth and also used as a type of code to prevent parents from understanding digital messages exchanged between technologically savvy kids.

So why not encourage young people to yield to their urges to explore online content, engage each other via social networking Web sites, and develop technical skills in using computers and IT devices? As most parents and adults know, the answer is very simple: children are curious by nature but their brain quite literally does not fully develop until after they have physically matured, rendering them incapable of consistently making sound decisions especially about risk-taking behaviors. In other words, their curiosity has not been tempered with an appreciation of context or abstraction. Elements of maturity are developed as functional tools that help the emerging young person to define his own experiences in terms of the world around him. Consider why elementary school students in fourth and fifth grades are not taught algebra. For the most part, children at these grade levels are not developmentally capable of understanding certain abstract concepts, especially those having to do with exceedingly complex dimensions of intimate human interactions.

Few adults would advocate for the unsupervised use of high powered motorcycles and handguns among impressionable young people. We can recognize that these technologies require the use of restraint and wisdom. Yet many adults fail to recognize inherent dangers in allowing unrestrained access to the Internet. The issue is complicated by the reality that parents tend to provide more freedom and extend greater **privacy** to their children as they age and demonstrate greater competencies using IT devices. By middle and high school age, youth who are naturally establishing their independence while expanding their social networks and technological savvy may resent what they regard as oversupervision or intrusions into their private matters.

Legal thinking in the United States has long reflected the need to protect children from harms they may inadvertently bring on themselves as well as harm that, sadly, is too often inflicted upon them by other people. As a self-governed people we recognize the importance of personal autonomy, but we affirm this value only to the degree that personal vulnerability is not exploited. The body of law that has emerged to address these vulnerabilities has identified certain activities as harmful in their very nature. Given the inability of children to discern potential for exploitation and **victimization**, the government invokes its authority to act on their behalf. Federal obscenity laws combined with case law rulings now prohibit the following:

(1) Depictions of real people (but not holographic images of human-appearing or cartoon characters) less than eighteen years of age, who are nude or engaged in explicit sexual activity (i.e., child pornography) may not be created, distributed or possessed; (2) obscene material (e.g., adult pornography depicting persons over eighteen years of age in nude, lewd or sexually explicit acts) may be restricted outside of private homes by local or state governments, but such material possessed inside of private homes is not illegal; and (3) creation or distribution of adult pornography even to individuals in their private homes and by any means may be criminalized or regulated by states and municipalities based on local community standards regarding what constitutes obscene material defined as that without serious literary, artistic, political or scientific value. (McQuade, 2006, pp. 321–322)

Specific examples of federal legislation intended to protect children from online pornography include the following (McQuade, 2006, p. 322):

(1) *The Child Internet Protection Act of 2001 (CIPA):* This Act requires schools and libraries in poor and rural school districts receiving federal support through the Federal Communication Commission's (FCC's) E-Rate Internet Funding Program to develop Internet safety policies and procedures, control Internet access, and monitor browsing by children, as well as to use filtering technology to block obscene content. American schools and libraries that do not participate in the E-Rate program are required under FCC regulations to implement and enforce a child oriented Internet safety policy.

(2) *The Prosecutorial Remedies and Other Tools to End the Exploitation of Children Today (PROTECT) Act of 2003:* This law provides

protections for children engaged in online browsing and chat by establishing programs such as AMBER alert and removing the statute of limitations on the abduction or physical/sexual abuse of a child. The Act affords law enforcement officers with easier attaining of wire taps warrants to monitor online activities suspected of involving child pornography or abuse, and affirmatively declares any obscene materials depicting children to be illegal. The Act also increased penalties for persons convicted in cases involving child pornography, cyberstalking or pedophilia, and encourages voluntary reporting of suspected child pornography found online. (McQuade, 2006, p. 322)

However on the basis of *United States v. Michael Williams,* the U.S. Supreme Court struck down portions of the *PROTECT Act* on grounds that it violated the First Amendment to the U.S. Constitution guaranteeing freedom of speech. As a result of the high court's ruling, law enforcement and prosecution agencies as of this writing have yet to resolve the controversial issue of child porn morphing in which images of youth, engaged in sex or displaying genitalia, but who do really exist, are created, distributed, or possessed via computer technology. (See encyclopedia entry titled **Computer Forensics**).

(3) *Controlling the Assault of Non-Solicited Pornography and Marketing (CAN-SPAM) Act of 2003:* This law renders it illegal to distribute email not identified in the subject title as an advertisement. The law also requires emails to include the physical address of the sender and a valid return email address, plus an opt-out feature through which people receiving **spam** to request additional messages not be sent. The law does not apply to spam sent from outside the United States.

In striking a balance between unrestrained personal choice and protecting members of society, people invariably make choices about the laws they collectively allow governments to enact. Nearly everyone in society abhors child pornography, though laws defining its creation, distribution, and possession vary among countries. However, Chapter 1, article 9 of the **Council of Europe Convention on Cybercrime** makes creating, distributing, or possessing child pornography illegal in signatory nations. This treaty also defines child pornography as any depiction of the following: "(a) a minor engaged in sexually explicit conduct; (b) a person appearing to be a minor engaged in sexually explicit conduct; (c) realistic images representing a minor engaged in sexually explicit conduct." Future challenges facing the international community include enforcing provisions of the Convention within nations that have agreed to its terms, and encouraging other nations to participate in the treaty and do likewise. It is also important to recognize that although many American youth who now access the Net receive unwanted pornographic images and solicitations for sexual chat or sexual encounters, large numbers of adolescents are also engaging in "pseudo child pornography" by taking and distributing pictures of themselves without clothes on or by possessing such photos of other persons under 18 years of age.

Suggested Readings: Christiansen, J. (2007). *Internet survival guide: Protecting your family* (1st ed.). Aliso Vieho, CA: Sheltonix; Infoplease.com. *History of censorship in United States.* Retrieved October 23, 2004, from http://www.infoplease.com/ce6/society/A0857225.html; Jenkins, P. (2003). *Beyond tolerance: Child pornography on the Internet.* New York: New York University Press; Sher, J. (2007). *Caught in the Web: Inside the Police hunt to rescue children from online predators.* Cambridge, MA: Da Capo Press.

Samuel C. McQuade, III and Kevin J. McCarthy

LAWS, ILLEGAL USES OF COMPUTERS AND IT DEVICES

Illegal use of information systems and computer technology includes many behaviors deemed harmful to individuals, groups of people, or organizations within society, as well as to society itself (see encyclopedia entry on **Information Assurance** particularly with respect to **critical information infrastructure**). For example, use of computers or other electronic devices to make unauthorized copies of literature, illustrations, architectural designs, photographs, diagrams, music, motion pictures, audiovisual assets, sculpture, and software is illegal. The practice of making copies of such copyright protected works is referred to as "**piracy**" and is usually committed by people in order to avoid paying royalty fees to the author and publisher or distributor of copyrighted materials. Courts in the United States have, with narrowly specified exceptions, ruled to uphold laws that provide protections against **copyright infringement**. Courts have also imposed steep fines and other penalties on cybercrime law violators. In addition to antipirating laws, several other categories of federal legislation have been enacted or amended (i.e., updated) to prohibit various types of **cybercrime** committed via computers or other types of IT devices used with the **Internet** or via other information systems.

Mail, Bank, and Internet Fraud

Before modern computers the federal government created the *Mail Fraud Act of 1948,* making it illegal to send postal mail only with a name or address. This law is actually a precedent to prohibitions against identify theft or using information systems to commit fraud including by way of delivery service such as those now provided by firms such as United Parcel Services (UPS) or Federal Express. "Fraud by wire, radio or television was criminalized by Congress beginning in 1952, and prohibited transmitting an electronic signal such as writings, signs, signals, pictures or sounds in order to obtain money or property under false or fraudulent pretenses" (McQuade, 2006, p. 312). Bank fraud specifically became illegal in 1984 as the use of computers became more common among financial institutions. Bank fraud involves implementing a scheme or creating false documents to get money not belonging to you from a financial institution. This can be attempted by trying to manipulate financial wire transfers, account funds, credit applications, assets held by banks, and securities (e.g., stocks, bonds, or mutual funds). According to 18 United States Code Section 1344, anyone found guilty of federal bank fraud may be fined up to $1,000,000 or imprisoned for up to 30 years, or both.

Computer Device Fraud and Abuse

The *Access Device Fraud Act of 1984* was the first genuine cybercrime law passed by the federal government. It prohibits creating, distributing, possessing, or using counterfeit-making devices to commit fraud. This includes computers, scanners, printers, and a wide variety of portable electronic devices, including cellular phones equipped with digital cameras. This law was strengthened in 1986 by the *Computer Fraud and Abuse Act (CFFA),* which prohibited computer hacking into computers containing classified government information. This included computers belonging to the federal government or financial institutions such as banks. The CFFA was later updated to include all "federal interest computers." This made it a "felony to hack into or exceed permissions within any computer system of the Federal Government, its contractors or grantees. Thus, for example, hacking into a computer system of a university funded by federal research grants is felony under the CFFA as amended, punishable by up to twenty years imprisonment" (McQuade, p. 312).

The CFFA was again amended by the *National Information Infrastructure Protection Act of 1996* to include all "protected computers" connected to the Net and used to support interstate commerce regardless of the Federal Government's possession, ownership or interest in data stored on an information system. In 2000, the Federal Circuit Court for the Western District of Washington ruled in *Shurgard Storage Centers v. Safeguard Self Storage,* that the CFFA applies criminally and civilly to disloyal or departing employees who use computers to reveal trade secrets information to competing firms (i.e., as in cases of insider **corporate espionage**). In 2001 Congress again amended the CFFA extending its reach to include computers located outside the United States involved in "interstate or foreign commerce or communication." More recently the CFFA has also been used by major IT corporations in combination with other laws to sue spammers. Hence, the CFFA remains among the most important, evolving, and expansive federal anti-cybercrime statutes" (McQuade, 2006, p. 313).

The *Violent Crime Control and Law Enforcement Assistance Act of 1994,* among its other provisions, created two new categories of insurance and telemarketing fraud. This was necessary after commercialization of the Internet in 1988 and increasing numbers of users equipped with personal computers who were wreaking online havoc by defrauding people online. The law increased punishments for telemarketing phone fraud that targeted elderly persons and made it illegal to tamper with credit card or financial access devices.

Economic Espionage and Electronic Theft

The *Economic Espionage Act of 1996* made it illegal to steal trade secrets by using any method or any type of technology. Prior to passage of this law, spying on corporations violated civil laws but did not risk imprisonment for offenders. The *Economic Espionage Act* also criminalized knowingly receiving or possessing trade secrets. For this reason, employees of firms who commission or condone spying are violating federal law. Further, corporations as a whole along with individuals can be charged with this crime. Firms claiming they were victims of spying must be able to demonstrate in courts of law an estimated value of items or **intellectual property** (IP) stolen and that reasonable efforts prior to the offense were taken to safeguard the trade secrets alleged to have been stolen.

The *No Electronic Theft Act of 1997* authorized fines and imprisonment of people convicted of intentionally distributing copyrighted works over the Internet. Many individuals guilty of pirating music, movies, or software are now serving prison terms for violating this law. In July 1999, the U.S. Department of Justice (DOJ) took steps to curb piracy and counterfeiting of intellectual property within the United States and in other countries. For example, DOJ prosecuted 17 defendants who were violating copyrights. Twelve of these defendants were allegedly members of the international pirating group called "Pirates with Attitudes."

Identity Theft

The *Identity Theft and Assumption Deterrence Act of 1998* reformed fraud laws pertaining to illegal use of credit cards and financial accounts.

> This law makes it illegal to knowingly: (1) produce or transfer a false ID; (2) possess five or more false IDs with intent to use them for a fraudulent purpose; (3) use a false ID to defraud the United States; (4) produce, transfer, or possess a device used for making false IDs or other documents with the intention of using it to create false identity documents; (5) possess an ID that is or appears to be an identification document of the United States which is stolen or produced without lawful authority knowing that [it was] stolen or produced without such authority; or (6) transfer or use, without lawful authority, a means of identification of another person with the intent to commit, or to aid or abet, any unlawful activity that constitutes a violation of Federal law, or that constitutes a felony under any applicable State or local law.

The *Identity Theft Act* prohibits the creation, transfer, possession, or use of a fake or real ID belonging to someone else

> in order to commit, promote, carry on or facilitate a crime, including acquisition of money, property or credit under an assumed name. The law pertains to any form of unique electronic identification, including biometric identification cards and verification technology. Persons convicted of identity theft or conspiracy to commit identity theft may be imprisoned for up to twenty years, especially if violations involve other serious crimes, such as drug trafficking or crimes of violence. (McQuade, 2006, p. 314)

Copyright Infringement

The *Digital Millennium Copyright Act of 1998* (DMCA)

> is a controversial law that makes it illegal to manufacture, distribute or sell technology that enables circumvention of copyright protections. Some additional highlights and

specific provisions of the Act are that it: (a) prohibits manufacture, sale, or distribution of code-cracking devices used to illegally copy software but cracking copyright protections to conduct encryption research, assess product interoperability, and test computer security systems; (b) provides exemptions from anti-circumvention provisions for nonprofit libraries, archives, and educational institutions under certain circumstances; (c) limits ISPs from copyright infringement liability for simply transmitting data over the Internet; (d) limits liability of nonprofit institutions of higher education when they serve as ISPs regarding copyright infringement by faculty and students; and (e) allows for reproduction of copyrighted materials under the *Fair Use Doctrine*. (McQuade, 2006, p. 314)

Spam

The *Controlling Assault of Non-Solicited Pornography and Marketing (CAN-SPAM) Act of 2003* became law in 2004 as a nationwide means to prevent **spam**. It prohibits sending commercial email without certain information about the sender and a way for users who receive spam to decline receiving more of it (see encyclopedia entry on **Spam** for more details). The Federal Trade Commission (FTC) is required to enforce this law but cannot apply it to spammers located in foreign nations. However, the Act does not prohibit the FTC, State Offices of Attorneys General, and Internet Service Providers from civilly suing spammers on behalf of consumers even if located in foreign countries. This is difficult, and success depends on legal relationships and treaties between the United States and other countries in which spammers are located.

Suggested Readings: Hawke, C.S. (2000). *Computer and Internet use on campus: A legal guide to issues of intellectual property, free speech, and privacy.* San Fancisco, CA: Jossey-Bass; Katz, J.E., & Rice, R.E. (2002). *Social consequences of Internet use: Access, involvement, and interaction.* Cambridge, MA: The MIT Press; Mathewson, J. (2002). Pirates of the new world: How about a new word for illegal software? (Insights). *Computer Use Journal, 20*(2), 8; McQuade, S.C. (2006). Cyber laws and regulations. In *Understanding and managing cybercrime.* Boston: Allyn and Bacon.

Samuel C. McQuade, III

LAWS, INFORMATION SECURITY REQUIREMENTS

The *Computer Security Act of 1987* was enacted after the *Computer Fraud and Abuse Act of 1986* to expand concepts of computer security protection involved. This law required all federal government computer systems containing classified or sensitive information to be supported with a special security plan that preferably included provisions for training of government employees who used the system. The *Computer Security Act* also required that information systems comply with security standards established by the National Bureau of Standards (now the National Institute for Standards and Technology, NIST), and required government agencies to develop their own standards and guidelines for federal computer systems with assistance if needed to be provided by the National Security Agency (NSA).

The *Information Technology Management Reform Act of 1996* requires that federal government agencies establish a chief information officer (CIO). A person holding this position is responsible for ensuring that information systems are properly managed and secure from threats of **cybercrime**. "This law also requires the Secretary of Commerce to create standards and guidelines to improve efficiency of computer operations, security and **privacy** of federal computer systems, and made the Office of Management and Budgeting (OMB) responsible for overall federal IT procurement, investment and security" (McQuade, 2006, p. 322).

The *Health Insurance Portability and Accountability Act of 1996 (HIPAA)* established new health insurance protections for millions of working Americans and their family members, including people who have pre-employment medical conditions that could cause discrimination against them in hiring decisions. For example, if a person changes jobs, HIPAA helps to ensure that their previous health care and health insurance information, including that stored on information systems, is protected against cybercrime and not unlawfully shared in violation of applicable privacy rules.

What HIPPA accomplished in the health services sector, the *Financial Services Modernization Act of 1999,* which is also known as the *Gramm-Leach-Bliley Act* (or simply "GLB"), applied to organizations within financial sectors. GLB

> repeals restrictions on banks of affiliating with securities firms and allows them to create a financial holding company to underwrite insurance and securities services. Provision of such services may be limited, suspended or repealed if the bank fails to pass financial or security audits. The law allows federal regulators to specify...safeguards for banks offering new financial services and removes FDIC assistance to bank subsidiaries and affiliates. (McQuade, 2006, p. 323)

As for **preventing cybercrime**, other provisions of the law require financial institutions to protect financial accounts information of customers who have checking, savings, or credit card accounts.

Financial institutions include banks, securities firms, insurance companies, and other entities providing various types of loans, financial assistance, or money-related services. Any firms qualifying as financial institutions as defined in the *Financial Services Modernization Act* are thus required to have information security policies and procedures in place, as well as technological capabilities to protect privacy of financial data.

The *Public Company Accounting Reform and Investor Protection Act of 2002* (also known as the *Sarbanes-Oxley Act,* named after the Senators who championed the legislation within the U.S. Congress) was enacted because of corporate misconduct involving abuse of information systems and securities fraud by officials within the Enron Corporation. This company specialized in brokering business deals and mergers of energy companies. It was famous during the 1990s for its technological innovation, which prompted many employees and other people to invest in the corporation. However, it was discovered that senior managers in the firm had falsely reported profits to drive stock prices up while using unconventional financial accounting methods to hide the truth from investors about looming debt owed by Enron. While many managers sold their interests in the company at inflated stock prices, most employees and other investors collectively lost over $1 billion dollars. It is important to understand that company officials got away with their crimes for a long time by abusing computer systems that contained financial data, along with the **Internet**, to report its false profits and conceal debt. The scandal resulted in Enron becoming one of the worst bankrupt cases in history and in the establishment of the Enron Fraud InfoCenter on the Internet. The law that resulted from the scandal strengthened regulatory authority of the Securities and Exchange Commission (SEC) to help oversee creation of public company accounting oversight boards, auditor independence, corporate responsibility, enhanced financial disclosures, analyst conflicts of interest, commission resources and authority, studies and reports, corporate and criminal fraud accountability, white collar crime penalty enhancements, corporate tax returns, and corporate fraud and accountability. (McQuade, 2006, p. 323)

Suggested Readings: Shostack, A., & Stewart, A. (2008). *The new school of information security.* Indianapolis, IN: Addison-Wesley Professional; Stamp, M. (2005). *Information security: Principles and practice.* New York: Wiley-Interscience; Whitman, M., & Mattford, H.J. (2007). *Management of information security* (2nd ed.). Florence, KY: Course Technology; Whitman, M., & Mattford, H.J. (2007). *Principles of information security* (3rd ed.). Florence, KY: Course Technology.

Samuel C. McQuade, III

LAWS, PRIVACY PROTECTIONS

What are our notions of personal privacy? How did we acquire a conceptual framework that allows us to actualize this concern into a meaningful construct. Is this concept shared by all humans, and how has it extended itself to the **Internet** environment that offers a cloak of transparent anonymity and a mystique of interpersonal detachment? Beware of the smoke and mirrors associated with **privacy** expectations and Internet-based transactions, no matter if they are commerce-based or recreational in nature. Understanding that there is a full spectrum of data-based information traps will help to lessen our personal anxieties and increase our level of computer sophistication as we encounter these experiences. We emerge each day to battle the great data extractor, which obtains information from online purchases or shopping, the use of credit online and offline, and messaging and emailing our friends and families. Even the advertising materials we receive and the hopeful calls from telemarketers are data-driven attempts to recognize our preferences and exploit our history of choices.

A simple activity like walking to my car in the evening after work may be videotaped and stored for later review. Is it any wonder that the progression of this technological advancement is the automated traffic violation system that utilizes video photography, governmental and informational databases, and even the U.S. Postal Service to acknowledge and correct my personal driving sins. No longer can one expect to speed and then hide in the privacy of personal anonymity. Technology seems to be making daily gains in unmasking these proclivities. Parking ticket recipients, a group that has formerly been occupied by scofflaws, have experienced a dramatic shift in enforcement techniques, given that local law officers can now use personal technology to identify the history of parking violations and unpaid fines and then adapt a response strategy, which may include towing the violator's car or affixing a "boot" to the tire until the owner takes care of his outstanding parking tickets. Oh for the good old days of being able to throw away a parking violation because one was driving a car with out-of-state plates and was thus protected by the shield of personal anonymity.

These life strategies have gone the way of the typewriter and carbon paper. Computer-based accountability procedures can be relentless in the pursuit of resolution and closure. Thus, we live in a world that embraces the fantasy of personal privacy while the reality of enhanced computer transparency continues to intrude upon our expectations. What a cognitive conundrum we have wrought. Movement toward embracing personal privacy produces the outraged cry that we are living in an IT stone age, while embracing the technological and informational leaps computers yield may result in our being data-naked and vulnerable to influences that seek to identify our personality characteristics in terms of potential for manipulation. This very dilemma goes to the heart of using legislative processes to establish a body of law governing Internet-based activities. At first glance such an agenda is likely to trigger a hue and cry from those concerned with freedom of choice and freedom of action, but a brief analysis of the potential pitfalls underscores the need for a legal framework to constructively pursue safe Internet access.

The potential for privacy infringement exists in nearly every aspect of our daily activities. Consider that an innocuous cell phone call can be used to place you geographically at a precise time and location. How will these data be used in determining your insurance rates, your attractiveness in potential hiring decisions, and/or your accountability to those utilizing this information to make business decisions about your risk or workplace effectiveness? It is common at this point to accept that employers implement keystroke-driven tracking systems to minimize inappropriate use of corporate IT resources. The other aspect of these efforts is to protect corporate assets from acts of intentional or unintentional harm. The insurance carrier has determined that your credit score and claim history should be a basic component in establishing their level of risk exposure and a practical assist in the determination of rates and available coverage. It becomes easy to feel powerless in an environment that seems to be dominated by computer technology. The sense of being overwhelmed can result from an experience working your way through multiple telephone menu selections, to the perfunctory (nonunderstanding) manner offered by some "customer service" representatives.

The most disrupting aspect of enduring this type of experience is the sense of aloneness resulting from an experience that offers no practical alternative. In many cases we just give up and yield our rights to the data ogre who threatens to ding our credit records with factually biased information. Or we just accept that "they" are the dominant partner in this transaction, so we wearily accept "their" rejection of our position. Winning the fight by wearing us down is still an effective business strategy and results in the annual displacement of monetary resources extending into the millions of dollars. Either way our privacy expectations vary contingent upon our exposure to environments that gather significant databases that are then used to peruse policies and/or predatory practices. Given these practicalities, laws and legal precedent has been established to equalize the David and Goliath experience and empower the consumer. Even these alternatives can carry the risk of being labeled a crank or a nuisance by virtue of the pursuit of resolution. No IT transaction is totally without some level of personal exposure.

Given these limitations within the current Internet environment, the government has sought to address the potential for disparity through identifying appropriate language that operationalizes a conceptual understanding upon which adequate legal standards can be developed. In terms of privacy legislation the government has produced the following sampling of laws that inform and guide the stream of enterprise emerging from computer-based activities and some of the concerns about their implications for national security.

Included within the provisions of these laws are some defining strategies that potentially impact every computer user in the United States:

The USA PATRIOT Act (2001)
The Homeland Security Appropriations Act (2005)
The CAN-SPAM Act (2003)
The Access Device Fraud and Computer Fraud Abuse Act (1984)
The Violent Crime Control and Law Enforcement Assistance Act (1994)
The Economic Espionage Act (1996)
The No Electronic Theft Act (1997)
The Identity Theft and Assumption Deterrence Act (1998)
The Digital Millennium Copyright Act (1988)
The Foreign Intelligence Surveillance Act (1978)
The Electronic Communication Privacy Act (1986)

The volume of critical legislation is only representative of current efforts to provide a uniform methodology either through the implementation of new laws and through a range of regulatory processes that function under the auspices of enabling federal legislation. In this catchment area of mandated control the individual is likely to find himself isolated and perhaps even suspect when attempting to maintain some sense of personal privacy amid the demands for universal transparency. Indeed, emotional integrity may demand a retreat to less threatening interactions, though they are not likely to be received with any depth of understanding or commiseration. Empathy is likely to be in short supply given the participant threats to our way of life. As we seek to redefine our roles in the global cybersociety, we are likely to be challenged on a personal and professional level to establish a new sense of worth given the multicultural effects of enhanced Internet communications. For some this will be an arduous experience invoking disgruntled and discomforted responses.

For those currently emerging into the realm of cybersociety, they are likely to have addressed this challenge at a personal level and are likely to wonder what all the fuss is about. Perhaps this leads us to the need to define an educational modality that can facilitate the cognitive transitions required by our technological advances. Within this context exists an opportunity to define and refine effective strategies for advancing interpersonal communications via the use of computer technology and IT applications. No longer do we have to frame our goals in terms of competitiveness, but perhaps the new currency of communication will embrace our willingness to be cooperative even if it hurts our "private selves" to stretch and accommodate new notions of privacy. When we have daily opportunities to peer into the homes of those who live halfway around the world, we can no longer hide behind a mask of disinterest or unconcern. Among the most challenging constructs that will emerge in the future are the redefinitions of the words "neighbor and community." Perhaps you will accept the premise set forth herein and find the strength to be disquieted for a while, even as you are in pursuit of life in the new world. Remember that Christopher Columbus's sailors were stretched pretty thin, both emotionally and physically, by the challenges that they experienced traveling upon unknown and uncharted seas. Are you up for the journey? You have just received your personal invitation!

Suggested Readings: Bennett, C.J. (1992). *Regulating privacy: Data protection and public policy in Europe and the United States.* Ithaca, NY: Cornell University Press; Boyd, C. (1998). *Information security and privacy: Proceedings of the Third Australasian Conference, ACISP'98, Brisbane, Australia, July 13–15, 1998.* Lecture Notes in

Computer Science. New York: Springer Publishing; Caloyannides, M.A. (2004). *Privacy protection and computer forensics* (2nd ed.). Norwood, MA: Artech House Publishers.

Kevin J. McCarthy and Samuel C. McQuade, III

LAWS THAT FACILITATE OR LIMIT CYBERCRIME INVESTIGATIONS

Several important laws designed to facilitate or limit cybercrime investigations began to be passed in the early 1960s as early computer systems were integrated into telecommunications switching technology that facilitated routing of telephone calls within the United States and internationally. This is when it was determined that organized crime organizations were increasingly using landline telephone ("wire") systems to carry out bank fraud and many other types of traditional crime long before *computer-related crime* and **cybercrime** were labeled as such. Federal laws subsequently enacted to facilitate or limit cybercrime investigation serve one or more of the following four primary purposes: (1) Protecting individual **privacy** while providing access to information held by the federal government, (2) securing information systems within the federal government, (3) ensuring national **critical information infrastructure** along with its availability and reliability, or (4) specifying illegal behaviors that involve using the **Internet**, information systems, or other electronic information technology (IT) devices.

The first major federal law created to crack down on organized crime was the *Racketeer Influenced and Corrupt Organizations Act* (RICO, pronounced "Reeko") of 1961. Since that year RICO has been applied by prosecutors to evaluate illegal activities of "junior associates involved in criminal organizations and leaders of criminal organizations without direct evidence of their being involved in any specific crimes." The implication is that cybercrimes that involve Internet communications between such individuals can be prosecuted under the RICO statute in addition to other specific violations of law. If a person is convicted of being involved in a criminal organization, his prison sentences can be dramatically increased. Certain hacker and pirating groups have been indicted for "racketeering," which essentially means a RICO violation.

RICO has aided in conceiving and enacting other laws that facilitate or limit cybercrime investigations, including the *Foreign Intelligence Surveillance Act (FISA) of 1978,* the *Wire and Electronic Communication Interception and Interception of Oral Communication Act* (also known as the *Federal Wiretap Act*), and the *Electronic Communications Act of 1986.* All these laws pertain in some way to procedures federal agencies must fulfill to secure a search warrant to conduct a wiretap (i.e., secretly listening to telephone or cellular phone conversations).

Later legislative developments produced the *Communications Assistance for Law Enforcement Act of 1994,* which required telecommunications carriers to actively assist in electronic surveillance initiated by law enforcement authorities. In the aftermath of the September 11, 2001, terrorists attacks, the U.S. government responded with the passage of the *USA PATRIOT Act,* which greatly expanded existing authority to conduct electronic counterterrorism monitoring and surveillance by law enforcement and intelligence gathering agencies. This act vastly expanded the ability of law enforcement officers to collect varied amounts and types of information through the use of phone taps, pen registers, and the utilization of trace technology to telecommunications including the routing and addressing of information. These provisions were secured under 18 USC Section 3121 (c). While constitutional guarantees have ensured the individual of the right against self-incrimination, provisions of the *PATRIOT Act* made it a crime to fail to cooperate with the appropriate authorities in investigations defined as matters involving national security. The law also prohibited business owners from consulting legal counsel in responding to these investigative demands. Later judicial action by the Federal Appeals Court nullified this aspect of the *PATRIOT Act* by ruling that it violated provisions of the First Amendment. The court's nullification restored the right to counsel while undergoing investigative proceedings.

In 2002 the *Homeland Security Act* authorized creation of the U.S. Department of Homeland Security, which today coordinates numerous federal law enforcement agencies to protect critical information infrastructure and national borders. The *Cyber Security Enhancement Act of 2002* increased potential prison sentences and fines for computer hackers whether they were first time offenders or repeat offenders. Other applications included the expansion of police powers to "conduct real-time Internet and telephone taps in cases of suspected threats to national security" (McQuade, 2006, p. 319). Expanded legislative authority was sought by the U.S. Department of Justice in 2003 in the form of the *Domestic Security Enhancement Act* (also known as "PATRIOT Act II" by people who worried about the potential of federal law enforcement abusing **government intelligence gathering**, surveillance, and monitoring responsibilities). Given its threatened draconian powers, it was eventually defeated through public protest. However, it was followed by the proposed *Vital Interdiction of Criminal Terrorist Organization Act,* which sought to establish a link between drugs and terrorism and thereby create a new category of terrorism labeled "narco-terrorism." This law attempted to address the transnational drug trafficking facilitated with Internet communications such as encrypted email, text messaging, and so forth. The *National Security Intelligence Reform Act of 2004* authorized the creation of a position entitled Director of National Intelligence (DNI), who had the mandated responsibility for coordination of intelligence gathering activities, analysis, and sharing of all counterterrorism information among federal, state, and local law enforcement authorities.

Suggested Readings: Casey, E. (2004). *Digital evidence and computer crime* (2nd ed.). Burlington, MA: Academic Press; Lessig, L. (2000). *Code and other laws of cyberspace.* New York: Basic Books; Reyes, A., Brittson, R., O'Shea, K., & Steel, J. (2007). *Cyber crime investigations: Bridging the gaps between security professionals, law enforcement, and prosecutors.* Rockland, MA: Syngress Publishing; Shinder, D.L., & Tittel, E. (2002). *Scene of the cybercrime: computer forensics handbook.* Rockland, MA: Syngress Publishing.

Samuel C. McQuade, III

LEETSPEAK

Leetspeak (written online as l337) is a text-based communication method primarily used on the **Internet** that uses combinations of ASCII characters to replace traditional Western-style Latin letters. The term is derived from the word "elite" reduced to "Leet" (written online as l33t) to initiate this specialized form of symbolic writing. There are several different dialects of Leet found on various Internet forums and message boards, but the basic syntax remains the same, allowing the intended meaning of words and phrases to be understood by users who communicate in this manner. Originally the word "Leet" was used as an adjective to describe the behavior or accomplishment of people who practiced this form of communication. In effect, they were considered elite Internet users because they could communicate online using symbolic syntax. Being able to communicate in Leetspeak is a badge of honor similar to the online status of someone who possesses excellent electronic gaming or computer hacking abilities. In other words, the ability to communicate in Leet is a technical skill that merits status depending on one's creative and expressive abilities using ASCII characters.

Historians of Leetspeak allege that it originated within bulletin board systems (BBS) in the mid-1980s. Having elite status on a BBS allowed a user to access file folders, games, and special chat rooms, which often included archives of pirated software, pornography, or text documents documenting topics such as how to construct explosives and manufacture illicit drugs. It is also thought that Leetspeak was developed to defeat text filters created by BBS or Internet Relay Chat (IRC) system operators of message boards to prevent discussion of forbidden topics such as cracking and **hacking**. Originally reserved for use by hackers, crackers, and eventually the more recent generation of so-called "script kiddies," Leet has entered the mainstream of MMORPGs and other forms of online gaming. It is often used to mock "newbies" (written online as n00bs, nub, or b00ns), a new player or someone inexperienced to a game or Web site community. More obscure forms of Leet involve the use of symbols exclusively, and continue to be used for its original purpose of encrypted communication (Mitchell, 2006).

Examples of Leet can be found in common chat communications. One of the simplest and most often used is LOL, meaning "laugh out loud" or "lots of laughs." This short series of letters indicates that the author is amused by something. There are similar acronyms and abbreviations that incorporate forms of LOL such as ROFL (rolling on the floor laughing), which is sometimes expanded into ROFLMAO (rolling on the floor laughing my ass off), or sometimes as LMAO (laughing my ass off) to signify a more humorous or sarcastic response to a statement or event. An overexclamation for emphasis on a topic, whether as surprise or outrage is OMG! (oh my God!). Other examples utilized for encryption of communications include the term "**warez**," which refers to pirated software. "Hax" and "crax" indicate software tools that were scripted for hacking or cracking legitimate software and Web sites. The term "sploitz" is often used to denote known exploits in an information system or in games.

With the expansion of Internet use in the early to mid-1990s, Leetspeak has become part of Internet culture. It is accepted slang by and among certain Internet users, especially gamers and forum members. As indicated above, Leet may also be utilized as a substitution cipher for personal communications or those related to illicit activities. Leetspeak styles of expression vary significantly among Internet users. Like slang terms used in other languages, Leet consists of odd expressions that may have particular meaning only among certain groups of Internet users. Loose grammar, just like loose spelling, encodes some level of emphasis, ironic or otherwise. A reader must rely more on intuitive parsing of Leet to determine the meaning of a sentence rather than the actual sentence structure.

In particular, speakers of Leet are fond of turning verbs into nouns and back again as forms of emphasis, e.g., "Austin rocks" is weaker than "Austin roxxorz," which is weaker than "Au5t1N is t3h r0xx0rz." Note that this latter Leet grammar is weaker still than something like "0MFG D00D /\Ü571N 15 T3H J00083Я 1337 Я0XX0ЯZ." In essence, all Leet expressions mean "Austin rocks." (Rome, 2001)

However, people unfamiliar or relatively less skilled in writing, reading, or understanding Leetspeak can easily misunderstand what is actually being communicated. This is analogous to visiting a region of your country or the world where people speak in an accent that you are not used to hearing, use unusual expressions that you do not know the meaning of, or speak a completely foreign language. Eventually, if you are exposed to it enough, you may pick up on the vernacular or start using it yourself.

In Leetspeak added words and misspellings often increase the writer's enjoyment as he develops his own expressive style and abilities. Leet, as in other hacker slang, also employs analogy in the construction of new words. For example, if "haxored" is the past tense of the verb "to hack" (hack → haxor → haxored), then "winzored" would be easily understood to be the past tense conjugation of "to win," even if the reader had not seen that particular word before (Rome, 2006). In order to overcome filtering and blocking software, curious adolescents will sometimes search for pornographic Web sites by using the Leet word "pr0n," which is a discrete and deliberate misspelling of "porn." This technique is also used to circumvent language and content filters on message boards as well as in chat programs, which would normally consider it **spam**. Another method would be to spell "pr0n" backwards so it appears as "n0rp" to obscure the meaning of the word. Yet the term is so common that entering it into a search engine will typically result in links to pornographic Web sites.

In conclusion, Leetspeak is a common though varied form of written communication historically used by skilled Internet users to express themselves in creative ways and achieve cultural status. The emergence and ongoing development of Leet is at least partially grounded in illicit if not cybercrime-related activities such as pirating, computer hacking, and cracking passwords. Millions of computer users, especially young people, use Leetspeak to communicate with each other. Several authors and a few researchers have written about the issue, and the subject is of increasing interest to scholars, to parents who may be concerned about what and with whom their children are communicating online, and to law enforcement officers who know that Leet can be a form of coded messages used in criminal activities.

Suggested Readings: Computer Hope. (2008). *Computer Hope help dictionary and advice.* Computer Hope Web site: http://www.computerhope.com/jargon/game.htm; H2g2. (2002). An explanation of l33t speak. BBC's *Hitchhikers Guide to the Galaxy: The Unconventional Guide to the Internet.* British Broadcasting Company Web site: http://www.bbc.co.uk/dna/h2g2/A787917; Mitchell, A. (2006, December 6). A Leet Primer. *Technology News.* ECT News Network, Inc. TechNewWorld Web site: http://www.technewsworld.com/story/47607.html?welcome=1209958401; Rome, J.A. (2001, December 18). *Relax we understand j00.* Sigma Tau Delta, The International English Honor Society, Case Western Reserve University, Beta Beta Chapter, Sigma Tau Delta Web site: http://www.case.edu/orgs/sigmataudelta/submissions/rome-relaxweunderstand.htm; Sterling, B. (1994). *The hacker crackdown: Law and disorder on the electronic frontier.* New York: Bantam Spectra Books.

Neel Sampat

M

MALWARE

Malware is a general term for a variety of harmful software specifically designed to attack computer systems, networks, or data. The term was derived by combining the words "malicious" and "software," and it is used to describe computer viruses, **Internet** worms, keystroke logging programs, rootkits, spyware, botnets, and the like. Malware can be the cause or the source of other types of attacks, such as **denial of service attacks**, **phishing**, and **spam**. While there are many different kinds of malware, all malware has one thing in common: its existence is *unwanted, unknown, or hostile* to the end user or owner of the computer system running it. A program that collects data on a personal computer can therefore be considered malware—but only if its existence is unwanted, unknown, or hostile. So while a spyware program that collects information on Internet activity without the knowledge or consent of the computer's owner *would* be considered malware, the "History" folder in the Windows operating system would not. And while keystroke loggers—programs that collect and store all of the keystrokes made on a computer—are commonly considered malware, many legal and legitimate software programs that offer parents the ability to monitor their children's computer habits would not be considered malware, even though they too may log and store keystrokes.

Most forms of malware become installed on computer systems after an inadvertent action of an unsuspecting computer user. Viruses, spyware, and rootkits can compromise a computer through an infected email or an email attachment being opened, or by an unsuspecting user visiting a phony Web site cleverly disguised as a legitimate site. Worms are the one type of malware that can propagate itself through flaws or holes in a computer's operating system, i.e., *without* any end user action at all. Most people use the term "virus" instead of "malware," and while viruses are a specific type of malware, not all instances of malware are viruses. Established and commonly known forms of malware now include the following:

Worms: Worms are a specific form of malware that propagates through a network of computers, usually by exploiting flaws in computer operating systems. As previously mentioned, worms are a unique form of malware in that they can pass through computer systems without any action by an end user. Many worms attempt to exploit flaws in the Microsoft Windows operating system because it is used on so many personal computers; however, worms can and have been developed to exploit weaknesses in other operating systems such as Linux, Unix, and Macintosh systems.

Viruses: Viruses are different from worms in that they require some user action to spread from one system to another. Viruses are most commonly spread through emails and email attachments, although they can be spread by other means. Many viruses operate by infecting one computer, then reading a user's address book to make subsequent emails look like they came from them. This tactic fools people into believing the malicious email came from a friend or acquaintance. On May 4, 2000, the "ILoveYou" virus was spread across the world in a matter of hours by emails with an irresistible "I Love You" in the subject line.

Rootkits: Rootkits attempt to take control of a computer system by attaching themselves to a portion of the operating system and then concealing their existence. Many rootkits modify a system's operating system in such a way that they often return when a system is rebooted, even after they appear to be removed. Rootkits are a particularly troublesome form of malware because they are so difficult to detect and clean.

Keystroke loggers: Keystroke loggers do what their name implies—they log or save the keystrokes made by a computer user in a file that can be accessed at a later time. Keystroke loggers can be used to steal credit card numbers, passwords, and personal information such as Social Security numbers.

Spyware: Spyware is used to collect information on the computer of an unsuspecting user for a variety of purposes. Some spyware will collect information on the Web sites a person visits; others will collect personal information such as Social Security numbers, passwords, etc. Excessive spyware can seriously degrade the performance of a computer by using up memory, CPU cycles, and other resources.

Adware: Adware or advertising-supported software is any software package that automatically plays, displays, or downloads advertising material to a computer after the software is installed on it or while the application is being used. It is separate from spyware in that it collects Web browsing history and then sends the data to a host to file browsing habits of an Internet user. More often adware is responsible for target pop-up ads that are geared towards the most popular interests that the browser user enters.

Botnets: A botnet is a network of infected computers that can communicate with each other to coordinate attacks or other actions. Many computers infected by bots do not appear to be infected at all because these bots often remain dormant for months or years before being activated. Computers infected with dormant bots are often called "zombies" because they can be used to attack other systems or networks without the computer owner even knowing they exist. Botnet networks can be used to send spam, propagate spyware, or launch denial of service attacks.

While malware is rampant on the Internet and cannot be completely prevented (short of disconnecting a computer from any network whatsoever, including the

Internet), some common steps can be taken to reduce the likelihood and impact of malware infections: First, keep operating systems patched and up-to-date. All operating system vendors commonly release security updates or patches to fix flaws and plug holes found in the system. Install a firewall. A firewall is either software or a device that controls what other systems can connect to a computer. While firewalls cannot completely prevent malware, computers without them are easier to find and infect. Run antivirus and antispyware software. Antivirus and antispyware software is special-use software that can find, detect, and clean malware from many systems.

Suggested Readings: Christodorescu, M., Jha, S., Maughan, D., Song, D., & Wang, C. (eds.). (2006). *Malware detection.* Advances in Information Security. New York: Springer Publishing; Harley, D., Bechtel, K., Blanchard, M., & Diemer, H. K. (2007). *AVIEN malware defense guide for the enterprise.* Rockland, MA: Syngress Publishing; Kleinbard, D., and Richtmyer, R. (2000, May 5). *The I love you virus sweeps the US.* Money.CNN.com. Retrieved from http://money.cnn.com/2000/05/05/technology/loveyou/; McMillan, M. (2006, May 23). Settlement ends the Sony Rootkit Case. *PC World* Web site: http://www.pcworld.com/article/id,125838-page,1/article.html; McQuade, S.C. (2006). *Understanding and managing cybercrime.* Boston: Allyn & Bacon; Skoudis, E., and Zletser, L. (2003). *Malware: Fighting malicious code.* The Radia Perlman Series in Computer Networking and Security. Upper Saddle River, NJ: Pearson-Prentice Hall.

Dave Pecora

MALWARE INCIDENTS

Malware incidents occur when malicious software, such as viruses, worms, spyware, or adware, is developed and spread between computers. These forms of attack have represented a threat to data and computers since the early 1980s, ranging from benign pranks to fraudulent criminal activities with the potential to harm the computers of individual users and organizations, as well as **critical information infrastructure**. Many significant malware attacks have occurred since the year 2000, especially as worms targeted the rapidly expanding network of inexperienced and unsecured **Internet** users. While exact damages are difficult to calculate, malware incidents have cost individuals and organizations throughout the world billions of dollars. Described below in historical order of occurrence are some of the most significant, well publicized, and highly damaging malware incidents.

The *Morris Worm,* developed and released by Robert T. Morris Jr., was the first Internet worm to gain major public attention. Launched onto the Internet on November 2, 1988, the worm infected approximately 6,000 DEC VAX servers connected to the Internet. At the time, this represented approximately 10 percent of the Internet, which was primarily composed of academic research computers. Estimates placed financial damages between $100,000 and $10 million. The Morris Worm, while not originally intended to cause damage, caused significant slowdown on each infected computer due to a programming flaw. Morris was later convicted under the newly legislated *1986 Computer Fraud and Abuse Act.*

On March 26, 1999, New Jersey resident David Smith released the *Melissa Worm* by using a stolen America Online account to post a message promising access to pornographic Web sites on the Alt.sex newsgroup. The worm infected vulnerable Windows 95, Windows 98, and Windows NT users. It also used email address books to send itself to other computers. The worm caused more than $80 million in damages. Smith was prosecuted and later pled guilty to violating state and federal computer crime laws.

Released on May 4, 2000, by a programming student in the Philippines, the *ILOVEYOU Worm* caused significant damage to computers running Microsoft Windows. Similar to Melissa, the worm spread extremely quickly through email messages containing a file attachment named, LOVE-LETTER-FOR-YOU.TXT.VBS. Once opened by a computer user, the worm attempted to email itself to everyone in the user's address book. The worm would then replace all picture, music, and video files with copies of itself. Affecting government systems and major corporations such as American Telephone and Telegraph (AT&T), Trans World Airlines (TWA), and Ford Motor Corporation, the estimated cost of damages caused by ILOVEYOU was placed between $100 million to over $10 billion.

Code Red was another worm originally released onto the Internet on July 13, 2001. It was designed to exploit a flaw in Microsoft IIS (Web page) servers, defacing Web sites, and performing a **denial of service (DOS) attack** on the Whitehouse.gov Web site as it spread from server to server. Because it required no user interaction to infect a computer, Code Red spread incredibly quickly, infecting more than 250,000 Web servers within a nine-hour period. This speed of "infection" not only contributed to the amount of damage done to web servers, but also served as an unintentional DOS attack as thousands of computers scanned the Internet for vulnerable hosts. A subsequent and similar worm, *Code Red II,* secretly installed a backdoor on infected servers, providing administrative access to those who knew how to use the software.

Upon its release onto the Internet on January 25, 2003, *Slammer* infected 90 percent of the computers vulnerable to its attack method within ten minutes. Demonstrating the need for increased awareness of patching and updating, Slammer exploited a flaw for which security patches were already available. Slammer drew public attention due to its interruption of critical information systems, including airport computers, automatic teller machines (ATMs), and information systems relied upon by a nuclear power plant. While the worm was not designed to cause any significant damage to computer systems, the financial impact was estimated between $1.05 billion and $1.25 billion.

The *Storm Worm* made its appearance in early 2007, infecting computers once again through an email attachment with the subject "230 dead as storm batters Europe." As an example of the increasing trend towards **cybercrime** for criminal profit, the malicious effects of the Storm Worm were not immediately apparent to computer users. Unlike previous malware threats, the Storm Worm does little to impact the host computer, making detection very difficult. Instead, this **malware** remains on a computer quietly installing a botnet client that allows the host computer to be controlled from a different location. Hundreds, thousands, and even millions of computers may conceivably be remotely controlled in this way. This malware also represents a constantly shifting target for antivirus corporations because the computer code that allows the worm to spread changes automatically every 30 minutes. Additionally, the control system for the Storm Worm botnet is fully distributed, making the network of infected machines impossible to shut down. Estimates place the number of infected computers anywhere between 1 million and 50 million, though the full extent of the Storm Worm may never be known. As of this writing, neither the programmers responsible for the worm nor those in control of the infected network have been identified.

Suggested Readings: U.S. Department of Justice. (2002, May 1). Creator of Melissa computer virus sentenced to 20 months in federal prison [Press Release]. Retrieved October 4, 2007, from http://www.cybercrime.gov/melissaSent.htm; Schneier, B. (2007, October 4). *The Storm Worm.* Retrieved October 12, 2007, from http://www.schneier.com/blog/archives/2007/10/the_storm_worm.html; U.S. Government Accountability Office. (1989). *Computer security: Virus highlights need for improved Internet management* (GAO/IMTEC-89-57). Washington, DC: John Carter; U.S. Government Accountability Office. (2000). *Critical infrastructure protection: "ILOVEYOU" computer virus highlights need for improved alert and coordination capabilities* (GAO/AIMD-00-181). Washington, DC: Jack L. Brock Jr.; U.S. Government Accountability Office. (2001). *Information Security: Code red, code red ii, and sircam attacks highlight need for proactive measures* (GAO-01-1073T). Washington, DC: Jack L. Brock Jr.; U.S. Government Accountability Office. (2006). *Internet infrastructure: DHS faces challenges in developing a joint public/private recovery plan* (GAO-06-072). Washington, DC: Keith A. Rhodes.

Nathan Fisk

MEETING AND FALLING IN LOVE ONLINE—BE CAREFUL!

People often desire to meet someone special to hang out with, become friends with, or even share their lives with for a time if not permanently as in marriage or in civil unions. For most of us, yearning for a significant other begins early in our dating years, which can last from only a few to many years in duration. Unfortunately, there are millions of people who are not able to find someone compatible with themselves through their daily activities. Oftentimes professional or personal circumstances interfere with meeting new people and expanding our social networks of friends. This is especially true when it comes to beginning long-term meaningful relations with someone who can share our dreams, hopes, and goals.

The **Internet** and World Wide Web now provide millions of people with new opportunities to meet and socialize online. People once socially isolated may turn to computers, *social networking* Web sites, and *computer-based dating services* to fulfill their dating needs. These sites and services can offer a method for initial encounters to meet interesting people and establish relationships that can lead to meaningful and even lifelong commitments. There are many people who are now involved in a long-term relationship that began online. However, there are risks to meeting and courting online, and many people have been the victim of crime as a result of initially socializing online. People who go online in search of companionship may be opening themselves up to being *socially engineered* and then a victim of *fraud,* **identity theft,** or worse. After all, the very factors that drive people to go online can make them vulnerable, including: (1) a strong desire for a new relationship, (2) the natural tendency of many to appear and be appealing, and (3) the need to share personal information with relative strangers.

Unfortunately, many people who engage socially online are deceived by the person or persons with whom they interact. Many people lie about their true name, their educational or income status, what they do for a living, the type of property they own, family background, and so forth. Some people initially do this in order to protect their true identities for fear of being victimized, then later become more honest as trusting relationships are built. However, this method is controversial—how can a trusting relationship be built around a false identity? What is more, one wonders about the integrity and honesty of a person who would deceive others just to meet them. Still, in this age of cybercrime, not posting certain kinds of personal information, including your real name, may be reasonable as a crime prevention strategy because, as indicated above, people can readily search the Net for personal details about someone using online search engines.

People who court online may also be relatively inexperienced in using computers, unfamiliar with **social engineering**, or unaware of certain ways in which **cybercrime** can be committed. They are particularly vulnerable to being taken advantage of when seeking online friendships. There are cases, though, where people not seeking new friends and associates online may find themselves in situations in which they are threatened or even "cyberstalked" for various reasons. Making an online purchase as a gift for someone you are fond of needs to be accomplished with caution. Consider the following examples of deceit and fraud that have occurred during the forming of relationships online.

A Nigerian man was investigated and subsequently prosecuted for gaining the romantic interest of a National Aeronautics and Space Agency (NASA) employee just so he could sneak **malware** onto her work computer. His intention was to steal passwords, banking information, and approximately 25,000 screenshots of sensitive government information. In April 2008 Akeem Adejumo, a 22-year-old Nigerian citizen, pleaded guilty and was sentenced to 18 months in prison by the Lagos State High Court in Nigeria. According to Jeff Taylor, the U.S. District Attorney for Washington, D.C., and an investigator at NASA's Office of the Inspector General, Adejumo first contacted the NASA employee in November 2006 on the online dating site Singlesnet.com. Adejumo posed as a man living in Texas. He used a phony picture and background information, and he courted the NASA female employee for several weeks before he sent an email to her work address that contained an attachment with his faked personal information. When she opened the attachment to see the picture, her system was automatically infected with a commercially available piece of spyware.

On May 8, 2008, three young girls from Auckland, New Zealand, became cyber-victims after an online sex predator enticed them to meet him in an adult chat room. Two of the girls indicated online that they were 18 and 16, when in actuality they were only 15 and 12 years old, respectively. This man physically met the three girls after sexually grooming them online for the in-person encounter. When authorities eventually contacted him, they found incriminating data on his computer including images of two of the girls involved. He was sentenced to 5 years in prison for unlawful sexual contact with the underage girls.

For every tragic story about making friends and courting online, there are as many and perhaps more success stories. People are increasingly turning to the online dating services to find and screen for suitable companions. For example, John and Christine Ozarchuck were reportedly tired of the "bar scene" and night life in their local communities. So in 2005 they posted their profiles onto online dating sites, which eventually resulted in their discovering each other. After four months of dating they became engaged and married a year later. Marriages and domestic partnerships that began as online interactions are common in the digital age of Internet supported computing and near instant communications provided by cell phone text messaging. People from all around the world are meeting, courting, and even falling in love online. If you participate in social networking, chat forums, blogs, or other online forms of communication, just be careful that you are not deceived and taken advantage of.

Suggested Readings: Ellison, N., Heino, R., & Gibbs, J. (2006). Managing impressions online: Self-presentation processes in the online dating environment. *Journal of Computer-Mediated Communication, 11*(2), 415441; Gaudin, S. (2008). *Nigerian gets 18 months for cyber attack on NASA employee.* Retrieved May 10, 2008, from http://www.computerworld.com/action/article.do?command=viewArticleBasic&articleId =9081838&intsrc=news_ts_head; Hitsch, G.J., Hortacsu, A., & Ariely, D. (2005). *What makes you click: An empirical analysis of online dating.* Cambridge, MA: MIT Press; McQuade, S. (2006) *Understanding and managing cybercrime.* Boston, MA: Allyn and Bacon; Murphy, J. (2006). Online dating success story. *WKYC NBC News.* Retrieved May 10, 2008, from http://www.wkyc.com/news/news_links/links _article.aspx?storyid=52413; Vass, B., & Mckenzie-Minifie, M. (2008). *Man met teen sex targets online.* Retrieved on May 10, 2008, from http://www.nzherald.co.nz/topic/ story.cfm?c_id=137&objectid=10509001.

Samuel C. McQuade III and Neel Sampat

MGM ET AL. v. **Grokster Ltd. et al.**

Metro-Goldwyn-Mayer Studios, Inc., et al. v. Grokster, Ltd., et al. was the 2005 landmark U.S. Supreme Court case ruling that decided creators of *peer-to-peer (p2p) file-sharing software,* such as Grokster, Morpheus, and KaZaA, can be held legally liable for **copyright infringement** committed by the users of their software as their products are designed in ways that induce users to violate copyright law. Thus, although creators of p2p software commonly used to illegally download music, movies, or other software did not violate copyright themselves, the court ruled that Grokster, Ltd. and several other co-defendant firms named in the lawsuit by MGM created "a device with the object of promoting its use to infringe copyright" (*Metro-Goldwyn-Mayer Studios Inc. et al. v. Drugstore, Ltd., et al.,* 2005, para. 4) and were therefore criminally liable.

The high court's ruling in this case disappointed technology developers and many other people and organizations concerned about interpretation of **intellectual property** (IP) and freedom of expression issues in the digital age. Among these was the Electronic Freedom Foundation (EFF) that defended StreamCast Networks (creator of Morpheus) on grounds that software creators named in the case relied on a U.S. Supreme Court ruling from 20 years earlier. In that case, known as *Sony Corporation of America et al. v. Universal City Studios, Inc., et al.,* controversy centered on Sony's Betamax Video Recorder (similar to the more popular VCR format that many people still rely on rather than DVDs to watch movies). Copyright holders of video content argued that video recorders were inherently illegal because they enabled individuals to record copyrighted content for other than personal use. However, the court decided that VCRs also provided for many legal uses of the technology that on balance benefited society. Thus, Sony and co-defendants in this case were not held liable for the copyright infringement of others using VCRs for illegal purposes.

It was on this basis that Grokster, StreamCast Networks, and other software creators involved in the more recent case hoped the court's prior reasoning and ruling would apply to p2p technology. However, judges became convinced that many p2p creators were fully aware that their software was being used primarily for copyright infringement and that software developers like Grokster were financially profiting from that infringement. Accordingly, the court decided that Grokster and other case defendants were contributing to the infringement. It is important to understand that in making this ruling the U.S. Supreme Court did not overrule its prior decision in the Sony case. Rather, it expanded legal issues that technology developers need to be concerned about, which now include inducement as well as contributory and vicarious liability.

The *MGM v. Grokster* case decision has several potential implications, including: (1) deterring software and other technology developers from undertaking certain kinds of research and development as they worry about ways in which consumers may illegally use their creations; (2) deterring investment funding in companies that may be perceived as being less profitable and more legally at-risk with regard to any new products they are developing; and (3) impairing economic development generally through loss of jobs and so forth. Specific effects of the *MGM v. Grokster* case ruling have varied. Grokster has stopped offering its application for download and posted a notice on their Web site announcing the court ruling. Company officials also posted information indicating that although there may be legal ways to continue offering their software, they did not believe they were safe and decided to end their creation instead. StreamCast Networks continued to fight in the courts, and at this writing a resolution to that firm's legal appeals and claims remains unknown. Developers of another popular p2p application, LimeWire, now require users to click on an agreement stating that they will not use the application for illegal purposes before downloading it.

The current legality of creating p2p software remains unclear depending on different interpretations of the *MGM v. Grokster* case ruling. With so much of the decision addressing the idea that Grokster and StreamCast desired to make a profit, it is unclear whether open-source or otherwise free p2p applications are entirely legal or merely "less illegal" under the court's ruling. Much appears to depend on motivations of p2p software developers, and the extent to which their products are knowingly if not exclusively used for illegal purposes. This remains controversial because developing and using p2p software for strictly legal purposes is not illegal. In fact, some college and university researchers along with other professionals employed in research and development firms routinely use p2p applications to legally exchange large data files they use in their work.

Suggested Readings: *Metro-Goldwyn-Mayer Studios Inc. et al. vs. Grokster, Ltd., et al.* (2005). 04 US 480; Electronic Freedom Foundation. (2007). Overview of *MGM vs. Grokster.* See http://w2.eff.org/IP/P2P/MGM_v_Grokster/; Wu, S. (2005). *MGM v. Grokster:* Background and analysis. See http://web.archive.org/web/20060111135013/ http://www.scotusblog.com/movabletype/archives/2005/03/mgm_v_grokster.html; Zeller, T. (2005, June 28). Sharing culture likely to pause but not wither. *New York Times.* See http://www.nytimes.com/2005/06/28/technology/28peer.html?pagewanted =1&ei=5090&en=41f5ea71b5f92739&ex=1277611200&partner=rssuserland&emc =rss&adxnnlx=1153411907-IhDfRpnMphZzBY9s4J9HUA.

Shaun M. Jamison

N

NAPSTER

The original Napster was a file-sharing program developed by Shawn Fanning while he was attending Northeastern University in Boston. Fanning wanted an easier method of downloading music than searching Internet Relay Chat (IRC) forums or Lycos. After creating Napster, Fanning decided to launch it as a business and established an office and executive team in San Mateo, California, in September 1999. The business was highly successful, and, at its peak, Napster had 80 million registered users. Napster is widely considered to be one of the first *peer-to-peer (p2p)* file-sharing systems available on the **Internet**. Technically, however, it was not a true p2p system because it utilized central servers to maintain lists of connected computers and to distribute music files that users of networked computers provided. In 2000, Napster became the focal point of a landmark legal case, which established that p2p companies and others could be held liable for the unauthorized distribution of copyrighted material.

As with the many p2p networks that have followed, Napster facilitated the transmission of MP3 files between and among its users. Napster dealt exclusively in music and allowed users to search for MP3 music files stored on the computers of other people located anywhere in the world. The p2p technology enabled the transfer of exact copies of digital music file contents among users without honoring copyright claims. Controversy ensued, however, when record labels and music artists such as Dr. Dre and Metallica discovered that users were distributing their music over Napster without paying royalties due—a clear case, as they saw it, of digital **piracy**.

In 2000, A&M Records and several other recording companies joined in launching a lawsuit against Napster for **copyright infringement** (see *A&M Records, Inc. v. Napster, Inc.*, 239 F. 3d 1004, 9th Cir. [2001]). The following year, the U.S. Court of Appeals for the Ninth Circuit ruled that Napster could be held liable for contributory infringement of the plaintiff's copyrights. This was the first major case to address the application of the copyright laws to p2p file sharing and was the ruling that established that p2p sites could be held liable for pirated material distributed through their networks (*A&M Records, Inc. v. Napster, Inc.,* 239 F. 3d 1004, 9th Cir. [2001]).

After a protracted legal fight, Napster was ordered to cease operations in March 2001 until all copyrighted material was removed from its server database. In July 2001, Napster shut down its entire network in order to comply with a court ordered injunction. On September 24, 2001, Napster agreed to pay music creators and copyright owners $26 million for past unauthorized uses of music and as an advance against future licensing royalties of $10 million. In the short term, Napster attempted to create a pay service, Napster 3.0 Alpha, but was unable to attain proper licensing for distribution (Carlson & Gustavsson, 2001).

On May 17, 2002, Napster announced that its remaining assets would be purchased by the German-based media firm Bertelsmann for $85 million. As part of the buyout agreement, Napster filed for Chapter 11 protection on June 3 under U.S. bankruptcy laws. On September 3, 2002, an American bankruptcy judge blocked the sale to Bertelsmann and forced Napster to liquidate its assets. Napster's brand and logo were acquired at bankruptcy auction by the company Roxio, Inc., which rebranded its Pressplay music service as Napster 2.0. Napster 2.0 is among several services collectively used by millions of people throughout the world to legally download music. The Napster ruling has frequently been cited as legal precedent imposing threat of liability against Web site authors for merely hyperlinking to copyrighted content.

Suggested Readings: *A&M Records, Inc. v. Napster, Inc.,* 239 F. 3d 1004 (9th Cir. 2001); Carlson, B., & Gustavsson, R. (2001). The rise and fall of Napster—An evolutionary approach. *Proceedings of the 6th international computer science conference on active media technology* (pp. 347–354). London: Springer-Verlag; Geisler, M., & Pohlmann, M. (2003). The social form of Napster: Cultivating the paradox of consumer emancipation. *Advances in Consumer Research, 30.* See http://www.markus-giesler.com/; Geisler, M., & Pohlman, M. (2003). The anthropology of file sharing: Consuming Napster as a gift. *Advances in Consumer Research, 30.* See http://www.markus -giesler.com/; Green, M. (2002). Napster opens Pandora's box: Examining how file-sharing services threaten the enforcement of copyright on the Internet.*Ohio State Law Journal, 63,* 799; King, B. (2002, May 15). The day that Napster died. *Wired.com.* Retrieved from http://www.wired.com/gadgets/portablemusic/news/2002/ 05/52540; McCourt, T., and Burkart, P. (2003). When creators, corporations and consumers collide: Napster and the development of on-line music distribution. *Media, Culture, & Society, 25*(3), 333–350.

Neel Sampat

NATIONAL CENTER FOR MISSING AND EXPLOITED CHILDREN

The National Center for Missing and Exploited Children (NCMEC) is a private non-profit organization started in 1984 in the United States under a congressional mandate. Primarily funded by the U.S. Justice Department, NCMEC performs the duties of a central point of contact for parents, children, law enforcement agencies, schools, and communities. NCMEC provides assistance to help facilitate the recovery of children who are kidnapped and to raise awareness of methods to prevent child abduction, molestation, and sexual exploitation. NCMEC services extend throughout the United States and internationally, and the organization coordinates with federal, state, and local law enforcement agencies on active cybercrime-related cases involving children who are missing or being exploited. Pursuant to its mission and its congressional mandates (see 42 U.S.C. §§ 5771 et seq.; 42 U.S.C. § 11606; 22 C.F.R. § 94.6), many of its program services address the prevention of **cybercrimes** that target children online.

The Congressional mandate leading to establishment of the Center was advocated by John Walsh, Noreen Gosch, and others as a result of frustration stemming from the lack of resources and coordination between law enforcement and other government agencies. John Walsh's involvement began with the abduction and murder of his son Adam Walsh. This abduction and murder case is perhaps one of the most famous child abduction cases. It is certainly one of the most frustrating. Over the years a grotesque serial killer confessed to the homicide but recanted several times. Over 25 years later, Adam's murder is still unsolved. In 1988 John Walsh was asked to host the television show, *America's Most Wanted,* which has been aired by Fox Broadcasting Company ever since. On May 2, 2008, the program celebrated the 1000th capture of a fugitive with assistance from viewers who watch the television show.

Currently NCMEC operates the CyberTipline that the public may use to report Internet-related child sexual exploitation including incidences of **child pornography**. Specific types of **Internet** content screened for includes nude or sexually suggestive photographs and videos that depict children, online enticement of children for sex acts, molestation of children outside the family, sex tourism for purposes of engaging in sexual activities with children in another state or country, child prostitution, human trafficking involving children, and unsolicited obscene material sent to minors.

NCMEC provides technical assistance to individuals and law enforcement agencies in the prevention, investigation, prosecution, and treatment of cases involving missing and exploited children. It also assists the U.S. Department of State in certain cases of international child abduction in accordance with the Hague Convention on the Civil Aspects of International Child Abduction. In addition, it offers training programs to social/human service professionals and teachers. NCMEC coordinates child-protection efforts with the private sector. It also networks with nonprofit service providers and state clearinghouses about missing-persons cases. And it provides information about effective legislation to help ensure the protection of children.

NCMEC has nine branch offices throughout the United States located in the following cities: (1) Tustin, California; (2) Naples, Florida; (3) Overland Park, Kansas; (4) Rochester, New York; (5) Buffalo, New York; (6) Utica, New York; (7) Columbia, South Carolina; (8) Lake Park, Florida; and (9) Austin, Texas. These field offices are deployed as regional centers for information regarding any of the aforementioned services. New York branch offices are closely coordinated out of the facility located in Rochester, New York, which is equipped with high tech training rooms frequently used by law enforcement agencies and other groups. The Southeast center, in Lake Park, Florida, operates as the central point for child-protection education and prevention.

Suggested Readings: De Becker, G. (2000). *Protecting the gift: Keeping children and teenagers safe (and parents sane).* New York: Bantam Dell Publishing Group; Goetz, E., &. Shenoi, S. (eds.). (2007). *Critical infrastructure protection (IFIP International Federation for Information Processing).* New York: Springer; Lewis, T.G. (2006). *Critical infrastructure protection in homeland security: Defending a networked nation.* New York: Wiley-Interscience; National Center for Missing & Exploited Children. (2008). NCMEC Home Page. Retrieved from NCMEC Web site: http://www.missingkids.com/;

Sullivant, J. (2007). *Strategies for protecting national critical infrastructure assets: A focus on problem-solving.* New York: Wiley-Interscience.

Neel Sampat and Samuel C. McQuade, III

NATIONAL WHITE COLLAR CRIME CENTER

The National White Collar Crime Center (NW3C) is a nonprofit organization supported with funds provided by the U.S. Department of Justice. With headquarters in Richmond, Virginia, this organization provides nationwide support to law enforcement, prosecution, regulatory, and other investigative organizations involved in the prevention, investigation, and prosecution of what it considers economic and high tech crimes. Although NW3C has no investigative authority itself, its job is to help law enforcement agencies better understand and utilize tools to combat crime, which it does through public education, convening professional training workshops and symposia, and posting onto its Web site research on many varieties of white collar crime. The NW3C has instituted the Internet Crime Complaint Center (IC3), which intakes, tracks, and refers complaints of telemarketing and Internet-based fraud among other types of crimes to authorities for investigation. NW3C sponsors a small amount of research through the White Collar Crime Research Consortium (WCCRC), a collective of more than 100 academic scholars and practitioners committed to promoting increased public awareness of white collar crime impacts on society. The organization also, through its board of directors, sponsors the National Cybercrime Training Partnership whose goals are integrated with other aspects of NW3C services.

Suggested Readings: Green, S.P. (2007). *Lying, cheating, and stealing: A moral theory of white-collar crime.* Oxford Monographs on Criminal Law and Justice. New York: Oxford University Press; National White Collar Crime Center. (2008). NW3C Home Page. Retrieved from NW3C Web site: http://www.nw3c.org/; Pontell, H.N., & Geis, G.L. (ed.). (2006). *International handbook of white-collar and corporate crime.* New York: Springer.

Samuel C. McQuade, III

NETWORK CENTRIC WARFARE

Indirectly related to **cybercrime** and having to do with managing cyber-related conflict and preventing conventional terrorism as well as **cyberterrorism** is the concept of Network Centric Warfare (NCW). Essentially, NCW refers to the capability of conducting high tech intelligence and military operations with information systems that link geographically dispersed technology and other resources and allow commanders to more efficiently carry out the objectives of peacekeeping and warfare when necessary. Greater use of *information technology* (IT) enables more effective tactical, operational, and strategic success on the ground, in the air, and at sea by military units that employ NCW principles and capabilities, many of which are classified and unknown to the general public. Yet it is commonly known that modern combat power is based upon real-time situational knowledge and enhanced command, control, and communications made possible through networked information technology.

Originally known as "information warfare" (IW), today's NCW has been developed since the mid-1990s as the end of the Cold War called for a transformation of

U.S. military forces. Whereas IW was a means of conducting or supporting military operations, NCW is a much larger, all-encompassing concept involving digital technologies interconnected via MILNET—the U.S. military's worldwide computer and telecommunications network analogous to the **Internet**. NCW began to really take shape after the first Gulf War in Iraq in which real-time intelligence gathering and analysis combined with innovative weapons platforms to change the ways in which battles were fought. Like its World War II German "Blitzkrieg" predecessor, the comparatively high tech nature of Operation Desert Storm in the 1991 conflict in Iraq demonstrated how NCW concepts and principles could be used to confound and ultimately defeat an otherwise capable enemy.

In addition to "battle space" engagements, NCW was and continues to be developed with inventions and innovations in information technologies, and on the basis of theories such as complexity theory and chaos theory, which help people to understand complicated and seemingly unpredictable behavioral patterns in nature. Thus, the development of NCW as a military concept emerged just as computing technology enabled these theories to be tested and further explored. By extension, digital age communications including land-based and satellite telecommunications networks provide efficient, accurate, and secure methods of communications along with opportunities for real-time data acquisition, analysis, and dissemination into decision cycles bearing on counterterrorism and military operations.

NCW has also taken on some of the organizational characteristics of information networks due to the underlying organizational effects of IT. Instead of battle lines and unit boundaries, the battle space (rather than "battlefields") are composed of "nodes," which are task-oriented military units (air-, land-, and sea-based). Nodes are interconnected by communication links and readily reconfigured for specific missions in real time. U.S. military branch services including the Army, Air Force, Navy, and Marines (which is actually a component of the U.S. Navy) refers to units organized in such a manner as "expeditionary." For example, the U.S. Army's Brigade Combat Teams are considered expeditionary, implying the ability to deploy combat personnel and equipment for specific purposes with speed.

Suggested Readings: Wilson, C. (2004, June 2). Network centric warfare: Background and oversight issues for Congress. Congressional Research Service report, http://www.mors.org/publications/phalanx/dec00/feature.htm; McCaffrey, B.R. (2000–2001, Winter). Lessons of Desert Storm. *Joint Force Quarterly,* 16; O'Rourke, R. (2001, June 6). Navy network-centric warfare concept: Key programs and issues for Congress. Congressional Research Service report for Congress, https://www.policyarchive.org/bitstream/handle/10207/3364/RS20557_20020603.pdf?sequence=3.

Joseph F. Hennekey

ORGANIZED CYBERCRIME

As its name indicates, organized crime involves many different types of illegal activities that are carried out in systematic ways to acquire market turf and make money. Since at least the mid-nineteenth century, organized crime has taken on different forms using available technology to accomplish these purposes. Ways in which the social and technological organizing of criminal activities has evolved has provided a rich historical basis for several great Hollywood movies that collectively help explain what is going on today with organized **cybercrime**. For example, the 2002 movie titled *Gangs of New York,* starring Leonardo DiCaprio, Daniel Day-Lewis, and Cameron Diaz, was a fictional account of the violent and criminal activities of people who historically band together for protection, political influence, and survival in the infamous Five Points District of New York City. This was a depiction of very early organized crime in America.

Another (1973) movie titled *The Sting,* starring Paul Newman, Robert Redford, and Robert Shaw, accurately dramatized real-life scenarios involving what was then (and still is) known as "the big con"—a reference to organized *confidence games* dating back to at least the beginning of the twentieth century. "Con games," as they are known, involve small-to-large-scale frauds that sometimes employ several role-playing perpetrators who work together to carry out "the con" against a chosen victim known as a "mark." Occasionally con games still occur at rural community and state fairs, but bigger schemes have historically been planned to occur in one city after another. In this way perpetrators can find new victims and reduce the chance of being caught by law enforcement.

People "marked for con" were targeted usually because of their wealth as well as on the basis of advance intelligence gathering by the fraudsters about their personal weaknesses, desires, and greedy tendencies if any. This information was then used to devise a promising "get rich quick" scheme that could actually involve setting up false offices, gambling establishments, or other places to validate appearances of legitimacy. When the time was right, the fraudsters would spring their trap and make off with the money. In the ideal big con the victims marked for the fraud never know they have been ripped off until it is too late. They also never know the true identities of the perpetrators. Although billed as a fictional crime-adventure-comedy that took place in 1930s Chicago (long before the advent of computers), many criminal methods portrayed in *The Sting* are still used today by high tech criminals. **Phishing** schemes, for example, socially engineer potential victims to click on Web sites appearing to be very legitimate in preparation for eliciting personal or financial information to be used for credit card fraud or identify theft.

The next chapter in the evolution of American organized crime has been the subject of several other movies including *The Godfather* (1972), *Scarface* (1983), *Once Upon a Time in America* (1984), and *Goodfellas* (1990). The hit fictional television series *The Sopranos* (1999–2007) also dramatized cultural fascination with organized crime figures and their sometimes ruthless methods. Frequently featuring generations of Italian and/or Sicilian families, Hollywood has correctly differentiated the stable illicit business activities of organized crime figures like Al Capone from the hit-and-relocate tactics of bank robbing gangsters like John Dillinger and the duo Bonnie Parker and Clyde Barrow. Whereas gangsters like Dillinger move about hoping to elude law enforcement, leaders and members of organized crime are traditionally physically bound to certain cities and regions in which they oversee highly structured groups, maintain combinations of legitimate and illegitimate businesses, and constantly reinvest (i.e., "launder") illicit money acquired through the sales of illicit drugs, illegal gambling and prostitution, loan sharking, community "protection" extortion, and skimming of organized labor union proceeds, among other racketeering practices. This model of organized crime existed from approximately 1910 to 1975, after which it was rivaled by transnational drug cartels, such as the infamous Columbian Cartel and Medellin Cartel, and huge race-based gangs that operate from within and outside of prison, such as the Black Guerilla Family, Mexican Mafia, and Aryan Brotherhood.

Computerization has greatly expanded the potential structuring, methods, and markets through which organized crime can profit. Gambling can now take place online and internationally, as can the sale of illegal pornography, sex-related services, tobacco, and alcoholic beverages. However, organized crime takes these and other classical means of profit to new sophisticated levels involving (1) encrypted, coded, and wireless communications; (2) Web-based data mining for intelligence gathering about potential targets; (3) creation and distribution of **malware** that can be used for online extortion or in bot-enabled distributed **denial of service attacks**; (4) **spam** or phishing schemes coupled with mass credit card fraud and **identify theft**; (5) password cracking along with computer hacking to facilitate all the above along with **corporate espionage** in search of trade secrets; and (6) theft of **intellectual property** including pirating and international sales of music, movies, and software.

Many combinations and variations of these methods and goals are now technologically possible and frequently involve offenders going to great lengths to disguise their identities. In 2005 the U.S.-led Operation Firewall arrested a clandestine group of **cybercriminals** known as "Shadowcrew." Authorities made 28 arrests and seized more than 100 computers in the United States, Russia, and other European countries. This crew of cybercriminals was alleged to have stolen more 1.7 million credit card numbers and took special efforts to hide their Internet protocol (IP) addresses, which investigators often use to associate offenders with particular computer devices and locations. It was further reported that although Shadowcrew operated similarly to traditional crime families, crew member involvement in the business changed periodically as offenders effectively came into and moved out of illegal activities online. Experts now agree that organized cybercriminals and threats are extremely difficult to identify much less defend against, investigate, and prosecute. This is especially true in nations where law enforcement capabilities are comparatively limited and priority is given to policing traditional street crimes.

Organized cybercrime is nothing new to the federal agencies such as the U.S. Secret Service, U.S. Department of Justice **Computer Crime and Intellectual Property Section**, and Federal Bureau of Investigation (FBI), which all investigate or prosecute its high tech activities. What is new, in addition to the methods described above, is the high tech ways in which organized crime organizations transfer and launder money on the **Internet**. Many transactions occur online via offshore financial accounts set up in countries that have no extradition treaties with the United States or that may even be hostile to U.S. interests. Major terrorist organizations such as Al Qaeda, Hamas, and other Asian terror groups qualify as another kind of organized crime enterprise. Frequently they target Western nations and carry out attack planning and logistical aspects of their operations online while also disguising their efforts through legitimate businesses or nonprofit fronts. They also create mergers with professional con artists and groups skilled in technical aspects of cybercrime.

Unlike traditional crimes such as murder, assault, robbery, and burglary in which law enforcement usually enjoys high percentages of solvability and prosecution success, complex cybercrimes require more technical skill and savvy by investigators and prosecutors. Organized cybercriminals tend to be very intellectual, disciplined, and focused on improving their high tech methods, making the investigation of their activities both tedious and complicated. U.S. and international law enforcement agencies such as **Interpol** are finding themselves increasingly challenged by the scale, complexity, and volume of organized cybercrime cases. Gone are the days when computer criminals were only lone teenagers hacking away on a home PC—today organized cybercrime is a very large and high tech business enterprise.

Suggested Readings: Brenner, B. (2007). *How Russia became a malware hornet's nest.* SecurityFocus Web page: http://searchsecurity.techtarget.com/news/article/0,289142, sid14_gci1275987,00.html; Krebs, B. (2006). Cyber crime hits the big time in 2006. *Washington Post* Web page: http://www.washingtonpost.com/wp-dyn/content/article/ 2006/12/22/AR2006122200367.html; Poulsen, K. (2005, February 17). *Feds square off with organized cyber crime.* SecurityFocus Web site: http://www.securityfocus.com/ news/10525; Reuters. (2002). *Cybercrime is getting organized.* Wired.com Web site: http://www.wired.com/techbiz/media/news/2006/09/71793; Williams, P. (2001). *Organized crime and cyber crime: Synergies, trends, & responses.* Global Issues Web page: http://usinfo.state.gov/journals/itgic/0801/ijge/gj07.htm.

Samuel C. McQuade, III and Michael J. Kozak

P

PHISHING

The term "phishing" is commonly believed to have been derived from the old expression "Let's go fishing to see what's biting!" In the technological world of **cybercrime**, phishing (pronounced the same as "fishing") by analogy means to cast "digital bait" onto the **Internet** to see who will bite. Thus, phishing is a type of **social engineering** that **cybercriminals** use when attempting to deceive potential victims into revealing private information about themselves or their computer accounts, such as usernames, passwords, and financial or bank account numbers. Information acquired through phishing is commonly used to carry out various types of cybercrimes. Gathering confidential data to carry out **identity theft** is among the most common goals of cybercriminals who employ phishing as an **attack vector**. Sometimes individuals or groups of people are specifically targeted for phishing attacks, perhaps on the basis of their online purchasing profiles or on the basis of their having been duped in a previous phishing attack.

Phishing emerged as an online form of abusing information systems and defrauding people as the World Wide Web was created and became widely used in the mid-1990s. In 1995–1996 phishing attacks occurred periodically through America Online (AOL). Hackers, posing as AOL administrators, tricked AOL users into revealing their credit card information by telling them that there was a problem with their billing. Phishing attacks against banks and other financial institutions were reported to authorities beginning in 2003. Until that time, many phishing emails were easily recognizable because of their poor grammar and spelling errors. However, phishing quickly became more sophisticated as attackers created more legitimate looking emails and began using other techniques. Today, phishing can occur in several different technical ways, but typically involves a cybercriminal sending a digital message that purports to be from a trusted source organization. This commonly happens when an attacker sends "spoofed" (i.e., faked) messages through email or instant messages that appear to be from a legitimate financial institution such as Chase Bank or a popular online retailer such as eBay or Amazon.

Typically the message will describe an urgent need for the recipient of the message, a possible cybercrime victim, to click on a Web link embedded within the text message in order to confirm or restore some aspect of a computer account they actually have. If the victim clicks on the hypertext link in the message, he will be taken to a Web site that appears to be that of the legitimate financial institution or retailer. Spoofed Web sites may actually contain digital images of the firm's logo and trademark, along with instructions for the victim to enter confidential information such as their bank or credit account numbers, usernames, passwords, or Social Security number (SSN). Ostensibly, this is done in order to verify the identity of the person before the underlying problem, about which the victim was contacted in the first place, can be resolved. If the victim provides this information, it will be used by cybercriminals, who then pretend to be the victim online.

Armed with the victim's confidential information, cybercriminals may then make illegal online purchases in the name of the victim by using their credit card numbers, withdrawing funds from financial accounts or receiving cash advances on lines of credit, or claiming government benefits using the victim's SSN. In some of the worst cases cybercriminals will take on the identity of the victim until their financial accounts and lines of credit are exhausted (i.e., "maxed out"). Sometimes cybercriminals will sell all or parts of the confidential information they have acquired about potential or actual victims to other cybercriminals who actually carry out the online financial thefts, fraud, or identity theft. This implies that as in traditional criminality, individual offenders can specialize in using particular forms of technological tools and methods to carry out their crimes.

Pharming is a phishing variant that does not require fraudulent emails. In these instances an attacker hacks into a domain name server (DNS) to change the *Internet protocol* address of targeted Web sites. This way, users attempting to access the legitimate Web sites of financial institutions or retailers they normally interact with are redirected to spoofed Web sites that can automatically capture their account names and passwords with spyware. Again, armed with confidential data, cybercriminals are free to carry out cybercrimes or sell the information so that other offenders can.

Since its onset in the mid-1990s, the technological sophistication and number of phishing attacks have increased dramatically. While some security professionals have estimated that a substantial proportion of emails may now be an unwanted form of **spam**, information security experts also estimated in 2007 that one of every 87 emails was a phishing attack. Thus, each year millions of phishing attacks are launched against computer users throughout the world. The phishing threat now extends to PDA and cell phone users who receive advertisements via email and instant messages, and this situation is worsened by the use of *botnets* now used by criminals to carry out various forms of cybercrime through remotely controlled computers. *Bot networks* can collectively launch millions of phishing attacks per day. In June 2007 alone, the Anti-Phishing Working Group (APWG) received 28,888 reports of phishing and subsequently identified 31,709 unique phishing sites, approximately 32 percent of which were determined to be hosted from within the United States. APWG also reports that 80 percent of phishing is conducted against 14 specific financial institutions. Estimates of consumer losses from phishing may be as high as $2.8 billion annually.

Although legislation intended to prevent or facilitate law enforcement efforts to combat crimes have historically lagged behind advances in information technology (IT) and criminal methods, several U.S. federal and state crime laws now prohibit phishing. Among these are the *Controlling the Assault of Non-Solicited Pornography and Marketing (CAN-SPAM) Act* of 2003. This law authorizes the Federal Trade Commission to prosecute people who engage in phishing or pharming. And since phishing as a specific form of social engineering is fundamentally about tricking people online, consumer awareness and education of IT device users are essential. Several government, nonprofit, and private entities actively provide professional training and education about phishing and how to protect against this form of cybercrime. Specific Web sites designed to educate consumers about the threats of phishing are those maintained by the U.S. Federal Trade Commission (FTC) OnGuard Online program, the Anti-Phishing Working Group, and the online MillerSmiles organization of the United Kingdom.

According to these and other organizations concerned about preventing phishing attacks, users should never click on links embedded within an email or instant message. Instead, users should type the universal resource location (URL) address into the address bar of their Web browser software application (e.g., Microsoft Explorer or Mozilla Firefox), or search for a financial institution's Web site on their own and navigate to the information they are seeking. Users are also reminded that given the phishing problem, reputable firms will seldom if ever contact their account users online. Instead, they will correspond via regular postal mail services. Users can also use the file/properties function in software to determine which Web site they are really on, and possibly to determine who or from where in the world the message was actually sent. It is also recommended that users look for the universal "secure Web site" symbol, especially when conducting online financial account activity or transactions. Secure Web sites use a technique called "SSL" (secure socket layer) that ensures the connection between users and the Web site they are viewing is private. This is indicated by "https://" instead of "http://" at the beginning of the URL address, *and* by a padlock icon that must be found either at the right end of the address bar or in the bottom right-hand corner of the browser window. A padlock appearing anywhere else on the page does not represent a secure site. The use of up-to-date spam filters may also head off many phishing attempts.

Suggested Readings: Anti-Phishing Working Group. Web site http://www.antiphishing. org, and, specifically, Phishing activity trends: Report for the month of June 2007, available at http://apwg.org/reports/apwg_report_june_2007.pdf, and Origins of the word 'phishing,' available at http://www.antiphishing.org/word_phish.html; Gartner Group. (2006, November 9). Gartner says number of phishing e-mails sent to U.S. adults nearly doubles in just two years. Gartner.com Web site: http://www.gartner.com/it/page.jsp?id =498245; McQuade, S. (2006). *Understanding and Managing Cyber Crime.* Boston, MA: Allyn and Bacon; Message Labs. (2007, September). Message Labs Intelligence: September and Q3 in review. A downpour of virus & phishing activity, in the wake of a storm worm surge." Available at messagelabs.com Web site: http://www.messagelabs. com/mlireport/MLI_Report_September_Q3_2007.pdf; National Conference of State Legislatures. (2007, February 21). 2007 State legislation relating to "phishing." NCSL Web site: http://www.ncsl.org/programs/lis/phishing07.htm; Richardson, R. (2007). CSI 2007 computer crime and security survey, from http://i.cmpnet.com/v2.gocsi.com /pdf/CSISurvey2007.pdf; U.S. Federal Trade Commission. (2008). OnGuard Online

Web site: http://onguardonline.gov/index.html; *Washington Post.* (2004, November 18). A brief history of phishing. *Washington Post* Web site: http://www.washingtonpost.com/wp-dyn/articles/A59350-2004Nov18.html.

Ben Woelk

PHREAKING

Phreaking is the unauthorized exploration and exploitation of telephone systems. Phreaking predates *computer hacking* and the use of modern cellular phones. However, the difference between phreaking and hacking has become indistinct as landline telephone and wireless satellite cellular networks have become interoperable and mainly controlled by computerized switches that route and connect phone calls made and received throughout the world. Phreaking was originally performed through a combination of **social engineering** and telephone tone generation (i.e., sounds unique to dial tones and specific numerals when dialing a telephone number). By recording and playing specific tones used for system control into a telephone, "phreaks" could navigate the telephone system in the same way that telephone company engineers could, albeit without authorization. Typical exploits included but were not limited to making and receiving free long-distance telephone calls.

Initially, phreaking was pioneered by blind teenagers in the late 1960s and early 1970s. Some of these teenagers, such as Joe Engressia (aka "Joybubbles"), had the ability to whistle tones into the telephone with perfect pitch. Using this and similar abilities, in combination with clever manipulation of telephone operators and engineers, Engressia and many other phreaks explored and exploited telephone networks throughout the world. Phreaking spread from blind teenagers as they contacted other young people with technical engineering and electronics skills for the construction of tone generating devices (Sterling, 1992). These "homebrew" devices were referred to as "boxes" and performed a variety of different functions. The most notorious of these was the "blue box" that was used to generate the same control tones that telephone operators had access to, allowing free telephone calls among other functions. Other commonly engineered and used boxes allowed users to accept phone calls free of charge to the caller (black box) or allow free phone calls from pay phones (red box).

In 1971, Ron Rosenbaum published "Secrets of the Little Blue Box" in *Esquire* magazine, placing phreaking into public view. The article included interviews with famous phreaks, including Joe Engressia and John Draper (aka "Captain Crunch"), who was renowned for his pioneering use of the little whistle that came in the breakfast cereal of that name to phreak. Afterwards phreaking methods were used increasingly for fraudulent rather than exploratory purposes, which led to federal agents arresting many phreaks, including some named in the *Esquire* article, including John Draper.

Similar to early hackers interested in exploring computer systems, many of the best phreaks desired only to explore telephone systems, rather than to exploit it for monetary gain. Traditionally, phreaks are generally more socially active in what they do with technology than comparatively recluse hackers. For example, a common phreaking activity would be to commandeer a telephone "bridge" to enable several phreaks to dial in to a common phone number and chat in a manner similar to a conference call. Prior to widespread broadband **Internet** access, much of hacking relied on phreaking to connect hackers to remote systems over long-distance telephone lines without incurring expensive charges from the telephone company. Although many perceive the phreaking "scene" to be dead, today's phreaks are continuing to explore a far more complex and much better secured telecommunications system. Many common technologies, such as voice mail box systems still provide targets for phreaks. Cellular phones and short message service (SMS) messaging are also becoming targets for phreaks particularly as use of cell phones and adoption of cellular technology for many purposes continues to rise.

Suggested Readings: Rosenbaum, R. (1971, October). Secrets of the little blue box. *Esquire,* 124; Gadaix, E. (2004, October 14). *Phreaking in the 21st century.* Presented at HITBSecConf2004, Kuala Lumpur, Malaysia; Sterling, B. (1992). *The hacker crackdown.* New York: Bantam.

Nathan Fisk

PIRACY

Digital piracy, sometimes referred as "bootlegging," is a form of **copyright infringement** and a method of obtaining and distributing software, games, video, music, and other media illegally via the use of computing and telecommunications devices. This includes the reproduction and distribution of copyrighted material in any form without the consent of the copyright holder. This material is often shared via the **Internet** over file-sharing networks and/or through peer-to-peer (p2p) networks, as well as on pirate servers. Each file provided by hosted servers can result in millions of downloads. Digital piracy takes place outside the Internet as well. For example, physical copies of pirated DVDs are illicitly sold in many cities.

Digital piracy has become a significant problem. In 2005, the Motion Picture Association of America (MPAA), a trade group for movie studios, estimated it lost $2.3 billion worldwide to Internet piracy (MPAA, 2005).

There are many legal ramifications of piracy, ranging from civil liability to federal prosecution. Federal statutes have long prohibited the unauthorized distribution of copyrighted works for personal gain. Under the *1996 No Electronic Theft Act* (NET Act), U.S. copyright law was broadened to allow for the civil and criminal prosecution of persons engaged in unauthorized distribution of copyrighted works without a profit motive as well. The NET Act altered the definition of financial gain to include bartering and trading of media, and facilitated the prosecution of members of "warez" groups as participants in a criminal enterprise (NET Act, 1997).

On October 4, 2007, Jammie Thomas, a Minnesota mother of two, was found liable for copyright infringement in the nation's first file-sharing case to go before a jury. Thomas was ordered by Judge Michael J. Davis to pay the amount of $222,000 in damages for sharing 24 songs on her personal computer (Kravets, 2007).

Digital piracy has its beginnings as an underground community. One of the first methods of file sharing was the physical goods trade. Before high-speed broadband connections, a person would create a copy of software or an application on a floppy disk for those who desired the software or application (Bennett, 2003).

In 1996, Hotline Communications Ltd. founded Hotline, a method of file sharing that used a tracker, server, and client that allowed a user to directly connect and transfer files. This greatly facilitated the transmission of various sorts of media and software, legal and illegal.

Other methods of distributing software and media developed during this period as well. In 1998 the emergence of instant messenger services such as Internet Chat Query (ICQ) allowed for a direct connection to be established between two users and transfer a file to either user. An alternative to using an instant messenger client was the use of a File Transfer Protocol (FTP) server to "host" a file on a server. FTPs were designed for file sharing as a file library or depository and lacked a user communication base, which prevented close online communities from evolving.

Current methods of digital piracy involve the use of file-sharing programs and services, such as p2p networks. A p2p network enables computers to connect directly to each other in order to distribute and copy files. There are many programs in existence such as BitTorrent, uTorrent, **Napster**, and Apple's iTunes. Many of these programs are legal and legitimate software that were developed for the open source community as a method of freeware distribution and licensed media distribution.

Suggested Readings: Bennett, H. (2003). *Understanding CD-R & CD-RW.* Cupertino, CA: Optical Storage Technology Association (OSTA); Kravets, D. (2007, October 4). RIAA jury finds Minnesota woman liable for piracy, awards $222,000. Retrieved October 5, 2007, from Wired.com: http://blog.wired.com/27bstroke6/2007/10/riaa-jury-finds.html; MPAA. (2005). *Internet piracy* [Fact Sheet]. Retrieved October 13, 2007, from http://www.mpaa.org/piracy_internet.asp; *The United States No Electronic Theft (NET) Act.* (1997). (H.R. 2265) 17 U.S.C. and 18 U.S.C.

Neel Sampat

PREVENTING CYBERCRIME

Anyone can be a victim of **cybercrime**. Every week there are news reports about data breaches and lost information in both the public and private sectors. The **computerization** of information, although it has made much information more accessible, has also led to an increase in **identity theft**, because *all* information an identity thief would need is stored online somewhere. You may even have personal identifying information (PII) stored on your own computer. Even if you do not have PII on your computer, it is your responsibility to stop criminals from using your computer to attack others. The increased use of broadband connections, coupled with the enormous growth in the use of wireless routers at home, has provided a treasure trove of information for the cybercriminal. Everyone who uses computers or other types of computerized devices is vulnerable to becoming a victim of cybercrime. The more often people are online, the more they are exposed.

Although your company or school may provide some protection for your computer at work (and maybe at home), keeping your computer safe is *your* responsibility? How much do you know about information security? Do you know how to keep your equipment and information secure?

Protection at Work or School

Although companies and schools provide some network-based protection for your computers and may require the use of specific security software and practices, they cannot stop you from doing something inadvertently that might expose information. If something goes wrong at work or school, you can call the help desk. Computer support people help keep your systems safe and functional. However, as individual users you are responsible and often held accountable for securing your computers and the data they contain. Users have always been the weakest link in computer security. At work, not only are you at risk from your own mistakes, you are at risk from what other users are doing as well. Many users access company or school networks from home with computer equipment not managed by your employer or school. Improperly managed computers provide an opportunity for **cybercriminals** to leverage weaknesses in home computers to attack the companies or schools to which you connect.

The Importance of Protecting Your Computer at Work, School, and Home

Every week, corporations, universities, and other organizations lose or expose PII. Noteworthy losses of PII in higher education (Privacy Rights Clearinghouse, 2005) include:

- A database compromise affecting 800,000 people (UCLA, October 2005 to November 2006).
- A database compromise affecting 197,000 people (University of Texas, April 2006).
- A server breach that exposed information on 300,000+ people (Ohio University, April 2006).

Altogether, 25 percent of universities and colleges have lost confidential information (Caruso, 2006, p. 10). In the private sector, T. J. Maxx exposed the PII of approximately 47 million customers (Vijayan, 2007, p. 1). These examples illustrate that good information security practices are critical. You would not want to be responsible for exposing other people's PII. And although you cannot control how other people handle your information, you *can* control how *you* handle your and others' information.

The problem is even greater for home users. A 2005 study by AOL and the National Cyber Security Alliance (NCSA) found that 81 percent of home users lacked core protection on their computers. Core protection is defined as recently updated antivirus software, a properly configured firewall, and/or spyware protection (AOL/NCSA, 2).

This entry provides information about both technical protection and best practices that will help you protect your computer and your personal information.

Basic Technical Protection

Your computer and other computerized devices require the following basic security protection.

Antivirus software

Antivirus software provides basic protection against specific and generic types of **malware**, including worms, viruses, Trojans, keyloggers, etc. Antivirus software is readily available for all types of computers and operating systems. Follow these guidelines when using antivirus software:

- Acquire antivirus software from a reputable source. Most information security vendors provide protective software for home users. These vendors include industry giants such as Microsoft, McAfee, and Symantec as well as smaller operations that provide free antivirus protections such as Avast.

- Make sure you install reputable antivirus products *before* you connect your computer to the **Internet**; otherwise your computer will be compromised even before you finish downloading needed product upgrades and patches. The U.S. **Computer Emergency Response Team** and Coordination Center (CERT/CC) provides a guide for home computer users titled *Before You Connect a New Computer to the Internet*, which provides excellent specific suggestions on this topic (CERT).
- Update the virus definition or signature files daily. Most antivirus software provides a way to do this automatically.
- Scan your system for viruses weekly.
- Enable any automatic protection, such as email scanning. Email is the most common **attack vector** for delivering viruses.

Use a Software or Hardware Firewall

A *firewall* regulates communication between your computer and the network, including the largest network of all, the Internet. It provides a set of access lists installed on a computer or coded into an appliance that protects a computer or network from intruders. If a worm or a hacker attacks your computer from the Internet, the firewall will block access to your computer. Some firewalls only regulate communications attempting to enter your computer (Windows XP); others also provide control over what leaves your computer (e.g., ZoneAlarm). Firewall rules can be configured to detect and deny intruder probes in various ways. Firewalls are available in both hardware (appliance) versions and as software. A properly configured router will also provide much of the protection of a firewall.

Firewalls provide protection from individuals who do not know the specific access credentials (such as passwords) to your computer system and will eliminate a good deal of risk from outside attack. Your company or school may use network firewalls to help protect the network, but these firewalls will not provide the protection needed for an individual computing device. A software firewall is sufficient for a single computer, but will not provide adequate protection and options necessary to protect a computer network. Use of a software firewall coupled with a router (at home) provides a good basic level of protection to an individual computer.

If your firewall provides an alerts feature, you will be able to see how often attempts occur to access your computer. You will be surprised at how often they take place. You may see hundreds of cyber probes pinging your firewall during any given work session, demonstrating the high frequency of attacks occurring. Every computer must have a personal firewall before connecting to the Internet.

Patches and Vulnerabilities

One method used by cybercriminals to attack your computer is taking advantage of vulnerabilities or weak spots. The vulnerabilities may be in your operating system or the specific applications you are using. Patches provide protection against software vulnerabilities. When a software vendor discovers a vulnerability, it will often make available a patch to address that vulnerability. Although most operating systems provide an automatic updating feature, some applications do not.

It is critical to apply patches as soon as possible. When a patch is released, cybercriminals will develop exploits for the respective vulnerability, often within hours.

Release of a patch provides both a fix for a vulnerability and a target for a cybercriminal. Cybercriminals will use an *exploit* to attack the specific vulnerability on computers whose users have not yet applied the patch. Patches may be released on a regular cycle. For example, Microsoft releases security patches every second Tuesday. Patches may also be released when vulnerabilities are discovered. (For example, Firefox and other non-Microsoft applications may release patches more frequently.) Even security software may need to be patched. Patching must become a regular part of your computer maintenance. Patching also is one of the chief defenses against worms.

Visit your software vendor's Web site or check the "Help" tab to find out if patches or updates are available. Some manufacturers send announcements of available updates to registered users of their products. If your software does not have an auto-update feature, you should check for new patches at least monthly or when you hear news of an exploit or attack.

Antispyware and Adware Software

Spyware has become the scourge of the Internet. Unlike other types of attacks whose effects may be obvious, spyware infestations are designed to run unobtrusively, capturing information about your Internet activities. Antispyware and adware software products will help you to detect and remove these types of malware from your system, may speed up system performance, and may provide protection when you visit malicious Web sites.

Use of antispyware products is not as straightforward as use of antivirus products. Although most antivirus products are interchangeable, different antispyware and anti-adware products will detect different types of spyware and adware. You must use more than one antispyware product to provide adequate protection. Antispyware is often free and available online. However, some spyware actually masquerades as antispyware, so use care when downloading from a company that is not a well-known security vendor. Spyware may even pose as a security scanner that actually installs spyware onto your computer. Typically these pop up while you are online to report something like the following: "PC running slow—Click here to have it checked."

Good Practices

Technology provides only part of the protection needed. How you use your computer will determine if you are successful in defending yourself against cybercriminals.

Use Strong Passwords

Passwords provide a means of limiting access to your computer use and to information stored on the computer or the network. A strong password provides a fundamental layer of protection. Passwords based on objects in your office, such as a picture of a Porsche, etc., provide little to no protection against a physical intruder. How do you know if you have a strong password?

For a number of years, a *strong password* has consisted of at least eight upper and lower case letters, symbols, and numbers. Because of advances in password cracking technologies, eight-character passwords may not prove to be sufficient. Ideally, a password should be 15 characters or longer, although not all systems will support a password of this length. How can you remember a password of this length? If you use a passphrase, it will make it easy to remember. Although using dictionary words in short passwords is not secure for passwords of less than 15 characters, they should never consist of proper names or words listed in a dictionary or encyclopedia. For a shorter password, it is easy to convert any name and word into a strong password. For example, the name "Einstein" can be converted to "E1nSt8n@". The password "E1nSt8n@g3Nius" is even better because it substitutes characters as in the first example but adds a second misspelled word in a way that is easy to remember. Now, the password combines several alphanumeric characters plus at least one other keyboard character in a very strong way.

A strong password should be intuitively associated with tangible items, pictures, or other intelligence known about the workstation or device owner. Using a strong password can eliminate significant risk of system manipulation and loss of data. Here are the basic rules for selecting a strong password:

- Make your password at least 8 characters long, consisting of a mix of lower and upper case letters, numbers, and symbols.
- Use a passphrase of at least 15 characters if at all possible. A good passphrase can include dictionary words, but should also include special characters, etc. An example of a good passphrase would be "IfI0nlyHad8Brain?".
- Do not use proper names or words from a dictionary or encyclopedia, including those printed in foreign languages.
- Make sure the password does not contain data of a personal nature, such as birthday, anniversary, street address, part of your social security number, or pet's name, etc.
- Change your password at least every 120 days.
- Do not repeat use of a password.
- Do not share your password.
- Do not write it on a sticky note on your computer or keyboard.

Password management

We all have multiple accounts that require passwords. Using the same password for accounts on critical systems does not provide sufficient protection. Here are some tips on managing multiple passwords:

- Although you do not want to use the same password for different critical accounts, it may make sense to try to reduce the number and complexity of passwords for less critical systems. Base the strength of your password on the value of the information you are trying to protect. Do not, however, use the same password to access work or banking resources or to sign up for a mailing list. In general, use as complex of a password as you can. Many Web sites provide ways to reset your password by answering specific security questions. Do not be afraid to use a difficult password and reset it when needed.
- Password management programs can help by storing and encrypting all other passwords and creating a single master password to access these passwords. Password management programs can facilitate easily accessing and backing up passwords. KeePass is a free/open-source password safe or manager that helps you to manage your passwords securely by storing your passwords in a database that is locked with one master key or a key disk. Various "smart" Universal Serial Bus (USB) drives provide password safe or access control functions for your computer. Some of these products use biometric authentication technologies.
- Networks may employ technology that forces users to change passwords on a regular basis and may enforce password complexity requirements as well.

Backup Your Data

There is an old saying that there are two types of users: those who have lost data and those who will lose data. It is important to back up important information on a regular basis. Some ISPs are starting to offer backup services. You may also back up information to a network storage device or to CDs or DVDs. The important thing is that you back up your data regularly to a safe place.

Use a Limited Account

Use of a limited account for everyday computer use provides another way to protect your computer from malware. Typically, home computers allow the use of two or three different account types: an administrative account, a limited account, and a guest account. These accounts have different purposes:

- An administrative account is used to install software and otherwise maintain your computer. It is not needed for typical activities such as Web browsing, emailing, and using most applications.
- A limited account or guest account does not have the ability to install software. The advantage a limited account provides when browsing the Web or opening an attachment is that if you are attacked by malware, it will not be able to install itself on your computer if you are using only a limited account. If you browse the Web using an administrative account, malware that attacks you will gain your privileges to install software on your computer.

I recommend use of a limited account for most activities. You will have to switch to an administrative account to install software, but the hassle of doing this is far less than the problem incurred from a successful malware attack.

Protecting Yourself When Using Wireless Devices and Access Points

Wireless networking allows you to connect to a network and often the Internet without using a cable. As more people purchase laptops, PDAs, and other mobile devices, wireless network access has become increasingly popular and convenient. Wireless access points must be set up properly to provide sufficient security. However, most wireless access points are set up in a manner that is extremely insecure. Without the proper precautions, wireless networking can place your **privacy**, your data, and your computer at significant risk.

When connected to an insecure wireless network, anyone within range of your computer and using the right tools can easily capture your traffic as it is transmitted across the network. This type of "listening in," known as sniffing, can be done with a laptop (or PDA), a wireless card, and some freely available software and is very difficult to detect.

Attackers may also use your connection for their own nefarious purposes. This could include anything from illegally downloading copyrighted files to posting **child pornography** on the Internet.

Follow these tips to use someone else's wireless connection safely:

- Avoid sending sensitive information over a wireless network.
- Encrypt your traffic.
- Provide sensitive information only to "secure" sites, i.e., sites that display https:// in the address bar and a padlock.

- Use virtual private networking (VPN) to encrypt all network traffic to and from your computer. If you have VPN access through your company or school, use it whenever you access a wireless network.

If you have set up your own wireless router or access point, you are responsible for ensuring that you have configured the router settings to provide sufficient security. Ensure that you have configured the following:

- Disable set service identifier (SSID) broadcasting. To make it easier to connect to a wireless network, access points broadcast the name of their network so that mobile devices can easily detect them. Disabling SSID broadcasting makes your wireless network "invisible" unless you already know the name of the network.
- Enable media access control (MAC) address filtering. Each wireless network card has a unique identification number known as a MAC address. By allowing only your network cards to access your wireless network, you can prevent other people from using your Internet connection without your permission.
- Enable Wi-Fi protection access (WPA) encryption. Enabling encryption on your access point serves two purposes. First, it prevents attackers from sniffing your traffic, which prevents them from watching what you are doing online. Second, it forces anyone attempting to access your wireless network to enter a password to gain access to your network.

Wireless routers provide a number of other ways to ensure only permitted computers are accessing the network. See your wireless router's user guide for details (RIT, 2006a).

Suggested Readings: Privacy Rights Clearinghouse. (2005, April 20; updated 2005, May 8). *A chronology of data breaches*. Retrieved May 11, 2008, from http://www.privacyrights.org/ar/ChronDataBreaches.htm; America Online and the National Cyber Security Alliance. (2005). *AOL/NCSA online safety study (December 2005)*. Retrieved May 11, 2008, from www.staysafeonline.info/pdf/safety_study_2005.pdf; Caruso, J.B. (2006). *Safeguarding the tower: IT security in higher education 2006: ECAR key findings*. Retrieved May 11, 2008, from http://connect.educause.edu/Library/ECAR/SafeguardingtheTowerITSec/41170; CERT Coordination Center. (2005). *Before you connect a new computer to the Internet*. Pittsburgh, PA: Software Engineering Institute, Carnegie Mellon University. Retrieved May 11, 2008, from http://www.cert.org/tech_tips/before_you_plug_in.html; RIT Information Security Office. (2006a, November). *Accessing wireless networks safely: Protection without wires*. Rochester, NY: Rochester Institute of Technology. Retrieved May 4, 2008, from http://security.rit.edu/docs/wireless-brochure.pdf; RIT Information Security Office. (2006b, November). *Web browsing safely: Avoid "getting caught" in the Web*. Rochester, NY: Rochester Institute of Technology. Retrieved May 4, 2008, from http://security.rit.edu/articles/webbrowsing.pdf; McQuade, S.C., III. *Understanding and managing cybercrime*. (2006). Boston: Pearson Education Inc.; Vijayan, J. (2007, March 29). TJX data breach: At 45.6M card numbers, it's the biggest ever. *Computerworld*. Retrieved May 11, 2008, from http://www.computerworld.com/action/article.do?command=viewArticleBasic&articleId=9014782.

Ben Woelk

PREVENTION EDUCATION

The need for greater education and computer literacy to fight **cybercrime** has long been acknowledged. In a 2000 speech before a U.S. Senate subcommittee, Attorney General Janet Reno formally stated that it was a cornerstone of the Justice Department's anticybercrime efforts (U.S. Senate, 2000). Cybercrime is distinctive, however, because it can be reduced through and caused by education. Educating the general population about ways in which IT can be abused and about information security technologies and methods can reduce society's vulnerability to existing forms of cybercrime, but this education can also spread knowledge about how to commit technological abuses among youth or other people who might be tempted to abuse computers and other types of IT. Indeed, many hacker magazines such as *2600* can be seen as empowering to both those who would abuse IT and those who would protect themselves from cybercrime. The result has been a proliferation of organizations devoted to raising public awareness about cybercrime and providing educational resources to prevent it.

Cybercrime education tends to take two forms: broad public awareness and specialist training. As the National Colloquium for Information Systems Security Education noted in 1998, "[O]ur nation needs an information-literate workforce that is aware of its vulnerability, as well as a cadre of information professionals who are knowledgeable of the recognized 'best practices' available in information security and information assurance" (CISSE, n.d., para. 2). By 2006 more than 50 online instructional resources geared toward kindergarten–grade 12 students, educators, and parents were available online. Among the most widely known and popularly used online instructional resources are the following: (1) I-SAFE (developed by i-SAFE Inc.), (2) NetSmartz (developed by the **National Center for Missing and Exploited Children**), and (3) I Keep Safe (developed by ikeepsafe.com).

Other online resources include, but are not limited to the following:

- Internet Crimes Against Children Task Forces
- Parent's Guide to Internet Safety
- FBI Safety Tips for Kids
- Cybercitizen Awareness Program
- Cyberethics for Teachers
- Childsafenet
- Technology in 4-H
- 4Girls Health
- Safekids
- NASA Explores Cyber Safety
- I Keep Safe
- Youth, Pornography and the Internet
- Parent's Guide to the Internet
- E-rate
- KidzPrivacy
- ChatDanger—Cyberspace Risks
- Copyright Kids—Copyright Society of USA
- CyberAngels—Guardian Angels, Inc.
- CyberNetiquette Comix—Disney
- CyberSafety—CyberSafety

- CyberSmart Curriculum—NSBA + others
- GetNetWise Online Safety Guide—GetNetWise
- GoCyberCamp—Univ of MinnesotaProtectkids.com—Enough is Enough
- Responsiblenetizen.com—Center for Safe and Responsible Internet Use
- Internet Safety for Teachers and Students—Stevens Institute of Technology
- Kidscomjr Internet Safety Game—Circle 1
- Netsafe Kids—National Academies of Sciences
- Play it Cybersafe—Business Software Alliance
- Safe Surfing Tips for Teens—Nemours Found
- Stay Safe Online—Nat Cyber Security Alliance
- WebMonkey—Lycos/Carnegie Mellon University
- WebWise Kids—WebWise Kids
- WiredSafety—WiredSafety
- Yahooligans Parents Guide—Yahoo

As the result of such efforts, along with those of several other organizations devoted to cyber education and prevention, gains are being made. Check out the following: (1) cyber tips provided by OnGuardOnline and annual government activities pertaining to National Cyber Security Month (October); (2) ongoing changes in state laws and school curricula; (3) cybercrime prevention efforts of civic and professional security organizations such as the Information Systems Security Alliance and Software Business Alliance; (4) private firms and nonprofit organizations such as i-SAFE, Inc. and the National Center for Missing and Exploited Children (NCMEC); (5) industry lobbying and protection organizations such as the Recording Industry Association of America (RIAA), Motion Picture Association of America (MPAA), and the Electronic Freedom Foundation (EFF); and (6) law enforcement agencies and organizations like the Anti-Phishing Working Group, International High Tech Crime Investigators Association (HTCIA), and the FBI's InfraGard program. Despite these efforts, much more needs to be accomplished.

Part of the difficulty that educators encounter is the diverse nature of the population that uses computers and widespread existing technological and human vulnerabilities to cybercrime, like **social engineering**. Issues such as socioeconomic status, access to technology, cultural expectations, attitude towards crime laws (e.g., those prohibiting **copyright infringement**), as well as technical computing vary enormously from user to user and all factor into cyber offending and **victimization**. In some cases, victims of cybercrime seek to educate others either directly through online and in-person peer groups or indirectly through word-of-mouth, online forums such as ScamFraudAlert.com, or social networking sites where they can tell their stories and issue warnings. Opportunities for information security and system administration specialist training in cybersecurity issues have also greatly increased in recent years, with a sharply rising number of professional certification programs and other credentials available from academic institutions and private firms. The Certification in Information Systems Security Protection is one such credential.

The National Security Agency and National Science Foundation have both sponsored a nationwide initiative to increase the number of trained information security experts. The Institute of Internal Auditors, SANS Institute, and Microsoft Corporation also provide professional training workshops and seminars. Professional training programs often focus on "nuts-and-bolts" technology issues like how to design and manage more secure networks, computers, and software. It is notable that many colleges and universities also sponsor undergraduate and graduate courses in areas of computer science, software administration, or network systems administration and security. People who take these courses are learning how to protect not only themselves and their personal information but also data residing on information systems of many different types of organizations.

In some cases the knowledge needed to make computers (or computer users) more secure is basic. Researchers at Carnegie Mellon University found that playing an educational "anti-phishing" video game for 15 minutes enabled study subjects to identify fraudulent emails and Web sites 18 percent more often. The effectiveness of educational programs can vary greatly and evaluation studies are very rare. In 2006 a formal evaluation of i-SAFE funded by the National Institute of Justice (NIJ) of the U.S. Department of Justice found that it had varying effects on student knowledge, knowledge retention, and behaviors related to cybercrime. A small number of evaluations about other prevention programs have also been undertaken, including those provided in Canada and Great Britain (see, respectively, Crombie and Tinneer, 2003; and Cyberspace Research Unit of University of Central Lancashire, 2002). The consensus at the 2007 Anti-Phishing Work Group (APWG) eCrime Researchers Summit reported "most current methods of user education are inadequate" (Montabano, 2007, para. 1).

Dr. Samuel C. McQuade, III of the Rochester Institute of Technology, a notable cybercrime researcher and former NIJ program manager, is also on record in publications and at numerous national conferences saying that **Internet** safety, information security, and cyber ethics education is sorely needed along with professional training, research, and evaluation in order to better understand and manage cybercrime challenges of society. Questions that remain largely unanswered through research include: (1) Which programs and blocks of instruction are most efficient to teach, most effective for knowledge retention, and actually empower decision making leading to cybercrime prevention? (2) What topics of instruction are not adequately addressed by available resources? (3) How effective are instructional tool developers at updating course content? (4) How can one best integrate topical coverage into existing curricula and educational settings to comport with mandated national and state education standards? (5) How can countries go about ramping up national teaching capabilities? (6) How can government and school districts garner parental, other adult, and more organizational engagement for informed supervision and role modeling in safe computing by youth?

Strategic challenges for education include the following needs to:

1. Recognize and accept that kids are offenders as well as victims, and they can flip-flop intermittently. All kids need cyber ethics and information security instruction.
2. Discern which instructional tools work, which are needed, as well as which work for whom (i.e., students, teachers, parents, and others).
3. Make these materials available in alternative useful forms.
4. Explore methods for "salting" content into existing curricula and standardized testing.
5. Create community-driven and supported initiatives while recognizing that schools alone cannot cope with the immense and complex challenges of cybercrime.
6. Create a nationwide "train the trainer" program for teachers.

7. Establish R&D and instructional development mechanisms to maintain quality of education in the face of technologically evolving cybercrime threats.
8. Provide opportunities and incentives for all sectors to participate, coordinate, and collaborate.
9. Focus federal government investments and leadership.
10. Establish acceptable universal standards for Internet safety education and adopt these into national and state education standards with financial assistance to schools as opposed to the legislating of unfunded mandates.

Society must also recognize that today's students are technologically savvy (see, e.g., encyclopedia entry on **digital youth culture**), but are not always able to recognize the implications of their actions and their access to the Internet. Today's students are society's emerging generation of tomorrow's workers, managers, and societal leaders. Physical and cyber security are intertwined and complicated by an increasingly mobile and digital society. Hence, we need to incorporate cyber topics into education generally.

Suggested Readings: CISSE. (n.d.) *History.* Retrieved from CISSE's official Web site: http://www.cisse.info/colloquia/cisse7/history.htm; Cyberspace Research Unit. (2002). *Young people's use of chat rooms: Implications for policy strategies and programs of education.* Lancaster: CRU; McQuade, S. (2006). *Understanding and managing cybercrime.* Boston: Allyn and Bacon; Montabano, E. (2007, October 10). Phishing education called inadequate. *IDG New Service.* Retrieved from http://www.pcworld.com/article/id,138243/article.html; United States Senate. (2000, February 16). Statement of Attorney General Janet Reno before the United States Senate Committee on Appropriations Subcommittee on Commerce, Justice, the State Judiciary and Related Agencies, February 16, 2000. Retrieved from http://www.cybercrime.gov/ag0216.htm; Sheng, S., Magnien, B., Kumaraguru, P., Acquisti, A., Cranor, L.F., Hong, J., & Nunge, E. (2007). Anti-phishing Phil: The design and evaluation of a game that teaches people not to fall for phish. Presented at the 2007 Symposium on Usable Privacy and Security (SOUPS). Available at http://cups.cs.cmu.edu/soups/2007/proceedings/p88_sheng.pdf; Yu, T., Zhang, M., Southern, L., & Joiner, C. (2001). E-commerce safety and security: A Statistical analysis of consumers' attitudes. *Issues in Information Systems, II.* Available at http://www.iacis.org/iis/2001_iis/TOC-IACIS-2001.htm.

Benjamin Wachs and Samuel C. McQuade, III

PRIVACY

Privacy refers to the general belief that certain things such as written materials, oral communications, and matters having to do with personal relationships are confidential and should remain so unless they are voluntarily divulged. However, in the digital age and given worldwide **computerization**, threats to privacy have grown substantially. Many people do not realize that whenever they use a computer or other information technology (IT), a detailed digital record of the data processed and/or transferred is stored on the hard drive of the device they used, on the server of the Internet Service Provider (ISP) if online usage was involved, and potentially on government or private sector databases (such as those that track Web utilization, financial transactions, employee performance, and telephonic communications). For example, digital footprints remain after one surfs the **Internet**, posts information to a Web site, or sends and receives email or text messages. Using a cell phone also leaves a digital trail of evidence revealing who may have placed the call, who was communicated with, how long they communicated, and where the call was made and received. All of these data, literally trillions of computerized records, are potentially valuable to investigations of traditional crimes and **cybercrimes** as well as for thwarting terrorist plots, but could potentially also be accessed in various ways by **cybercriminals**. The data could also be accessed by others, either intentionally or perhaps even inadvertently.

Threats to privacy are becoming an increasingly serious issue because detailed records of computerized device usage are also increasingly being stored online. For example, property records, residential and business addresses, voter lists, and court documents are being digitized in greater numbers by local and state governments and then made available as public records on the Internet. The online storage of emails, photos, banking and financial information, Social Security numbers, and many other types of information has also increased substantially. However, the information is not always stored in secure locations.

Increased personal information online means increased opportunities for someone to use that information in an inappropriate manner. This unauthorized use of information may then be used for abusive or criminal purposes such as **identity theft** or *harassment*. Certain practices of Internet companies that maintain Web sites that routinely use browsers to mine data for personal information are also significant threats to Internet privacy. As consumers perform Internet searches and disclose personal information online, companies can record and store data that may be personal or describe online activities. Further, Internet-based companies often require user registration that involves submitting information that enables identification techniques. Similar practices can extend to online purchases and product warranty procedures forced on consumers. Personal information can also be revealed through online activities such as using email and managing financial accounts. *Spyware* commonly downloaded or installed by unwary consumers also constitutes another threat to online privacy because it forwards personal data to third party strangers without the user's knowledge or consent. Information forwarded in this manner can range from computer or financial account usernames and passwords to the URLs of Web sites visited, and names, email addresses, and phone numbers of persons listed in contact lists.

The security of online information has been called into question in the wake of such security breaches as the 2006 incident in which America Online (AOL) accidentally released the search data of 658,000 users. Also in 2005, ChoicePoint, one of the largest data collectors and resellers in the United States, paid $10 million in civil penalties and $5 million for consumer redress due to an unprecedented data breach. In this case, criminals posing as legitimate business customers used the Internet to access the records of 163,000 consumers and obtained personal information such as Social Security numbers and dates of birth with the intent to commit identity theft.

In America privacy concerns have historically included debate as to how far the government may go in accessing and analyzing data about citizens and residents. Recently, in order to better combat terrorism, the *Uniting and Strengthening America by Providing Appropriate Tools Required to Intercept and Obstruct Terrorism Act of 2001* (i.e., *USA PATRIOT Act*) greatly expanded the authority of law enforcement officers and other government officials to monitor emails, online communications, and phone calls of people. Considerable controversy about this law, however, and particularly concern about the authority of certain U.S. government agencies to carry out their national security responsibilities in cases involving domestic rather than international communications, remains a huge concern for many people. While many people agree with the need for such a law, others see it as a violation of the Constitutional provisions against unreasonable searches and seizures, as well as a threat to privacy.

Laws protecting online privacy and communication are still evolving and vary depending on the type of communication. For example, it has been held in court that an expectation of privacy in an email is reduced once the message is received by another person; see *United States v. Kenneth Charbonneau, 979 F. Supp. 1177 (S.D. Ohio 1997)*. Therefore, a person receiving an email has control over the email, may forward it to others, and cannot be subject to a privacy claim. Similarly, courts have held that users have no reasonable expectation of privacy for information posted to bulletin boards or sent in chat rooms (Collier, 2007). The same has been held true for social networking sites because information is willingly disclosed on these sites. Overall, since the Internet exists as a means for information sharing and exchange, the result is a lessened expectation of privacy. Therefore, once information is shared on the Internet, the user essentially loses control of that information.

Federal online privacy laws are still developing. The *Federal Trade Commission Act* (FTC Act) was enacted to protect against unfairness and deception by enforcing how companies collect, use, and secure the personal information of consumers. Also, the *Children's Online Privacy Protection (COPPA) Act of 1998* safeguards the rights of children by restricting the types of information that commercial Web sites can collect from children who are younger than age 13. The law also contains a provision requiring parental approval for registration to commercial sites such as the popular social networking sites. This law is difficult to enforce because it is difficult to verify the accuracy of the ages of those who attempt to sign up to use the site. Although not specifically listed in the U.S. Constitution, the right to privacy as a basic human right has been established by the Supreme Court under the Ninth Amendment (Collier, 2007).

Suggested Readings: Brodkin, J. (2007). *ChoicePoint details data breach lessons. PC World* Web page: http://www.pcworld.com/printable/article/id,132795/printable.html; Collier, B.P. (2007). Privacy on the Internet: What is reasonable in a wired world? *The Practical Lawyer, 10,* 17–23; Honeycutt, J. (2004). *How to protect your computer from spyware and adware.* Microsoft Web page: http://www.microsoft.com/windowsxp/using/security/expert/honeycutt_spyware.mspx; Larkin, E. (2006, June). New privacy threats. *PC World, 24*(6), 20–22; McQuade, S.C. (2006). Privacy infringement, In *Understanding and managing cybercrime* (pp. 247–264). Boston: Allyn & Bacon; Privacy International. (2007). A Race to the bottom—Privacy ranking of Internet services. Privacy International Web page: http://www.privacyinternational.org/article.shtml?cmd%5B347%5D=x-347-553961; SearchCRM.com. Web page: http://searchsecurity.techtarget.com/; Simpson, M.D. (2007, April). Savaged in cyberspace. *NEA Today, 25*(7), 23; Totty, M. (2007, January 29). Technology (a special report): How to protect your private information: Your life is an open book; it doesn't have to be. *Wall Street Journal, 01,* 1–5; Willard, N. (2006). *Cyberbullying and cyberthreats: Responding to the challenge of online social cruelty, threats, and distress.* Eugene, OR: Center for Safe and Responsible Internet Use.

James P. Colt

R

REGULATORY AGENCIES WITH CYBERCRIME OVERSIGHT RESPONSIBILITIES

Regulatory agencies are an important part of the U.S. government and state governments. Sometimes they are part of the executive branch of government and ultimately report, respectively, to the president of the United States or the governor of a state. In other instances, regulatory agencies are established as independent commissions. Typically, a law passed by the legislative branch of government will authorize the creation of a regulatory agency in order to oversee particular government or business practices. After a regulatory agency is created, it tracks future laws passed by the legislative branch to promulgate specific rules governing what agencies and firms can and cannot do. These rules are referred to as regulations, which have the full force of government law.

> This means that government regulatory agencies can take enforcement action against corporations, public utility and transportation companies, and other types of proprietary firms and subsidiary contractors, etc. if they violate regulations, such as those required to comply with standards for information systems security technology and practices. (McQuade, 2006, p. 307)

Laws and regulations are a matter of public record and are created after input is received by key stakeholders with particular interests in matters of security, public safety, commerce, transportation, and telecommunications policies, among many other subject areas of public concern.

> In many instances, regulatory agencies have legal power to impose steep fines, issue stop work orders, mandate reforms and revoke business/operating licenses held by corporations, public utility and transportation companies, and other types of private and non-profit organizations. Regulatory agencies also coordinate investigations with law enforcement agencies in cases involving suspected violations of regulations and crime

laws. Examples of federal agencies with regulatory authority relating to potential computer abuse, cybercrime violations and information security issues including protection of critical infrastructure and information infrastructure include the following: (McQuade, 2006, p. 307)

Federal Aviation Administration (FAA), the Federal Communications Commission (FCC), the Federal Deposit Insurance Corporation (FDIC), the Federal Elections Commission (FEC), the Securities Exchange Commission (SEC), the Federal Trade Commission (FTC), and the U.S. Nuclear Regulatory Commission (NRC).

Suggested Readings: Federal Aviation Administration. (2008). Federal Aviation Administration (FAA) Home Page. Retrieved from http://www.faa.gov/; Federal Communications Commission. (2008). Federal Communications Commission (FCC) Home Page. Retrieved from http://www.fcc.gov/; Federal Deposit Insurance Corporation. (2008). Federal Deposit Insurance Corporation (FDIC) Home Page. Retrieved from http://www.fdic.gov/; Federal Elections Commission. (2008). Federal Elections Commission (FEC) Home Page. Retrieved from http://www.fec.gov/; U.S. Securities and Exchange Commission. (2008). United States Securities and Exchange Commission (SEC) Home Page. Retrieved from http://www.sec.gov/; Federal Trade Commission. (2008). Federal Trade Commission (FTC) Home Page. Retrieved from http://www.ftc.gov/; U.S. Nuclear Regulatory Commission. (2008). United States Nuclear Regulatory Commission (NRC) Home Page. Retrieved from http://www.nrc.gov/.

Samuel C. McQuade, III

RESEARCH ON CYBERCRIME

Since the mid-1970s researchers associated with colleges, universities, government agencies, professional membership associations, and other entities have accomplished several important studies about computer abuse, computer-related crime, and cybercrime issues. Looking back, we can now see that their discoveries helped society to understand the evolving nature and extent of what today we now recognize as **cybercrime**. Researcher Donn Parker began this effort by studying early forms of computer abuse, which he described in his 1976 book titled *Crime by Computer.* Parker found that computer abuse was increasing markedly, and he forewarned that younger generations of computer users were likely to engage in fearsome levels of offending.

Parker's research inspired additional research in 1984 by the American Bar Association (ABA) and by the American Institute of Certified Public Accounts (AICPA). The ABA project surveyed approximately 1,000 organizations, including many then regarded as Fortune 500 firms. These included many banking and financial institutions, which were among the first types of organizations to feel the effects of computer crime. Only 283 organizations responded to the ABA survey. Many (48 percent) reported they had experienced a computer abuse or crime incident within the prior year with estimated losses ranging from $145 million to $730 million. Thirty-nine percent of organizations that responded to the survey indicated that perpetrators were not able to be identified. The survey conducted by the AICPA was much larger, involving 5,127 banks and 1,232 insurance companies. A relatively small number of banks (105, or 2 percent) and insurance companies (40, or 3 percent) reported experiencing fraud as a consequence of electronic data processing.

In 1985 President Ronald Reagan's Council on Integrity and Efficiency found after surveying numerous federal agencies that computer fraud and abuse existed within the U.S. government. The study discovered 172 cases with estimated losses ranging up to $177,383 and that most instances ranged from $10,000 to $100,000. The following year, in 1986, Forbes Fortune 500 companies surveyed estimated that throughout the country banks lost from $70 million to $100 million annually in financial wire transfers. In 1987, the ABA conducted another survey, this time of 300 corporations and government agencies. Twenty-four percent reported they had experienced computer crime within the previous year with losses ranging from $145 million to $730. In 1989 the Florida Department of Law Enforcement completed a survey of 382 law enforcement agencies, 20 state attorney general offices, and 898 other organizations within the public and private sectors. Findings included that 25 percent of organizations had been victimized by computer crime within the year preceding the survey, and that monetary losses exceeded $1,000,000 in some cases. This string of research studies clearly indicated that **computerization**, despite its advantages, was also bringing about increasing incidences and prevalence of computer-enabled crimes and potential financial losses from abuse of computer systems. Note that it was not until 1986 that the U.S. government passed the *Computer Crime and Abuse Act,* making hacking and certain other types of computer abuse illegal. Several states also passed computer crime laws beginning in the 1980s as research demonstrated the need for this.

Richard Hollinger of the University of Florida is credited with undertaking the first computer crime study involving college students. His study conducted in 1989 focused on pirating and accessing computer accounts without authorization. Results revealed that 10 percent of students had pirated software and 3 percent had accessed a computer account without permission. Hollinger also reported that male students were about twice as likely as female students to engage in these activities and that, if study results were applied to the general population of students surveyed attending the southern university, there could be thousands of felony crime cases committed each semester via campus computer networks.

A 1991 survey later reported on by the United Nations Commission on Crime and Justice (in 1997) found that among 3,000 **Internet** address sites located in North America and Europe, 72 percent had experienced a breach of information security within the preceding year, and 43 percent of these breaches were of an illegal nature. Then in 1993, inspired by Hollinger's earlier study, William Skinner and Anne Fream conducted another study of college students. Their survey of 581 students focused on software **piracy**, guessing passwords, gaining unauthorized access to systems merely to browse data or manipulate it, and writing or using virus-like programs. The study found that nearly half the students surveyed had committed one or more of these activities, a clear sign that computer abuse and crime committed by college students was increasing just as the Internet was changing to support the World Wide Web.

In 1996 David Carter and Andra Katz of Michigan State University completed their national study of 600 corporate security directors, all members of the American Society of Industrial Security (now known as ASIS International). Nearly all 151 respondents to the survey (98 percent) revealed that their firms were victimized by computer-related crimes, with nearly one in three indicating their firm had been victimized 25 or more times primarily by insider employees. Carter and Katz also discovered that the principle asset targeted in the attacks was **intellectual property** such as trade secrets information.

The year 1997 marked the beginning of research interest in computer-enabled crimes committed against youth online. In this year the U.S. Congress provided funds through the **National Center for Missing and Exploited Children** (NCMEC) to the University of New Hampshire Crimes Against Children Research Center. Researchers David Finkelhor, Kimberly Mitchell, and Janis Wolak subsequently published their report in 1999 of findings from the National Youth Internet Survey. The report described survey findings from telephone interviews with 1,501 randomly selected youth ranging in age from 10 to 17 and their parents. Results revealed that within three years of the World Wide Web becoming widely used, approximately 1 in 4 youth were exposed to pictures of naked people or individuals having sex; 1 in 17 was harassed or threatened online; 20 percent of youth surveyed had been solicited for sex within the preceding year; and 3 percent had been asked online to meet someone in person, or received a phone call, mail, money, or some type of gift from someone they had communicated with online. The survey also revealed, however, that about 48 percent of all unwanted solicitations for sex were believed to have been communicated by other youth (i.e., persons less than 18 years of age). This study was repeated five years later. In 2006 researchers from the Center reported that little had changed: Youth were still being victimized online by adults and by other youth despite several new laws intended to prevent and deter cybercrimes (see **Laws, Children Online**, **Laws, Illegal Use of Computers and IT Devices**, **Laws, Information Security Requirements**, **Laws, Privacy Protections**, **Laws That Facilitate or Limit Cybercrime Investigations**).

In 2003 the Federal Trade Commission released the first national study of identify theft. The report concluded that over 23 million Americans had been victims of **identify theft** within the preceding five years, with approximately 10 million of these people having been victimized within the year preceding the survey. (This study established the foundation for the later enactment of the *Identity Theft and Assumption Deterrence Act* in 1998.) From 2004 to 2006 Samuel C. McQuade, III and colleagues associated with the Rochester Institute of Technology (RIT) in New York State completed a series of college student surveys pertaining to use of the Internet, computer, and other types of information technology (IT) devices. Findings from this research revealed that college students were often victims and also offenders of online abuse and cybercrimes, such as cheating on assignments, papers, and examinations; pirating of music, movies, and software; making online threats and stalking; credit card fraud and identity theft; and computer hacking or password cracking among other forms of IT-enabled abuse and crimes.

In 2008 McQuade and numerous colleagues affiliated with RIT and The (Rochester, New York Regional) Cyber Safety and Ethics Initiative completed a survey of 40,079 kindergarten–grade 12 students along with hundreds of parents and teachers from 14 school districts. Titled the "RIT Survey of Internet and At-Risk Behaviors," this study concluded that (McQuade, 2008)

- Most kindergarten-age children use the Net and are exposed to content which makes them feel uncomfortable, yet one in four do not report disturbing incidents or materials to grownups.
- Cyber bullying begins in second grade at the same age when eight percent of children report seeing or being told private things about the bodies of other people while they are online.

- Illegal pirating of music, movies and software via p2p networks begins in fourth grade as does children sharing of personal information about themselves with friends and strangers online.
- By middle school (grades 7–9) approximately eleven percent of students report defeating of Internet filtering/blocking software installed on home computers by parents. They engage in many forms cyber-enabled offending spanning academic dishonesty to purchasing illegal and prescription drugs online, among other types of IT-enabled abuse and crime. They are also victims of many types of online abuse and crime, not limited to those of a sexual nature, and many youth are victimized in more than one way every year. (McQuade, 2008)

RIT's research is also revealing that this general trend continues through high school and into college years; that cybercrime involves much more than adult sex offenders targeting adolescents online; and that most online abuse and crime involving youth goes unreported and undetected. Indeed, youth often victimize each other online even as they are victimized by adults, and they often know offenders beforehand. (McQuade, 2008)

The preceding descriptions of research studies essentially track the emergence of cybercrime and various ways in which information systems, computers, and other types of IT devices are increasingly used to cause harm. Despite the importance of these and other studies, considerably more research is needed to better understand cybercrime and ways to prevent and deter it. Historically researchers have had very little money with which to undertake cybercrime-related research. In addition, they have been hampered by several other things including: (1) a primary focus by criminologists and criminal justice agencies on traditional forms of crime not involving the Internet and IT devices; (2) statistical reporting systems that include limited data on ways in which IT-enabled crimes occur; (3) reluctance by financial institutions and other types of organizations to report monetary and data losses out of fear about losing consumer or investor confidence; and (4) relatively few researchers being interested or trained in technology and cybercrime issues. As the number, variety, and consequences of cybercrime increases, society must overcome these historical barriers to research about high tech ways in which people violate laws and cause harm via the Internet.

Suggested Readings: American Bar Association. (1984). *Report on computer crime.* Washington: The Task Force, 51, 12, 6 p. HV6773.A44; Carter, D.L., and Katz, A.J. (1996). *Trends and experiences in computer-related crime: Findings from a national study.* Paper presented at the annual meeting of the Academy of Criminal Justice Sciences, Las Vegas, Nevada; Finkelhor, D., Wolak, J., & Mitchell, K.J. (2000, June). *Online victimization: A report of the nation's youth.* Washington, DC: National Center for Missing and Exploited Children; McQuade, S.C. (2007). We must educate young people about cybercrime before they start college. *Chronicle of Higher Education, 53*(14), B29; McQuade, S., and Sampat, N. (2008). *Survey of at-risk behaviors.* Available at http://www.rrcsei.org/ RIT%20Cyber%20Survey%20Final%20Report.pdfParker, D.B. (1976). *Crime by computer.* New York: Charles Scribner's Sons; Skinner, W.F., and Fream, A.M. (1997). A social learning theory analysis of computer crime among college students. *The Journal of Research in Crime and Delinquency, 34*(4), 495–519; Synovate. (2003). *FTC identity theft survey report.* Washington, DC: Federal Trade Commission.

Samuel C. McQuade, III

S

SCIENTIFIC AND PROFESSIONAL MISCONDUCT

Scientific and professional misconduct pertains to fraud committed by researchers and other professionals engaged in the management of studies, business operations, or government or other nonprofit services. This is an important cybercrime issue because such fraud, including faking of research findings, mismanagement of finances, and/or violating **intellectual property** (IP) rights, increasingly involves using computerized devices and networks.

At a minimum, scientific and professional misconduct typically violates *codes of ethics* if not also organizational policies and criminal laws prohibiting *fraud* among other types of *financial crime*. The Office of Research Integrity, which is part of the U.S. Department of Health and Human Services, has created standards regarding "fabrication, falsification or plagiarism in proposing, performing or reviewing research, or in reporting research results" (Weiss, 2005, p. AO3). Nonetheless, in surveys scientists conducting research in human health and other issues admit they fake aspects of their research. In what has been reported as "the most extensive scientific misconduct case the National Institutes of Health (NIH) has seen in decades...[Dr. Eric Poehlman] admitted in court documents to falsifying data in 15 federal grant applications and numerous published articles" (Kintisch, 2005, p. 1851) and to defrauding the U.S. government of millions in sponsored research dollars. For his crime Dr. Poehlman received more than a year in prison and a $250,000 fine, and he was banned from receiving future research funds from the U.S. government.

Since the **Internet** was transformed into the World Wide Web in the mid-1990s making the Net much easier and more popular to use, scientific and professional misconduct has occurred with greater frequency. Among the notorious private sector cases are those involving crimes committed by senior managers and executives of large businesses like Enron and also WorldCom. Both of these cases involved investigations by the U.S. Securities Exchange Commission into *securities fraud* (i.e., manipulation of company stock market prices). The crimes were determined to have occurred over long periods of time, on a grand scale, involving billions of dollars and resulting in thousands of people losing their investments in these companies. Fines and prison sentences were imposed on several senior individuals in these companies, who exemplified ways in which lack of professional ethics, cyber abuse, and **cybercrime** often involve using computer and other information systems including the Internet to manipulate accounting data in order to carry out finance-related crimes.

Suggested Readings: Chang, K. (2002, October 15). On scientific fakery and the systems to catch it. *New York Times,* F1; Kintisch, E. (2005). Scientific Misconduct: Researcher Faces Prison for Fraud in NIH Grant Applications and Papers. *Science, 307*(5717), 1851; Kintisch, E. (2006). Poehlman Sentenced to 1 Year of Prison. *Science* magazine Web site: http://sciencenow.sciencemag.org/cgi/content/full/2006/628/1; McQuade, S.C. (2006). Scientific misconduct. In *Understanding and Managing Cybercrime* (pp. 92–93). Boston: Pearson Education, Inc.; Moore, J.W. (2002). Scientific misconduct. *Journal of Chemical Education, 79*(12), 1391; U.S. Office of Research Integrity Web site: http://ori.dhhs.gov/education/, and specifically "2005 Press Release—Dr. Eric T. Poehlman," viewable at http://ori.dhhs.gov/misconduct/cases/press_release_poehlman.shtml; Weiss, R. (2005). Web sites of SecuritiesFraud-FYI, specifically http://www.securitiesfraudfyi.com/enron_fraud.html and http://www.securitiesfraudfyi.com/worldcom_fraud.html.

Samuel C. McQuade, III

SECURITY MANAGEMENT RESPONSIBILITIES

Information assurance within organizational settings is the responsibility of all system users because, as an old saying goes, "a chain is only as strong as its weakest link." However, managers who oversee information systems security in organizations have several administrative and technical responsibilities that ordinary system users will not have the needed expertise to accomplish. Depending on the size of the organization and the number of managers involved in system administration responsibilities, special duties may include the following: (1) conducting security assessments to record security measures already in place; (2) designing and implementing security controls; (3) recommending and possibly overseeing technology purchases to improve security measures when warranted; (4) managing teams of technical personnel to provide assistance to system users; (5) outsourcing technical services when in-house personnel do not have sufficient knowledge, skills, or abilities to accomplish information security changes or objectives; (6) conducting risk and threat analyses to determine forms of **cybercrime** the organization may be especially vulnerable to; (7) ensuring due diligence, which refers to implementing information security policies, procedures, and technologies that are consistent with sound and best practices within the organization's industry or employment sector; (8) establishing data and operational recovery plans and business continuity plans to keep the organization functioning even amidst a devastating event such as a natural disaster or cybercrime that cripples critical information systems; (9) facilitating internal and external security audits to detect accounting and security-related improprieties; and (10) effecting leadership to bring about needed cultural reforms within the organization to influence attitudes and behaviors among users for better security practices. There is much to understand about each of the topics listed above, which could easily fill an entire chapter in a book devoted to information systems security management. Here we will briefly describe technical concepts that pertain to managing information security within organizations.

An information system consists of combinations of hardware and software that can be used to manipulate data. Information systems can be installed in facilities or vehicles of any kind. Determining the level of protection that an information system should have may be specified by government laws or regulations, technology standards, and/or best practices for due care and diligence. Security domains are generally hierarchical in nature, implying one level of security is cleared to see information at a lower level of security. For example, government information categorized as "Top Secret" is more sensitive and requires higher levels of security than "Secret" or "Classified." Levels of information systems security depends on the nature of data contained within the system and accessible via hardware and software components. Revealing the salary of employees in the private sector is not nearly as serious as allowing classified government data to be hacked into or lost as the result of losing a laptop computer or storage media containing such data. The value of particular information determines standards of protection that must be applied and will also guide the thoroughness of periodic systems checks and audits.

In all organizations information assurance is a combination of ensuring the confidentiality, integrity, and availability of data contained on information systems. *Confidentiality* refers to keeping sensitive data nonaccessible to people who do not have authorization to view the data. *Integrity* refers to protecting data against unauthorized modification or destruction. *Availability* pertains to how accessible data are to users who are authorized to view the data. Additional technical concepts related in information assurance include the following: (a) *authentication,* which means to verify data stored, transmitted, or received has not been manipulated; (b) *nonrepudiation,* which refers to a sender of data or source of an information security problem not being able to later claim they were not responsible; and (c) *audit trail,* which includes records of user activities that occur on an information system and are in their own right to be considered sensitive data in need of relatively high levels of protection. For example, during software testing a technology developer may send test messages through a security boundary device to validate that the number of messages sent is the same as the number of messages received. An audit trail of this test that shows an unequal number of messages sent and received within an information system may reveal a security flaw.

The audit mechanism of a computer system has five important security goals. First, the audit mechanism must allow examiners of data processing to review patterns of access to information systems, software, and files. Second, audit mechanisms must discover users' and outsiders' attempts to bypass information security protections. Third, computer audit mechanisms must identify instances in which users exceed their authorized permissions. Fourth, computer audit capabilities should deter authorized users and outsiders from misusing or abusing an information system. Fifth, audits should reinforce principles of information assurance in the minds of authorized users (i.e., by putting them on notice that use of information systems via computers or other electronic devices is recorded and discoverable). Thus, even if an attempt to bypass an information security protection is successful, an effective audit trail will document the activities (e.g., keystrokes) and enable investigators conducting a forensic analysis to trace the event.

Suggested Readings: Caelli, W., Longley, D., and Shain, M. (1991). *Information security handbook.* New York: Stockton Press; Director Central Intelligence. (2000, May). *Protecting Sensitive Compartmented Information Within Information Systems.* Washington, DC: Government Accountability Office. Available at http://www.fas.org/irp/offdocs/dcid-6-3-manual.pdf; Guttman, B. (1995). *An introduction to computer security: The NIST handbook.* Darby, Pennsylvania: Diane Publishing Company; McQuade, S.C. (2006). Preventing cybercrime with information security. In *Understanding and managing cybercrime* (Chap. 10). Boston, MA: Allyn and Bacon; Committee on National Security Systems. (2006, June). National Information Assurance (IA) glossary. *CNSS instruction 4009.* Washington, DC: Government Printing Office. Available at http://www.cnss.gov/Assets/pdf/cnssi_4009.pdf

Rob Paisley

SOCIAL AND ECONOMIC IMPACTS OF CYBERCRIME

For every form of crime there exist one or more *victims* consisting of individuals, groups of people, and/or organizations such as business or government agencies. This reality applies to all types of **cybercrime** and *online abuse.* Consequently, anyone who uses computers or portable electronic devices such as laptops, PDAs, and cell phones is vulnerable to being harmed in some way. Each year millions of people throughout the world who live, work, or go to school and use these and other types of *information technology (IT)* devices are victimized by one or more types of cybercrime or online abuse such as computer hacking, **identify theft**, online threats and harassment, and theft or destruction of data to name just a few. Some victims of cybercrime experience destruction, manipulation, or denial of access to valuable data; others suffer loss of time, money, computer equipment, and/or other resources; still others become fearful of having their systems attacked again or experience other types of emotional harm. Depending on the type(s) and sophistication of cybercrime or online abuse of *information systems* involved, people may not even realize what has occurred until damages have been done, if ever.

All forms of harm experienced by victims of crime, including cybercrime, may be qualified and understood in terms of their social and economic impacts. Whereas social impacts pertain to adverse personal consequences experienced by people such as becoming fearful or having their interpersonal relationships negatively affected, economic impacts refer to financial losses experienced by members of society or organizations. In theory social and economic impacts are inseparable because while financial value may be associated with personal harm and suffering, loss of money or other types of financial assets including valuable data may result in social consequences such as compromised **privacy**, family strife, loss of employment or academic standing, and so forth.

Criminologists (i.e., experts who study crime-related issues), law enforcement officers, government officials, insurance agents, and other members of society concerned with the social and economic impacts of cybercrime periodically attempt to measure the prevalence and/or incidence of cybercrimes and the effects of these on people affected. This is typically accomplished with specialized research involving the surveying of crime victims or systematic analysis of police investigation reports possibly combined with economic impact studies. For example, on an ongoing basis the U.S. Bureau of Justice Statistics (BJS) in partnership with the U.S. Census Bureau surveys people living in the United States about crimes they have experienced and the impacts of these on their lives. The Federal Bureau of Investigation, also in partnership with BJS, annually gathers and reports information about the number and impacts of crime that occurs throughout America. Economic impacts of crime studies are often based on these and similar survey research reports.

Current estimates of the social and economic impacts of cybercrime vary widely depending on the type of cybercrime and population of victims studied, time period involved, and value placed on losses experienced by victims. For example, in 2007 the Consumer Reports National Research Center, on the basis of a survey of more than 2,000 households with **Internet** access, estimated that in the two years prior to the study being undertaken U.S. consumers lost $7 billion as the result of computer viruses, spyware, and **phishing** schemes (Prince, 2007). Also in 2007, researchers at the Rochester Institute of Technology (RIT) found in a survey of several thousand K–grade 12 students found that children begin using the Internet at very young ages (McQuade & Fisk, 2007). When they do, most students use their home computers, cell phones, and other mobile devices without parental supervision, positive role modeling, or school instruction in how to be safe, secure, and responsible online. Consequently, perhaps millions of children throughout the United States and in other nations are increasingly engaged in offending behaviors while online and are also victims of many types of high tech crime and abuse.

Specific RIT research findings reveal the following: (a) Most kindergarten-age children use the Net for relatively long periods of time and are exposed to content that makes them feel uncomfortable, yet one in four do not report disturbing incidents or materials to grown-ups; (b) cyber bullying—intentionally embarrassing, harassing, intimidating, or threatening other people online—begins in second grade at the same age when 8 percent of children report seeing or being told private things about the bodies of other people while they are using the Internet; (c) illegal pirating of music, movies, and software via peer-to-peer networks begins in fourth grade as does online sharing of personal information with friends and strangers that can lead to crime **victimization**; (d) by middle school (grades 7–9) 8 percent of students report defeating Internet filtering or blocking software installed on home computers by parents. As a group, middle school students engage in many other alarming behaviors online including but not limited to dishonest communications, academic cheating, illegally purchasing prescription or illicit drugs, computer hacking, password cracking, and violating copyrights. Many times the victims of cybercrimes and online abuse are friends of juvenile offenders. This general trend continues through high school and into the college years with the variety and amount of cyber offending and victimization corresponding with use of IT and time spent online. In addition, most online abuse and crime involving children is not reported and goes undetected. RIT's research also reveals that children often victimize each other online even as they are victimized by adults, and they often know their offenders beforehand (McQuade & Fisk, 2007).

Several things prevent accurate estimates of the amount of cybercrime as well as the social and economic impacts of any particular type of cybercrime. These include, but are not limited to, the following: (a) people not realizing they have been victimized, (b) reluctance of crime victims to report crimes to authorities, (c) inconsistent categorization of cybercrimes by law enforcement agencies, and (d) relatively few criminologists who are interested and also able to research cybercrime issues. In reality there are very few reliable estimates of social and economic harms caused by cybercrime. Fortunately, this situation is beginning to change as more research is undertaken and reported to the public, thereby making more and more people aware of the worldwide cybercrime problem, its impacts on society, and the ways in which it can be prevented.

Suggested Readings: McQuade, S.C. (2006). The social and economic impacts of cybercrime. In *Understanding and managing cybercrime* (Chap. 6). Boston: Pearson Education, Inc.; McQuade, S., and Fisk, N. (2007). *High tech adolescent offending and victimization: A new paradigm for crime and deviancy research.* Presented at The National Institute of Justice Conference on July 23, 2007, in Arlington, VA. Available at http://www.rrcsei.org/rrcseicontentresearch.pdf; Prince, B. (2007). *Survey: Cost of cybercrime reaches $7B.* Retrieved August 10, 2007, from http://www.eweek.com/article2/0,1759,2167203,00.asp.

Samuel C. McQuade, III

SOCIAL ENGINEERING

Social engineering is the act of manipulating a person or persons into performing some action. In the realm of computer abuse, this most commonly takes the form of, but is not limited to, convincing victims to divulge personal, financial, or security-related information or to grant access to computer systems or physical environments where such information is stored. Use of trickery and fraud is common in such attacks (McQuade, 2006).

Attacks can take place in person, over the phone, through the **Internet** (including email, instant messaging, and the like), through hard copy correspondence, or through any other means of communication.

While computer crime is often thought of in terms of purely technical exploits, this mind-set is dangerous and shortsighted. As legendary cybercriminal and current security expert Kevin Mitnick has pointed out, humans are generally the weakest link when it comes to securing information. In *The Art of Deception,* his 2002 book on the subject, Mitnick describes many of his own exploits using social engineering.

Social engineering plays a role in many different kinds of computer abuse and crime and is a popular **attack vector**, or means of attack, among hackers and others. A common example is the practice of **phishing**, where an attacker or attackers send out email, instant messages, voice mails, or other communiqués disguised to look like they came from a legitimate source, such as a credit card company, bank, or business. The fraudulent message generally requests that victims "verify" personal information such as account numbers or passwords and often direct them to enter such information into equally fraudulent Web sites. The attacker can then use the personal information to commit fraud, **identify theft**, and other crimes (McQuade, 2006).

Not all social engineering techniques require a technological component, however. Another common example of social engineering is pretexting. Pretexting involves the use of an invented identity and/or scenario (the pretext) to persuade a person to provide sensitive information or access to sensitive computer systems and the like. An attacker calling a victim and pretending to be from his bank or calling an employee of the bank and convincing them that he is, in fact, the victim would be two examples of this type of attack. Pretexting is generally conducted over the phone and requires prior research on the part of the perpetrators (FTC, 2006).

Pretexting is often used to convince businesses to release customer information and is sometimes used by private investigators to obtain things like banking records, phone records, and other personal information (Bangerman, 2006).

Obtaining a person's phone records through pretexting was outlawed by the U.S. Congress in 2006. This law carries fines of up to $250,000 and as many as 10 years in prison for violators. Companies caught pretexting can be fined as much as $500,000 (Bangerman, 2006). Obtaining a person's financial records through pretexting was outlawed by Congress in 1999.

Phishing is also illegal under the *Controlling the Assault of Non-Solicited Pornography and Marketing (CAN-SPAM) Act of 2003,* which authorizes the Federal Trade Commission to prosecute phishers (McQuade, 2006).

According to noted computer security expert Donn Parker, effective social engineering techniques involve one or more of the following:

- Using appropriate, often official-sounding jargon, such as that used by a specific company or agency.
- Mentioning, or "name dropping," persons in authority in such a way as to imply relationships with that party.
- Reading online bulletin boards and the like as a means of gathering intelligence on a victim or victims.
- Reading initial log on screens to learn basic contact information, such as help desk numbers.
- Mixing lies and truths to make requests seem more plausible.
- Exaggerating or minimizing the importance of receiving certain information.
- Asserting authority, "pulling rank," or pretending to be someone in authority.
- Using intimidation and threats to manipulate subjects.
- Using praise, sympathy, and flattery to manipulate subjects.
- Repeatedly causing false alarms in order to get a subject to disable security safeguards. (McQuade, 2006)

Social engineering attacks generally follow a distinct pattern. In the first step, the perpetrator identifies the people, facilities, or information system to be attacked. In the second step, the attacker conducts research and collects intelligence on his or her target in order to discover security weaknesses. In the third step, the attacker develops rapport with persons who control access to the targeted information, computing system, or facility. In the fourth step, the attacker violates the trust of those persons, and in the fifth step, uses the information collected to commit one or more abuses or crimes (McQuade, 2006).

Suggested Readings: Bangermam, E. (2006, December 11). *Congress outlaws pretexting.* Available on the Ars Technica Web site: http://arstechnica.com/news.ars/post/20061211-8395.html; McQuade, S.C. (2006). *Understanding and managing cybercrime.* Boston: Allyn & Bacon; FTC. (2006). *Pretexting: Your personal information revealed.* Federal Trade Commission Web site: http://www.ftc.gov/bcp/conline/pubs/credit/pretext.shtm; Mitnick, K., Simon, W.L., & Wozniak, S. (2002). *The art of deception: Controlling the human element of security.* New York: John Wiley & Sons.

Eric Walter

SPAM

Spam is unsolicited commercial messages sent electronically, usually to many people at once, often through email. Spam generally contains advertising in one or more forms such as offers to sell prescription drugs, stock tips, links to online dating services or pornography Web sites, or various business opportunities often of questionable legitimacy. A person who sends spam is called a "spammer."

The word "SPAM" has been in use almost 70 years, long before it described advertising related email. "SPAM" was first coined (and trademarked) in 1937 as the brand name of a canned pork product that is still made by the Hormel Foods Corporation. Hormel's official SPAM Web site recommends that capital letters be used when referring to its meat product, and that lowercase letters (i.e., "spam") should be used to refer to unsolicited advertising emails.

How "spam" came to mean unwanted advertising-related email is unclear. One theory comes from the British television series *Monty Python's Flying Circus.* In a well-known skit from that show, Viking warriors chanted "*Spam!*" repeatedly, drowning out all other dialogue, in the same way that spam messages drown out other communication. It has also been suggested (and widely debated) that "spam" is an acronym for such terms as "simultaneously posted advertising message" or "single post to all mailboxes." While no evidence exists that definitively answers this question, support for the Monty Python link was noted in an episode of NPR's *All Things Considered* (See "At 30, Spam Going Nowhere Soon," 2008). Today, the word "spam" has become part of the lexicon of cyber culture, usually referred to in disgust by users who dislike receiving unwanted email sent by advertising agencies or other types of firms.

Creating spam is not difficult. The process involves first creating an enticing email message, embedding links to additional online sources of content, and then distributing the email simultaneously to as many users as possible. In the early days of the **Internet**, spam messages were posted in online chat sessions and newsgroups where many users would see it due to the open nature of those conversational formats. The first spam message was allegedly sent in 1978 to about 400 people in order to sell computers. Throughout the 1980s and 1990s, as more Internet users established personal email accounts, mass lists of email addresses were gathered and used to send spam messages to multiple individuals at once. Today, one common method of distributing spam is through **botnets**, which are networks of computers that have been secretly taken over by hackers or others and are remotely controlled in ways that are not obvious to their users. These "**zombie computers**" send spam messages to emails that are contained either in the computer's own address book or on massive external lists of email addresses.

These address lists are obtained in various legal or illegal ways. For instance, address lists can be purchased from legitimate companies going out of business or from firms that do not maintain **privacy** policies for protecting personal information of their customers. Email address lists can also be stolen through hacking into information systems or socially engineering people into giving up client or customer account information. It is also possible to acquire massive email lists from legitimate publication customer lists or by harvesting personal information off of the Internet using special software designed to systematically search Web sites for email addresses or other contact information. The legality of such measures is frequently unclear.

In the United States, the sending of spam may be illegal in some cases. The *2003 Controlling the Assault of Non-Solicited Pornography and Marketing (CAN-SPAM) Act* makes it a crime to distribute spam that lacks a subject line identifying it as an advertisement, a legitimate physical address to the individual or group sending it, a valid return email address, and an opt-out feature by which users can prevent future emails. The legislation does not affect spammers outside the United States, however.

A substantial amount of email now being sent and received may be considered spam. In a May 2004 Congressional hearing, the email filtering company Postini Inc. estimated that 83 percent of the email it handed for its mostly U.S.-based customers was spam. India, a country whose Internet presence has grown substantially in recent years, has experienced an explosion of spam with as much as 90 percent of all email traffic sent to Indian PC users in 2004 identified as spam.

Spam can be dangerous. For example, **malware** can be embedded within or attached to an original email message, which can cause damage to an operating system or software applications installed on a computer hard drive. Spam can also take the form of a Trojan horse malware program to cover its harmful contents and can also damage computers when massive amounts of email are sent to a single or limited number of computers in a tactic known as "mail bombing," which can be a form of **denial of service** or **distributed denial of service attacks**. In one case, a teenager from the United Kingdom flooded a server with junk emails causing it to crash. There are many examples of spam slowing down computer networks and disrupting the pace of Internet traffic.

Spam is not limited to computer email messages. It is now also being sent via text messages to mobile phones, in a process commonly known as "spimming." Each year, unwanted spam costs consumers and businesses billions of dollars in time and productivity losses. In 2004 economic losses within the United States were estimated at over $21 billion; however, this amount may be increasing. Each year estimates of financial harm caused by spam on a worldwide basis increase. In 2007 Nucleus Research estimated that the costs of spam exceeded $71 billion worldwide. The organization attributed losses to the following: (1) businesses needing to purchase anti-spam technology; (2) lost productivity by employees who waste time to delete spam or who take company time to check out spam messages or embedded Web links; (3) wasted storage space on information systems; (4) increased Internet connectivity service fees that are passed along to customers; and (5) confusion surrounding what is related to **cybercrime** and real economic issues versus deceptive information relating to financial matters such as business investment opportunities.

Suggested Readings: At 30, Spam going nowhere soon. (2008). *All Things Considered:* National Public Radio; Hormel. (2006). *SPAM and the Internet.* Hormel Web site: http://www.spam.com/legal/spam/; IT Security. (2008). The real cost of spam. IT Security Web site: http://www.itsecurity.com/features/real-cost-of-spam-121007/; ISPs charge to deliver mass e-mails. (2006, May/June). *The Information Management Journal, 40*(3), 20; Kirk, J. (2006, May 22). Alleged e-mail "bomber" faces trial after ruling. *ComputerWorld, 40*(21), 18; McQuade, S. (2006). *Understanding and managing cybercrime.* Boston: Allyn and Bacon; Miller, C. (2005, August). Mobile spam: Coming to your mobile phone? *Law Enforcement Technology, 32*(8), 44, 46–49; Rockbridge Associates. (2005). *2004 National technology readiness survey.* Retrieved from http://www.rhsmith.umd.edu/ntrs/NTRS_2004.pdf; Spam invades India. (2006, May/June). *The Information Management Journal, 40*(1), 16.

Kelly Socia

T

TECHNOLOGIES COMMONLY USED FOR CYBERCRIME

In order to understand technologies used in cybercrimes, it is first important to understand various forms of **cybercrime** and ways in which they are carried out online. Each type of cybercrime may require a particular set of skills, knowledge, resources, access to particular data or information systems, and motive. Collectively these factors are known as "SKRAM" (Parker, 1998). It is also true that while the SKRAM of individual and groups of **cybercriminals** vary, so does the intensity of their motivations, which has to do with how driven they are to accomplish their crimes. Therefore, regardless of whether the cybercrime involves **child pornography**, "click fraud," *computer trespass,* **copyright infringement**, *cyber stalking,* denial of service/extortion, **identity theft**, cyber threats or harassment, **intellectual property (IP)** theft, creating and distributing **malware**, masquerading (including **phishing**), marketplace or disaster *fraud,* unsolicited email (**spam**) or instant messages (*spim*), etc., the people behind these and other forms of cybercrime all possess unique SKRAM that drives their choice of information systems, tools, and techniques to carry out the types of cybercrime that they tend to specialize in.

Most cybercrime has come about as the result of **computerization**, which is rapidly expanding the scale, complexity, connectivity, and affordability of information services and information technology (IT) devices. In general, **Internet** service and IT costs are declining, and this allows more and more people to begin using computers and other devices in deceitful, harmful, and criminal ways. Technological advances always provide benefits and possibilities of risk and harm to society. Just as cars allow people to drive around comfortably, conveniently, relatively quickly, and safely, it is also true that cars can be driven in negligent or reckless manners risking property and the lives of everyone who shares the roadway. Cars are sometimes also used deliberately to carry out crimes. This is analogous to users of IT devices who navigate the cyber superhighways of the Internet. With adequate knowledge and skill they can choose to "drive" their computers or other electronic devices on the Internet in safe and responsible ways or in negligent, reckless, and even criminal ways that cause harm to other people. Users who would responsibly use IT are constantly battling with unseen cybercriminals, some of whom use their computers to conduct thousands of calculations per second just to scan for security vulnerabilities on information systems.

In reality, responsible IT users and cybercriminals can use the same information systems, devices, and software to accomplish information security or cybercrime objectives. The same technology that enables people to put an entire human resources database in their pocket for emergency access purposes enables a disgruntled employee to walk off with it and later sell the data to identity thieves. The root of these weaknesses is the lack of security representation in organizations that produce software and in the mind of the software consumer. Who asks for security features in the software they use? When using email or instant messaging software, who wants to make sure that persons with whom they are interacting really are the persons intended? For some businesses and government agencies this precision of knowledge is critical, especially if financial data or other types of sensitive information need to be exchanged online. But most consumers do not see it as important, or they see the steps that need to be taken for obtaining and checking digital signatures as inconvenient.

New forms of IT can result in new opportunities for cybercriminals. Products now being designed to enable photos taken with digital cameras to be automatically and directly transferred to social networking Web sites are a prime example. The danger lies in the connection "handshake" between servers possibly being intercepted, as well as photographic content becoming publicly available and subsequently used without authorization for criminal purposes. Many of the municipal network wireless projects suffer from the same design flaw, no real identification or authentication of users logging into the system, and possibly connecting through unsecured ports (see **wardriving**). Open Internet access processes, so-called "just sign-on" connections lacking identification and authentication safeguards make it easy for criminals to act anonymously.

Another important technology concept to understand is "depth of defense," which is also known as "layering" of information security protections. This is the idea of designing the equivalent of several concentric fences, walls, locked doors, security personnel, and surveillance camera systems along with other forms of physical and cyber protections such as firewalls around valued facilities and data. However, the expression "defense in depth" also coined by security professionals also applies to the thinking of cybercriminals. This is especially when it comes to protecting their identity. Even though a computer account registration might indicate an address in London, network traces to the IP address could actually identify the system user being in Sydney, Australia. Using false names and contact information is very common, despite being illegal for certain individuals, such as registered sex offenders living in the United States or people applying for banking or credit card accounts.

Acquiring the real names, addresses, and established cyber/banking account numbers is critical to accomplishing many forms of cybercrime, and it is absolutely fundamental in identity theft cases. In other words, cybercriminals often pretend to be someone online not only by using handles, screen names, or usernames, but also by using information about someone else in order to assume part or all of his identity. Taking over a computer and turning it into a *bot* to be used for criminal purposes is like stealing a car to pull off a bank robbery: Even if witnesses get the license plate number and a description of the getaway car, police, upon finding the car, will still not have the driver who robbed the bank! Kevin Mitnick allegedly used up to six intermediate computers from around the Internet in order to work on a computer he intended to compromise.

Cybercriminals who wish to remain anonymous are now also using "the onion router" (TOR) method, which is a network of peer computers that will scatter traffic in near real time to routing hosts. That means that a person can set up a computer system to go through TOR capable of routing traffic through another TOR site. By routing traffic through a series of onion router connections being hosted in different countries, cybercriminals can elude law enforcement or other investigators by diverting their real whereabouts and identity. TOR systems can be configured to transmit data very quickly and retain it for only short periods of time, while also changing connection interface requirements. So the "state" of where an offender is and how they are able to transmit traffic back and forth and all around the world is kept for only a short time and changes constantly. Consequently, a cyber attack launched through TOR may appear to be coming from all over the Internet. As was mentioned above, TOR has legitimate uses, where people in countries with oppressive regimes are able to access more accurate information from outside sources without being traced.

Weakness in the design of identification systems abounds. The foundation of email transfer, the Simple Mail Transfer Protocol (SMTP), trusts the user to say who he is, but accepts all sorts of usernames (e.g., DancingDiva4187). However SMTP does not restrict the number of accounts that any single person can have. This is not unlike postal mail: a person can send and receive mail and packages from many different physical address locations. Another vulnerability inherent to Internet technology is epitomized in "spidering" methods used in Web browser search engines such as Google, Yahoo, Ask.com, and Lycos. If cleverly used by cybercriminals, these tools can be a power source for intelligence gathering about information systems, organizations targeted for economic espionage, or people whose confidential information will then be used to make them victims of identity theft. While so-called "Google hacking" to acquire information through the Web is an ethically controversial practice, millions of people conduct searches online each day in order to find out information about persons, places, things, and processes—all of which can potentially be used for good or for causing harm and committing crimes. Using search engines to find design flaws in operating systems and software applications is also common practice by computer hackers and crackers. Vulnerabilities, exploits of those vulnerabilities, information used in **social engineering**, anonymous relay sites or networks, information on countries where cybercrime is not addressed, and Web hosting services in those countries are all part of the vast repository of Internet information made easy to use through search engines.

The Design Flaws of Ease of Use

There is no security advocacy in terms of managing complexity. Most users want things simple, but also want all sorts of bells and whistles. That is why most users agree to the End User License agreement (EULA) without reading it. It is also why users do not bother to check software packages for spyware, or even for reliability. So hackers can and have bundled malware with useful products, and have included in license agreements that software and agents can be installed along with the desired software. Users click past the EULA and hope that their antispyware and antivirus packages catch it, not realizing that the protective software may also introduce bugs into overall software load at a rate of 100 per 1000 lines of code (Epstein, 2001).

The Design Flaws in Error Handling

Most scanners that are used by systems administrators and hackers alike operate off of some sort of decision tree. As soon as the type of operating system in use can be determined (e.g., Windows®), then tests for another operating system are unnecessary (e.g., Mac OS X®). The design flaw that enables effective fingerprinting of operating systems and applications is often the lack of standardization of error messaging. For example, one server may respond with the message "Authentication required" and another may say "Please Login" when presented with a blank username. Requirements embodied in standards often specify what needs to be done to handle legitimate requests, and often say what is an error condition, but can stop short of describing the exact text or format of the returned message. Cybercriminals and the technology they employ often look not only at bending legitimate traffic to their use but even use responses to illegitimate traffic to make their attack more effective.

Attacking Weaknesses in Implementation

Lack of universal validation of input is a common and persistent problem. Non-validated input can lead to a condition called "buffer overflows." Computers execute instructions processing data of some sort. Both the instructions and the data are stored in memory. If data are allowed to overwrite programs waiting for execution, then the malware can be placed in the execution area as part of a larger stream of data.

Some operating systems do not allow processes to write to memory allocated to another process. Others create "execute only" zones in memory that report an error if there is an attempt to write to them with data. Windows Vista supports Address Space Load Randomization (ASLR), so that it is more difficult to know where administrative tasks reside. McAfee AVERT® Labs reports that concerted efforts are underway to map or predict the randomized addresses. If the technology seems to be strong, it is within limits. Again, ease of use and flexibility have given rise to "plug-in modules," "snap-ins," interpreted languages, and other data-driven forms of execution, where the code is at some point "data" to an application that has the ability for dynamic extension of functionality.

Buffer overflows are usually patched by the vendor. However, as soon as a patch is released, malware and exploit writers use reverse engineering techniques used in code debugging to isolate what is being patched. After finding the vulnerability, and creating an exploit, it is merely a matter of time before finding the systems that are not well maintained.

Attacking Weaknesses in Validation and Verification

Validation and verification (or V&V) is the place in software development where testing is done to ensure quality of the product. Validation and verification is a step that costs money and slows down shipping software. But from economic analysis, it is usually worth it, as there is less cost to fix the problems before the software is deployed than after it has been deployed. For individual contributors involved in open source projects, the primary risk management tool is the peer review in the design and implementation phases. Validation and verification for some open source software can consist only of alpha and beta tests, where it is released to select groups for utilization. In commercial validation and verification, data fuzzing is used, among other techniques. Hackers frequently employ these tools and techniques on software to look for the same things testers are after, software flaws.

Attacking Weaknesses in Maintenance

Most of the exploitation that turns up as computer incidents still involve computers, networking gear, or applications that are in the maintenance phase. It is amazing how many examples of technology are either not maintained (because of lack of time or money) or have dropped out of support by the vendor. What hackers take advantage of here is that change is costly. Even if the change has a benefit (like an operating system patch), it still requires resources to install and test.

Although some zero-day exploits exist for which there is no patch to prevent exploitation, there is still a great variety of places around the Internet where the systems administrator has been out with a broken leg, or where the budget was cut, and the systems admin position eliminated.

Poor system maintenance procedures provide rich opportunities for exploitation by means that are already known.

Finishing Exploitation?

People do not get rich by just attacking computers, networks, or applications. Exploitations often involve unauthorized use of compromised resources or theft of information.

Unauthorized use of resources is most common in the form of a remote control program or "bot." These programs could be used to string together intermediate systems or to act as relays for stolen data. The common use today is to make the computer's resources for hire, so that other programs, like scanning programs or spamming programs, can operate. Often times, rootkits, which hide processes and files from the user and from anti-malware programs, are combined with the remote control software and the programs run from it, so that users think that their computer is just a little slow.

Theft and sale of information is hot in two markets, identity-related information and intellectual property information. Identity information can be found by scanning the files on the computer, either with specialized scanners or with general purpose pattern matching utilities. Sometimes that is not necessary. Desktops and directories have become so big and cumbersome that desktop indexing and search utilities are becoming popular, Google Desktop® being a prime example. Windows Vista® does aggressive indexing too. User names and passwords are also valuable identity-related information. Keystroke loggers steal credentials used to login by intercepting the information before it ever has a chance to be encrypted. Screen scrapers are the opposite, but rely on the fact that you often are presented with information in your browser that is sensitive and has come through an encrypted channel. If you get close enough to the user, on input or output, the information has to be decrypted. The screen scraper code can be run in a browser so that the Web pages are scanned for patterns or words, and if they are present, a cached copy of the Web page is saved for later transmission.

Intellectual property may be harder to find, but criminals will often do the types of searches described above, but for keywords like "research," "product launch," or even classification terms like "confidential," "secret," or "restricted." These types of searches are necessary only if the searcher does not know anything about the target. More often they will have done research to determine likely areas of valuable information.

With information-based crimes, there is always the issue of getting the data back to the criminal, in order to offer it for sale. Once again, Web ports are rarely closed, and SSL encrypted e-commerce ports pass encrypted contents, so the data can be easily siphoned off through the encrypted Web ports in environments that do not monitor all Web traffic.

Social Engineering

Although social engineering has its own entry, a brief technology overview is necessary to complete the picture. Social engineering attacks target the user, and not the technology. They ask the user to give away something that they should not. Social engineering can be personal or delivered through technology. Phishing emails and phishing Web sites are examples where people are taken to believable Web sites that impersonate their bank or the IRS. Another technology-enabled social engineering method has to do with caller ID spoofing. Caller ID information is just data, and with the right equipment can be spoofed so that an external number looks like an internal number. Though not an example of technology enabled crime, users were asked to exchange their passwords for a chocolate bar, and 64 percent did (Kelly, 2007). A higher tech version of the same came when a penetration tester was engaged by a bank. Thumb drives with a Trojan installed were scattered in a break area outside the bank. Many people picked them up, walked inside, and plugged them in to see what was on them.

One other technology used in social engineering has to do with audio and video data gathering. It can also support information-related crimes, although the technique is the same. People often buy a webcam and a microphone for online live video and audio. That works well as long as you are in control of your computer. If it has been compromised, and there is not a physical "On/Off" switch on the device, it can be used to gather information about you, what you are working on (if at work), or special relationships in your life. All of this gathered information can be used to gain your trust, for further exploitation.

More to Come

This is just a sampler of some of the technologies, and how they are used. The Australian government produces a periodic report on how the nature of technology enabled crime changes, which in its most recent version is 166 pages long (Choo et al., 2007). There is also much speculation on how spam email will transition to instant messaging and Internet telephony. Anti-malware vendors are extending product lines to mobile devices, as they become more capable. "Web 2.0" is under attack because it mixes fantasy with identity, and is, as yet, incredibly open. One only has to do a Google search of an educational Web site for drugs used for sexual enhancement, and you will find a lot of spam embedded in the blogs. The other aspect of "Web 2.0" that makes it ripe for abuse is its scale. With millions of members, and massive numbers of people online, all sorts of crime can take place in the shadows.

Suggested Readings: Choo, K.-K. R., et al. (2007). *Future directions in technology-enabled crime: 2007–09.* Retrieved December 30, 2007, from http://www.aic.gov.au/publications/rpp/78/rpp78.pdf; Epstein, K. (2001, September). Analysis: Data infrastructure. *Ziff Davis CIO Insight.* Retrieved on January 5, 2008, from http://www.cioinsight.com/c/a/Trends/Analysis-Data-Infrastruture/; IT Compliance Institute. (2007, September 19). *Cybercrime surpasses illegal drug trade in terms of global value.* Retrieved December 30, 2007, from http://itcinstitute.com/display.aspx?id=4202; Kelly, M. (2007, April 16). Chocolate the key to many company PCs. *ENN.* Retrieved January 22, 2008, from http://www.electricnews.net/article/10038156.html; Long, J. (2005).

Google hacking for penetration testers. Rockland, MA: Syngress Publishing, Inc., ISBN 1931836361; *McAfee® Avert® Labs top 10 threat predictions for 2008.* (2007, November 16). Retrieved December 30, 2007, from http://www.mcafee.com/us/local_-content/white_papers/threat_center/wp_avert_predictions_2008.pdf; Null, C. (2004, March 3). Google: Net hacker tool du jour. *Wired Magazine.* Retrieved January 3, 2008, from http://www.wired.com/techbiz/it/news/2003/03/57897; Parker, D. (1998). *Fighting computer crime: A new framework for protecting information.* New York: Wiley Computer Publishing, ISBN 0471163783; Richards, Dr. C.W. (1993, January 29). *Riding the tiger: What you really do with OODA loops.* Retrieved January 25, 2008, from http://www.belisarius.com/modern_business_strategy/richards/riding_the_tiger/tiger.htm.

Jim Moore

THEORIES OF CYBERCRIME

A theory may be defined as "an interrelated and testable set of propositions that explain a phenomenon" (McQuade, 2006, p. 141). This is not as complicated as it reads. Simply put, theories help us to understand and explain things. Over time thousands of theories have been developed by people to explain things of the world and even of the universe. For example, in the sixteenth century men such as Copernicus and later Galileo Galilei, with the aid of his homemade telescope, proved that the Earth revolved around the Sun rather than the other way around. This new scientific discovery changed human understanding of the solar system and led to many other pioneering ideas about our planet. But also during the period in history in which Galileo lived, and for a long time afterwards, theories about why crime occurred were limited to choices that people made.

Known generally as *choice theory,* this explanation of crime asserts that people commit crime because they chose to and that they are deterred only by the certainty, swiftness, and severity of punishment. Suppose, for instance, in this era of cybercrime that a person understands that hacking into a computer system or exceeding their network permissions is against the law, that if do this they are likely to be swiftly identified, prosecuted, and severely punished with fines and/or imprisonment, but they choose to hack into a computer system anyway. In that case their actions could be explained with choice theory. Although choice theory came about through the thinking and writing of Cesare Beccaria in the mid-seventeenth century, it is still widely relied on to explain why people break laws against many types of traditional crime and **cybercrime**.

Beginning in the nineteenth century new scientific methods led to discoveries having to do with *trait theory.* This group of theories basically argues that people commit crimes because of their biological and/or psychological characteristics, rather than moral choices they make about what is right versus wrong and whether or not to obey societal laws. Notions that a person may be genetically predisposed or may experience uncontrollable impulses to behave in irrational, violent, or otherwise harmful ways is rooted in concepts of trait theories. Today the concept of so-called "Internet addiction" is based on the belief that people can become excessively aroused by playing computer games or engaging in other online activities to an extent that is harmful to themselves.

In the twentieth century several additional general theories of crime came into being. One of these was *social process theory,* which posits that people commit crime as the result of how they are raised, educated, and acculturated in society. In this view of crime causation family and other social bonds as well as school, religious, recreational, and professional activities that people participate in, along with learning from others, greatly determine whether they fall into criminal lifestyles. A modern example of applying this theory to cybercrime could involve pirating of music, movies, or software. Research now reveals that adolescents often learn from friends or family members how to steal such **intellectual property** using peer-to-peer networks on the **Internet**. In the process they associate this behavior as being normal and with being accepted socially. Individuals with a weak sense of computer ethics and personal responsibility are especially vulnerable to being influenced and slipping into crime in this or other ways.

Whereas social process theory places responsibility for committing crimes on individuals, *social structure theory* asserts that people commit crimes because of the way society is organized. For example, students living in poor families or who receive inferior education may be systematically deprived of their ability to become wealthy or successful in other ways. As a result, according to social structure theory, "the system drove them to commit crime." Perhaps the strain to become wealthy and keep up appearances entices some people to commit **identify theft** or another type of online fraud. Or perhaps the systematic breakdown of families and other institutions of society, due to cyber rather than in-person relationships and business dealings, contributes to the onset of criminal behaviors.

Conflict theory takes social structure theory to another level of understanding and has to do primarily with control of wealth and utilization of power in society for the benefit of oneself and to some extent for "lesser" people who are needed for menial or bureaucratic jobs in society. In this explanation of crime who you are, who you know, what you do for a living, and how rich you are matter a great deal in whether or not you contribute to crime society. When it comes to cybercrime, conflict theorists might claim that very wealthy people with power over how computers and the Internet are used in society may inadvertently contribute to other people rebelling and abusing their IT devices in ways that cause harm.

In reality, most *criminologists* today agree that none of the above general theories of crime and cybercrime can adequately explain why crime occurs. Instead, researchers are increasingly coming to understand that some combination of these general theories and their subcategories must be considered in individual crime cases. For this reason integrated theory also emerged beginning in the 1970s to explain causes of crime. Integrated theory combines one or more aspects of choice, trait, social process, social structure, and choice theories to provide a broader and hopefully more reasonable explanation for why crimes by individuals as well as groups in society occur. Of importance is the new **Theory of Technology-Enabled Crime, Policing, and Security**, which may provide the best overall explanation for why crime evolves technologically.

Suggested Readings: Akers, R.L. (1998). *Social learning and social structure: A general theory of crime and deviance.* Boston: Northeastern University Press; Jacoby, J.E. (ed.). (1994). *Classics of criminology* (2nd ed.). Prospect Heights, IL: Waveland Press, Inc.; McQuade, S.C. (2006). Theories of IT-enabled abuse and crime. In *Understanding and managing cybercrime* (Chap. 5). Boston: Pearson Education, Inc.; Rogers, M.K. (2001). A social learning theory and moral disengagement analysis of criminal computer behavior: An exploratory study. PhD diss., University of Manitoba, Winnepeg Manitoba, Canada. Available at http://homes.cerias.purdue.edu/~mkr/cybercrime-thesis.pdf;

Schmalleger, F. (2004). *Criminology today: An integrative introduction*. Upper Saddle River, NJ: Pearson–Prentice Hall; Siegel, L.J. (2000). *Criminology* (7th ed.). Belmont, CA: Wadsworth Publishing; Skinner, W.F., & Fream, A.M. (1997). A social learning theory analysis of computer crime among college students. *The Journal of Research in Crime and Delinquency, 34*(4), 495–519.

Samuel C. McQuade, III

THEORY OF TECHNOLOGY-ENABLED CRIME, POLICING, AND SECURITY

The Theory of Technology-Enabled Crime, Policing, and Security combines several categories of criminological theories (see encyclopedia entry **theories of cybercrime**) to help society better understand why cybercrimes co-evolved with computer and telecommunications technologies to become among the most complex and difficult forms of crime to prevent, investigate and control. The theory explains how (McQuade, 2006, pp. 176–179):

- Technologies are combinations of tools, techniques [and systems] ranging from simple-to-complex in their design, materials, construction, manufacturing processes, adoption, social implementation, technical/systems integration and applications. Criminals, police and security professionals employ a full range of technologies that are available to them for similar and countervailing purposes.
- New forms of deviance, social abuse or crime, that is *new crimes,* are committed through innovative use of technology. Initially new crime is not well understood, and is therefore relatively complex, because investigative experts tend not to be able to explain how criminals are using technologies to other investigative experts across time and distance.
- Faced with relatively complex crime and attendant management problems, police, security professionals and prosecutors innovate with countervailing technologies to overcome and if possible stay ahead of technological gains made by criminals. With increased understanding and law enforcement interdiction, new crimes transform into better-understood *adaptive crimes,* and laws making criminally adaptive behaviors explicitly illegal begin to be enacted.
- The process of formulating and enacting new crime laws and regulations raises public awareness of crime problems threatening to society. Combined with media attention about these issues, attitudinal and behavioral changes emerge in ways that precipitate arrest and prevention of adaptive crimes.
- Eventually, adaptations of laws are widely adopted and diffused as a form of legal/social technology that leads to increased investigation and prosecution. When this happens, once new and then adaptive crime transforms into *ordinary crime* that is much better-understood, routinely recognized and responded to, and may be systematically targeted for prevention.
- Enhanced enforcement, combined with continual technological advances in society, compel smart criminals intent on getting away with ordinary crime to adopt new technologies. This begins anew the cycle of technological competition between criminals and the police (i.e., the emergence of deviance/social abuse, new crime, adaptive crime, and ordinary crime).
- Criminals that do not adopt new technologies are at greater risk of being caught unless and until their technological capabilities exceed those of law enforcement

and security professionals. Similarly, law enforcement and security professionals must consistently develop, adopt, and diffuse new technologies or risk falling behind in their crime fighting capabilities. Over time, recurring criminal and police innovation cycles have a "ratcheting-up effect" akin to a civilian [and military] arms race.

- Crime and policing become increasingly complex as a function of increasingly complex tools and/or techniques available in society and employed by criminals, police or security professionals. The result is perpetually complex, technology-enabled crime, policing and security management—a never-ending competition in which police and security professionals will, in general, react to criminological innovation.

- Tools and techniques once developed, adopted, and understood tend to remain in use by criminals, police and security professionals because of their continuing functionality and/or constraints to technology development or adoption. The result is a full range of relatively simple (ordinary) to relatively complex (new) forms of crimes and countervailing investigation and protective methods.

- Criminals and police are always wondering about their adversary's activities, and each group may not fully understand the consequences of their own operations (i.e., use of technology). This can result in unintended positive and negative spin-offs effects. Over time, technology employed in crime, policing and security management is better understood, thus relatively less complex, and in the case of crime (hopefully) more manageable, except to the extent that criminal innovations disrupt relatively stable technological competitions between law abidance and violating forces of society.

The forgoing hypotheses provide a framework for understanding all forms of criminality and especially those that are evolving with computing and telecommunications technology inventions and innovations. Developed initially as a concept paper by the author (McQuade, 1998), the theory was later expanded and provisionally tested by him in doctoral dissertation research that triangulated findings using three research methods, including: (1) content analysis of purposive expert interview transcripts, (2) history construction of the technology of money laundering as a proxy for several forms of increasingly complex IT-enabled crimes, and (3) archival records examination comparing federal money laundering prosecution cases for evidence of increasing technological complexity before and after the onset of the World Wide Web (i.e., 1986–1992 and 1993–1999).

Suggested Readings: McQuade, S.C. (1998). Towards a theory of technology-enabled crime. Unpublished manuscript: George Mason University; McQuade, S.C. (2001). *Cops versus crooks: Technological competition and complexity in the co-evolution of information technologies and money laundering.* Fairfax, VA: George Mason University; McQuade, S.C. (2005). Technology-enabled crime, policing and security. *Journal of Technology Studies, 33*(1), 32–42; McQuade, S.C. (2008). Cybercrime: New conundrums and challenges in the paradigm of evolving criminality. In Michael Tonry (ed.), *Handbook of criminal justice.* New York: Oxford University Press.

Samuel C. McQuade, III

U

UNITED STATES V. LAMACCHIA

United States v. LaMacchia can be seen from many vantage points across the broad spectrum between the defendant's perspective of his activities as freedom of speech all the way to the government's contention that it is a criminal act to facilitate $1 million in lost revenue by distributing copyrighted software. It is important to consider along with the decision itself, the impact that the *United States v. LaMacchia* decision had on society, polarizing some of the undecided to the extremes, while enticing others to think of "open source" in new and expanded ways. In order to see the effects on society, it is important to know the issues were being raised inside and outside the courtroom, set in the context of technology of the day.

An overview of the case and how it developed suggests that the government, by indicting David LaMacchia under the Wire Fraud Statute, 18 U.S.C. § 1343, avoided the difficulty of proving that Mr. LaMacchia had the intent to personally profit from the scheme to defraud as required by the criminal copyright statute, 17 U.S.C.S. § 506 (a). However, that approach was not without risk. David LaMacchia filed a motion to dismiss citing two reasons. The first was that the bulletin board that he was operating was a free speech issue, and that he could no more be held accountable for its use for illegal purposes than a library could be held responsible for someone using the information in a book for illegal purposes (Gallagher, 1995). The second argument that is referred to frequently in the Memorandum of Decision is that the Wire Fraud Statute is not as broadly applicable to rights conferred by statute as it is to property rights. It was the second argument that featured prominently in the decision by the presiding United States District Judge Richard G. Stearns (Stearns, 1994).

Understanding the players, the technology, and the circumstances will facilitate the analysis of the issues. David LaMacchia was a 20-year-old engineering student at the Massachusetts Institute of Technology (MIT) when he was indicted under the Wire Fraud Statute for distributing software on an electronic bulletin board where bulletin board users could download copyright protected software. Also in the language of the indictment was that he was in conspiracy with unknown persons, which can best be interpreted as the users of the bulletin board. In the background are MIT, Microsoft, and the other vendors of the software that was being distributed through the bulletin boards that he was operating.

Setting the technological framework of 1994 is useful in documenting what actually was done, in the context of the culture that rewarded the behavior. The primitive state of **Internet** technology showed that those who downloaded software from LaMacchia's bulletin board had to be resourceful, patient, and able to persevere to obtain the prize of no cost software.

"Bulletin boards" predated what we know today as the Web. Web browsers were in their infancy. Although search capabilities did exist on the Internet, at that time they were primitive. Gopher focused on search and retrieval of documents and WAIS (the Wide Area Information Server) provided full text searches of databases. David LaMacchia's bulletin board existed and prospered largely through "word of mouth." People both had to be looking for no cost software and had to be telling others where to find it. Still, finding it at MIT on the "Cynosure" bulletin board took some effort and resourcefulness. Undoubtedly, more people were looking for no cost software than found it on his bulletin board.

The bandwidth used by his "Cynosure" and "Cynosure II" bulletin boards was what attracted the attention of MIT and federal authorities. In 1994, it was not uncommon for well-connected entities to have network bandwidths less than 1 Megabit per second for their Internet connection. Consider as well the consumer side. The fastest modems available in the 1993–1994 time frames were capable of transferring data at most at 28.8 Kilobits per second (Kbps). Many users of that era had 1,200 bps, 2,400 bps, 9,600 bps, or 14.4 Kbps modems. Downloading was slow and tedious, especially for multimegabyte files, such as Excel 5 and WordPerfect6, which could be found on Cynosure. So it was quite an accomplishment to cause an estimated revenue loss of more than $1 million.

The estimated loss was viewed by some as indicative of the growing focus of individuals on what it cost them, rather than what it might cost society and software producers in terms of lost revenue, or what it might cost professional software developers in terms of layoffs and lost jobs.

Others subscribed to the "hacker ethic" of the 1980s and 1990s, which focused on doing no harm, but doing all that you could do. The ethic permitted the use of computers and software that did not belong to you as long as no one was harmed. The line of reasoning extended to the use of copyrighted software. If you used software that you would not have purchased otherwise, then no sales were lost, and no harm was done. From this perspective, there was no $1 million loss. Some took it full circle, claiming that charging for software resulted in a net loss to society, when compared to a society where all software was free (Stallman, 1994).

Both of these perspectives continue to be held today to varying degrees. Recent research suggests that some computer users, especially among the young, have the disposable income to buy copyrighted works, but will not. From research conducted at RIT during the 2004–2005 academic year, 40 percent said that they would not pay 1 cent for a song or movie if they were able to illegally download it (McQuade, 2005). The survey asked the question in the context of entertainment, and not software, but the pattern suggests the LaMacchia decision and subsequent laws seeking to criminalize sharing of copyrighted material have had little effect on the normalization of **intellectual property** theft in the areas of music, movies, and software.

The best results in society, it seems, are toward dialog and collaboration as can be seen in the open source community. Segments of the open source community recognize the need for software developers and the companies for which they work to both earn income. Software developers, as well as intellectual property owners, also recognize that by giving a little of time, effort, and resources, many can be helped, and more can prosper. It was seen at first in the Linux community, which recognized that Red Hat should be able to make money by distributing and supporting the Linux. It was also companies like IBM and Sun Microsystems that ended up putting some of the software that they developed into the open source community.

What ruled the day for the actual LaMacchia decision centered heavily around the arguments for applying the Supreme Court's decision in *Dowling v. United States* to the LaMacchia case. In the Dowling case copyrighted material and the Wire Fraud Statute were also central to the case (Blackmun, 1985). The Supreme Court held that the rights of conferred by reason of statute were different from property rights for "physical 'goods, wares [or] merchandise.'" Justice Blackmun drew a further distinction as to the "rights" on which to focus in his opinion. "The primary objective of copyright is not to reward the labor of authors, but to promote the Progress of Science and useful Arts." In his decision, Judge Richard G. Stearns speculates that the progress of the science and the useful arts might be affected adversely by the broad criminalization of copying software, even once, for private use.

The pivotal issue, carried forward from the Dowling case, was that Congress had very carefully considered the position and application of criminal penalties in the spectrum of remedies available for copyright holders. Justice Blackmun assumed that Congress had been intentional and precise in crafting the statutes protecting copyright. Judge Stearns followed that line of reasoning to affirm the motion to dismiss.

In the dismissal opinion, Judge Stearns did note that what David LaMacchia did was wrong, just not criminal, stating,

> This is not, of course, to suggest that there is anything edifying about what LaMacchia is alleged to have done. If the indictment is to be believed, one might at best describe his actions as heedlessly irresponsible. and at worst as nihilistic, self-indulgent, and lacking in any fundamental sense of values.

In December 1997, Congress did react to the same perception that Judge Stearns did, and the *No Electronic Theft Act* amended the provisions of titles 17 and 18, U.S. Code, to make it illegal for anyone other than the copyright holder, assignees, or their agents to distribute copyrighted software over the Internet. Under provisions of the act, violators could face up to 5 years in prison and fines up to $250,000.

Suggested Readings: Blackmun, H.A. (1985, June 28). *Dowling v. United States Certiorari to the United States Court of Appeals for the Ninth Circuit.* Retrieved October 23, 2007, from http://caselaw.lp.findlaw.com/scripts/getcase.pl?court=US&vol=473&invol=207; Gallagher, D.A. (1995, Summer). *Free speech on the line: Modern technology and the First Amendment,* 3 Comm. Law Conspectus 197, 198; McQuade, S.C. (2005, October 20). *Understanding and managing cybercrime.* Boston: Allyn & Bacon; Stallman, R. (1994). *Why software should not have owners.* Retrieved October 23, 2007, from http://www.gnu.org/philosophy/why-free.html; Stearns, R.G. (1994, December 28). *United States v. LaMacchia Memorandum of Decision.* Retrieved October 23, 2007, from http://www.loundy.com/CASES/US_v_LaMacchia.html.

Jim Moore

V

VICTIMIZATION

For every form and type of crime there is at least one crime victim. A crime victim may be an individual or an organization, such as a business or government agency, who has experienced physical or emotional harm, theft or damage to property, or loss of money, time, professional reputation, and so forth. However, not all victimization stems from criminal acts. People can also be harmed and thus victimized as the result of improper civil interactions, such as a breach of contract. In actuality, many victims have been harmed by both criminal and civil wrongdoing. This is why many perpetrators of crime are also sued in civil court and end up having a financial judgment ordering them to pay victims money for their losses in addition to receiving sentences consisting of fines and/or incarceration for their crime(s).

Victimization is the process by which an act causes harm or loss to one or more people. Cybercrime victimization refers specifically to the process of some person or organization being harmed by a **cybercrime**. It may also be referred to as a process of criminal victimization, because the behavior that caused the harm or loss was illegal and may have taken place over a period of time and in many separate locations. There are three main types of criminal victimization—primary, secondary, and tertiary— which depend on who experiences harm or loss. In *primary victimization* the victim is the direct target of the crime. The victim is harmed as a result of experiencing the criminal act and consequences firsthand. For example, a person whose computer becomes infected with a virus or the organization whose servers are hacked into would be primary victims. *Secondary victimization* occurs when a victim is the indirect target of the crime. The victim is harmed due to an association with the primary victim who experienced direct harm (e.g., as a family member, friend, or associate), but is not otherwise immediately involved or injured. For example, an employer of a primary victim of **identify theft** may be secondarily affected by the crime because the primary victim's job performance decreased as the result of stress or missing time from work to attend to crime-related matters. *Tertiary victimization* refers to society at large experiencing indirect "ripple effects" of crime. For example, when consumers are required to pay higher prices for goods and services due to shoplifting of music CDs and online **piracy**, tertiary victimization has occurred. Higher insurance rates and taxes and fear of crime may also be considered tertiary effects of crime.

There are also four main categories of loss or harm that crime victims can experience involving physical, financial, and/or emotional harm. *Physical harm* includes death and bodily injury caused by gunshot or stab wounds, bruises, cuts, broken bones, and so forth. *Emotional harm* includes loss of mental health or psychological impairment as a result of the crime attributable to anxiety, depression, post-traumatic stress disorder, anger, and fear of future victimization among other issues. *Financial harm* includes theft of money or other forms of financial assets (a common goal in several *types of cybercrime*), as well as damage to property such as computer hardware or software. Financial harm may involve direct ("out-of-pocket") expenses (e.g., to pay medical bills and repair or replace damaged property) or indirect expenses as the result of purchasing crime prevention items such as *anti-malware software* and support services to prevent future cybercrimes. Other indirect expenses could include legal costs, increased insurance rates, and lost wages from time out of work. Social and/or professional harm may also occur as the result of cybercrimes, as when a company must go out of business after losing all their customer and financial account information in a computer *hacking* incident, or when a student is excluded from her friends as the result of **cyber bullying**. In general, primary crime victims may experience physical, emotional, financial, and either social or professional harm; secondary victims may experience emotional, financial, and either social or professional harm; and tertiary victims as members of society at large may experience financial harm.

Victimization initially occurs at the time of the original crime. However, *revictimization* may occur as the result of how a victim is treated by criminal justice system officials after the crime has been reported to authorities. As noted by Gulotta (1984, p. 87), "a victim of crime, more often than not, also becomes the victim of the criminal justice system." Situations that can contribute to feelings of revictimization include the following: insensitive questioning by law enforcement officers; lack of information about the status or outcome of the case; police or prosecutor attitudes suggesting the victim is to blame; lost wages due to time spent away from work in order to cooperate with investigations or testify in court along with takng time off from work; problems finding transportation or child care in such instances; general stress, fear of future crime, and anxiety about testifying in court; contact with the offender "on the streets" or in court; or lengthy time delays that occur as the case makes it way through the criminal justice system (Tomz & McGillis, 1997). All these issues may apply to victims of cybercrime as well as traditional crimes that do not involve computers, other types of information technology (IT) devices, and the **Internet**.

Better training of law enforcement officials, improving relationships between prosecutors and victim-witnesses, and making more advocacy programs available to help victims at all stages of the criminal justice process may decrease this feeling of revictimization. This is especially important given the illusive nature of many cybercrimes and the reality that perpetrators of cybercrimes may never be located, arrested, brought to trial, or spend any time in jail. In these cases it becomes all the more important for victims of cybercrimes to be treated with compassion by criminal justice authorities.

Compared to traditional forms of crime, cybercrime victimization is somewhat different. First, there is a concern about crime seriousness. Traditional person-to-person crimes, especially violent offenses, often cause physical harm to the victim. Cybercrime, on the contrary, could result only in indirect physical harm because it generally lacks interpersonal contact between victim and offender. Because physical injury is a very obvious sign that a crime has occurred, a cybercrime may not be as viewed as having harmed its victim at all. This view does not take into account the other losses (i.e., emotional or financial) that a cybercrime victim may experience, even though they might be just as devastating. Second, attacks that occur via the computer may also cause "information" losses to victims in the form of theft, manipulation, destruction, or denial of access to valuable data stored on computers. Normally financial losses refer to money, financial assets, or tangible property. But in today's world, in which money can also be in digital form (e.g., as bank and credit card account data), financial information stored on computers is especially prized by many **cybercriminals**. Similarly, personal, proprietary, and computer network account data are also highly valued by cybercriminals, regardless of the media they are stored on, provided they can attain access to the device (e.g., a PDA, flash drive, data CD, etc.). Once valuable data fall into the wrong hands, they can be used to commit any number of cybercrimes.

Over 20 years ago, Bloombecker (1985, p. 7B) commented that not only can "everyone…become a computer crime criminal, everyone can [also] become a computer crime victim." As the use of computing and Internet technologies increases, it is incumbent that protective security measures be adopted, and good user practices followed, to prevent widespread, future cybercrime victimization.

Suggested Readings: Bloombecker, J. (1985, October 21). Hackers erode confidence about privacy of data. *USA Today;* Gulotta, G. (1984, January). New approaches to victimology. *International Review of Applied Psychology, 33*(1), 87–95; Kerber, R. (2007, January 18). TJX credit data stolen; wide impact feared. *Boston Globe,* A1; McQuade, S.C. (2006). *Understanding and managing cybercrime.* Boston: Allyn & Bacon; Tomz, J.E., & McGillis, D. (1997, February). *Serving crime victims* (2nd ed.). U.S. Department of Justice, Office of Justice Programs, National Institute of Justice. Washington, DC: U.S. Government Printing Office.

Sara E. Berg

W

WARDRIVING AND WARDIALING

In order to access the **Internet** using mobile devices such as laptop computers and PDAs, users on the move need to find open network access points, which are nothing more than physical locations at which a wireless signal can be received. Common methods of finding an open wireless network access point are referred to as "wardriving" or "warwalking" or "warbiking," respectively, depending on whether the user is in a vehicle, on foot as a pedestrian, or riding a bicycle. These activities are also sometimes referred to as "network spoofing" or "network pirating" or "net-leaching." Typically, wardriving, for example, is accomplished by one or more people in a vehicle with a laptop computer or other device equipped with GPS capabilities and mapping software. As open (unsecured) wireless access points come into range of the wireless antennae, the access point location is documented by the GPS-equipped device and the mapping software. If GPS or mapping technology is not used, wardrivers will commonly mark the access location by drawing symbols (often with chalk) on a public place such as a sidewalk or on a mailbox or the side of a building. In this way they can easily find it again as can other people who periodically engage in wardriving. It is interesting to note that special warchalking symbols developed over several years have been used by some commercial enterprises offering wireless connection services.

"Wardialing" is similar to wardriving-like activities but is the term used for locating a dial-up modem network. Wardialing involves using a dial-up modem to dial several phone numbers in search of a modem that can potentially provide indirect access to the Internet (i.e., via further access to the system or network behind that modem or access point).

There are two types of wardriving, active and passive. *Active wardriving* occurs when a wireless device is used to contact the wireless access point that it is searching for. Once contact is made, the device then becomes associated with and recognized by the wireless network. *Passive wardriving* occurs when a device only attempts to detect (listens for) a wireless access point without actually joining or communicating with the network system device transmitting a signal. Often, directional antennas can be used to detect wider signal ranges and thereby locate a greater number of available access points within a geographic area.

Wardriving is very common throughout the United States and in many other countries that provide for wireless Internet connections. Millions of unique Internet access point locations have been identified and made publicly known. Certain Web sites even specialize in revealing Internet access point locations and promote wardriving as an acceptable aspect of the contemporary **digital youth culture**. According to *The Register,* unauthorized use of wireless networks is commonplace in countries such as China, where 54 percent of survey respondents admitted to either accessing a neighbor's wireless connection or logging onto unauthorized connections in public places. Similar rates of unauthorized wireless network connections have been reported in Germany (46 percent) and in South Korea (44 percent). Once an attacker is connected to a residential wireless network behind an open access point, he has effectively bypassed a system router that should be a first line of defense against computer hacking. Having gained such access, it may be much easier to penetrate the residential user's PC to obtain confidential and valuable information.

Wardriving, warwalking, and warbiking are controversial. Some legal experts claim that these activities amount to theft of services, that by detecting and accessing open Internet access points without paying for the connection service, those who connect without permission are breaking the law in ways analogous to people who dispose of their trash in commercial dumpsters without permission. This is especially true if the device used while wardriving or other means locates a Dynamic Host Configuration Protocol (DHCP) IP address from an access point and then connects to a particular fee-for-service network. Proponents of wardriving, however, argue that publicly available access points should not be restricted, especially if network administrators do not take steps to control wireless access ports on their network devices. Referring back to the trash bin analogy, proponents further argue that so long as the network is able to accommodate more connections simultaneously, akin to more room in a trash bin, there is no harm in people connecting even if they are not authorized and do not pay for the connection.

Another concern about wardriving, warwalking, and warbiking has to do with connections being used for illicit or illegal purposes independent of connecting to a wireless network in the first place. For example, in 2003 police in Toronto, Canada, arrested a man who was wardriving within a residential neighborhood. After connecting to the Internet through a wireless access point being transmitted from a nearby house, he downloaded **child pornography**. If it were not for the investigation conducted by police, the illegal activity could possibly have been erroneously attributed to the homeowner whose unsecured wireless Internet connection was transmitting the signal out to the neighborhood street. Depending on the strength of the wireless signal, architectural features of the buildings in the immediate area, and other geographic factors along with weather conditions, residential wireless connections may broadcast nearly one-quarter mile.

To guard against **cybercrimes** and network abuse over wireless networks municipalities, shopping malls, airports, and other public or private facilities, system administrators need to consider and incorporate network security standards and practices into the wireless network or information systems they are responsible for. Even wardialing, despite relatively slow speed of dial-up modem connections, remains a threat despite increasingly widespread broadband or high-speed Internet connections. This is partially because many information systems still rely on traditional dial-up modems for backup access to other networks and the Internet when primary connection problems arise. Unfortunately, such backup systems often do not have the same or higher level of information security standards in place as the primary higher speed network connections. Companies with unauthorized modems connected to their information system networks are a commonly overlooked security flaw.

Prevention also involves following several best practices, such as changing the default password of a wireless router or access point regularly. Users should not broadcast the SSID (service set identifier) of their router or access point. A MAC address filter may be enabled on the access point to allow only your wireless card to connect via wireless. Additionally, at least WEP (wireless encryption protocol), WPA (Wi-Fi protection access), or WPA-2 encryption should be used with a strong passphrase of at least 12 characters. In addition, strong passwords and passphrases for network access should be used, as well as logging of all network traffic of computer activities. Warning banners and full use of call-back features when available should be implemented.

Suggested Readings: Leyden, J. (2007, August 23). A wardriving we will go! *The Register* Web page: http://www.theregister.co.uk/2007/08/23/mobile_security_survey/; McQuade, S.C. (2006). *Understanding and managing cybercrime* (pp. 80–81; 433_435). Boston: Allyn and Bacon.

Paul Lepkowski

WAREZ GROUPS

Warez groups are organized bands of software pirates. Warez groups illegally obtain, crack, and make copies of copyrighted software, movies, and music. These files are known as "releases" in the warez community. The groups are not typically motivated by financial profit. Instead, warez groups compete with one another to be first in releasing pirated software onto the **Internet** and to the community of users who participate in "the warez scene." Releasing illegally acquired (i.e., pirated) software is considered a game among group members. Winners gain respect and prestige.

The term "warez" was originally slang for software, but later expanded to include music and movies. Warez groups have been commonplace since the early 1980s and have used a variety of different file transfer technologies. Initially they used electronic bulletin board systems to share releases. Later, as Internet access became available to the public, other methods such as Internet Relay Chat and USENET newsgroups were used. Currently, releases most commonly are provided to end users through peer-to-peer software.

Warez members are typically categorized according to their primary role within the group. *Leaders* manage and direct other group members, determining which types of software, music, and movies to crack and release. *Suppliers* locate and provide copies of releases. Releases are more highly valued by warez groups if they have not yet been made available commercially. *Crackers* remove the copy protection from the release. This allows the release to be used without a legitimate license.

If the release is a movie or music file, *encoders* compress the raw movie and music releases into smaller files, such as MP3s or AVIs before release. *Packagers* compress the release and split it into smaller files to make it easier to transfer online. Packagers also add additional information about the release in .nfo (pronounced "info") files that can include group name, file size, and license information. *Couriers* then enter information about the release into a group database for tracking prior to distributing the releases between top-level servers.

Many people distribute illegally acquired music, movie, or software files on their own, independent of any warez group, but are still considered part of the warez scene. There are a wide variety of different types of warez groups, many specializing in different types of software. *Razor 1911* is widely considered to be the oldest surviving warez group, having been established in 1985. In contrast, the warez group known as *Drink or Die (DoD)* was disbanded after an anti-online **piracy** campaign known as *Operation Buccaneer* was carried out by the U.S. Department of Justice in December 2001. Prior to this, the *Pirates with Attitude (PWA)* group were rivals of DoD and became well known for releasing Microsoft's Windows 95 operating system software before its commercial release. PPWA was also later disbanded after members were prosecuted under the federal *No Electronic Theft (NET) Act of 1997.*

Suggested Readings: About The Scene. (2007). *Releasegroup structure.* Retrieved October 10, 2007, from http://www.aboutthescene.com/releasegroup/structure.html; U.S. Department of Justice. (2002, July 2). *Member of "DrinkOrDie" warez group sentenced to 41 months* [Press Release]. Retrieved from U.S. Department of Justice Web site: http://www.usdoj.gov/criminal/cybercrime/Pattanay.htm; Defacto2. (2006). *The scene archives.* Retrieved October 11, 2007, from http://www.defacto2.net/groups.cfm?mode=detail&org=pwa.

Nathan Fisk

RESOURCE GUIDE

Important Books on Cybercrime-Related Subjects

Computer and Intellectual Property Section–Criminal Division. (2002). *Searching and seizing computers and obtaining electronic evidence in criminal investigations.* Washington DC: U.S. Department of Justice.

Cuéllar, M., et al. (2001). *The transnational dimension of cyber crime and terrorism.* Abraham D. Sofaer and Seymour E. Goodman (Eds). Palo Alto, CA: Leland Stanford Junior University, Hoover Institution Press.

Girasa, R.J. (2002). *Cyberlaw: National and international perspectives.* Upper Saddle River, NJ: Prentice-Hall.

Goetz, E., & Shenoi, S. (Eds.). (2007). *Critical infrastructure protection (IFIP International Federation for Information Processing).* New York: Springer.

Himanen, P. (2001). *The hacker ethic and the spirit of the information age.* New York: Random House, Inc.

Hugh, S.A. (2006). *Computer and intellectual property crime: Federal and state law.* Arlington, VA: BNA Books.

Levy, S. (1984). *Hackers: Heroes of the computer revolution.* New York: Doubleday.

Lewis, T.G. (2006). *Critical infrastructure protection in homeland security: Defending a networked nation.* New York: Wiley-Interscience.

McCue, C. (2007). *Data mining and predictive analysis: Intelligence gathering and crime analysis.* Boston, MA: Butterworth-Heinemann.

McQuade, S. (2006) *Understanding and managing cybercrime.* Boston, MA: Allyn and Bacon.

National Academy of Engineering. (1985). *Information technologies and social transformation.* Washington, DC: National Academy Press.

National Research Council. (1991). *Computers at risk: Safe computing in the information age.* Washington, DC: National Academy Press.

Popp, R.L., & Yen, J. (Eds.). (2006). *Emergent information technologies and enabling policies for counter-terrorism.* IEEE Press Series on Computational Intelligence. New York: Wiley-IEEE Press.

Prosise, C. (2001). *Incident response: Investigating computer crime.* New York: McGraw-Hill Companies.

Raymond, E. S. (1996). *The new hacker's dictionary.* Cambridge, MA: MIT Press.

Richards, J. R. (1998). *Transnational criminal organizations, cybercrime, and money laundering: A handbook for law enforcement officers, auditors, and financial investigators.* Boca Raton, FL: CRC Press.

Schneier, B. (2000). *Secrets and lies: Digital security in a networked world.* New York: Wiley Computer Publishing.

Segaller, S. (1999). *Nerds 2.0.1: A brief history of the Internet.* New York: TV Books, L.L.C.

Splichal, S., et al. (1994). *Information society and civil society: Contemporary perspectives on the changing world order.* West Lafayette, IN: Purdue University Press.

Sullivant, J. (2007). *Strategies for protecting national critical infrastructure Assets: A focus on problem-solving.* New York: Wiley-Interscience.

Tapscott, D. (1998). *Growing up digital: The rise of the net generation.* New York: McGraw-Hill.

Toren, P. (2003). *Intellectual property and computer crimes.* Intellectual Property Law and Business Crimes Series. New York: Law Journal Press.

Websites

Computer Crime and Intellectual Property Section
  http://www.cybercrime.gov/
The Cyber Safety & Ethics Initiative
  http://www.rrcsei.org/
Department of Homeland Security
  http://www.dhs.gov/index.shtm
Federal Aviation Administration (FAA)
  http://www.faa.gov/
Federal Communications Commission (FCC)
  http://www.fcc.gov/
Federal Deposit Insurance Corporation (FDIC)
  http://www.fdic.gov/
Federal Elections Commission (FEC)
  http://www.fec.gov/
Federal Trade Commission (FTC)
  http://www.ftc.gov/
Information Systems Security Association (ISSA)
  http://www.issa.org/
InfraGard
  http://www.infragard.net/
National Center or Missing & Exploited Children (NCMEC)
  http://www.missingkids.com/
NetSmartz Workshop
  http://www.netsmartz.org/
Nuclear Regulatory Commission (NRC)
  http://www.nrc.gov/
OnGuardOnline
  http://onguardonline.gov
Securities and Exchange Commission (SEC)
  http://www.sec.gov/

Feature Films

Movie	Year	Director	Synopsis
Antitrust	2001	Peter Howitt	This movie has some strong points about it. Two idealistic computer whiz kids graduate from Stanford, and one of them enters the world of private sector programming. Sure enough, these two programmers find themselves in the middle of cybercrime scandals.
Die Hard 4	2007	Len Wiseman	Leave it to Bruce Willis to save the world from uber hackers. Macintosh advertising personality, Justin Long, plays the reluctant programmer caught up in an digital terrorism scheme. Like *Swordfish,* this movie has over-the-top violence and outrageous action sequences.
Enemy of the State	2001	Tony Scott	The 2001 treatment of the story was designed as a modern techno thriller and has some tremendous special effects and satellite surveillance sequences.
Foolproof	2003	William Philips	A lower-budget movie about hobby bank robbers, this was a delightful surprise to many viewers. Ryan Reynolds and his friends "virtually" rob banks for fun, but are blackmailed into doing a heist for real.
Goldeneye	1995	Martin Campbell	In this James Bond film, two computer programmers fight for control of a Russian satellite weapons platform while Bond tries to find the mastermind behind it. This over-the-top movie follows the path of hackers trained by a government who fight each other over the Web.
Hackers	1995	Iain Softley	Well, this story was really weak, and the hacking scenes were nowhere near reality. But you have to watch this just to say you did.
Mission Impossible	1996	Brian De Palma	While many people no longer like Tom Cruise, his first MI movie did have IT and computer hacking sequences.
Office Space	1999	Mike Judge	A classic, four disgruntled employees catch wind of downsize, devise a very probable scheme of "salami slicing" corporate accounts, and leave with a very nice pension.
Pirates of Silicon Valley	1999	Martyn Burke	This is the flawed storytelling of how Apple and Microsoft came to be. While this movie got mixed reviews, many people have commented they loved it.
Sneakers	1992	Phil Alden Robinson	While dated, this movie was groundbreaking at the time it was made and is still charming to this day. The story revolves around two college buddies who take different paths in life. One becomes an ethical hacker, and the other…well, he is not quite so noble.

Movie	Year	Director	Synopsis
Swordfish	2001	Dominic Sena	Over-the-top violence, preposterous situations, sexy women, and outstanding special effects make this a great popcorn rental. No, do not bring your brain to watch this, but if you like techno-thrillers, definitely rent this.
Takedown	2000	Joe Chappelle	This is the sensationalized story of famous phone phreaker, Kevin Mitnick.
The Italian Job	2003	F. Gary Gray	Modern heist movies always involve some sort of hacking. This particular heist movie is extremely entertaining, especially when the supposed true inventor of "Napster" is the main hacker.
The Matrix	1999	Andy Wachowski, Larry Wachowski	This was such a groundbreaking adventure in reality and existentialism. No, you will not learn how to break into a Linux server by watching Trinity port-scanning with "nmap."
The Net	1995	Irwin Winkler	Sandra Bullock plays a software engineer who loses her identity to digital thieves. Filmed during the fanatic years of the then-novel World Wide Web, this film is now cliched. Nevertheless, fans of Sandra Bullock will still enjoy watching this B movie.
The Score	2001	Frank Oz	Edward Norton and Robert De Niro are fabulous in this heist flick. In a clever plot to rob a Montreal customs house of some royal artifacts, Norton and De Niro must break into the security systems with the help of a socially awkward hacker who lives in his mother's basement.
The Thirteenth Floor	1999	Josef Rusnak	A very extreme version of "The Sims," this movie is about scientists who create a virtual world where participants plug in and take over a computer character's life. The characters are unaware of their puppet existence, but then a real life murder shakes the foundation of the game.
TRON	1982	Steven Lisberger	A hacker is transported into the digital universe inside a computer and must survive combat as a cyber gladiator in order to stop the villanous Master Control.
WarGames	1983	John Badham	A pivotal film calling attention to threats posed by computer hacking and limitations of computer technology. A young man finds a back door into a military computer that is linked to the nuclear defense grid of the United States. A preposterous plot, and yet compelling commentary on nuclear war and the destruction of the human race.

Documentaries

Title	Year	Director
Revolution OS This documentary tells the story about the Linux operating system, and how it forwarded the philosophy of "open source" and free intellectual property. Not an action movie, but definitely interesting for people who want to learn more about why computer culture is the way it is.	2001	J. T. S. Moore
Untitled Hacker Documentary Film describes cybercrime and computer abuse methods used by terrorists, computer security activists, and malicious youth. It also features of activities of The Cult of the Dead Cow and the malware program called "Back Orifice 2000" that is infamous for its ability to seize control of an unprotected computer running a Windows operating system when connected to the Internet.	2006	Sam Bozzo
Can You Hack It? This film explores the origin of true hackers vs. today's computer criminals by following the adventures of Adrian Lamo and other well-intentioned hackers, who found security holes and pointed them out so they might be fixed, only to eventually be arrested. Commonly thought of as computer criminals and vandals, a true hacker is an innovative thinker able to "hack" himself out of a given problem or situation, whether it be computer related or not. Historically, hackers have accounted for mankind's greatest inventions and discoveries and yet have repeatedly been persecuted for their new ideas by the powerful and fearful. Experts on cyberterrorism also examine our societal view of the hacker and debate as to whether or not we should recruit and utilize the skills of the helpful hackers to fight future cyber wars, instead of continuing to punish what we do not understand.	2008	Sam Bozzo
The History of Hacking This film features interviews with Steve Wozniak, John Draper, and Kevin Mitnick, who describe their contributions to information technology, Internet culture, and perceptions about cybercrime and cybercriminals.	2006	Discovery Channel
Hacking Democracy—HBO A highly acclaimed film exposing major problems of election and voting fraud in relation to technical security problems with electronic voting machines combined with abusive use of computers and other types of	2006	Sam Bozzo

Title	Year	Director
information technology (IT) devices. This fast-moving film also reveals hacker motivations and methods to attack everything from home computers to information systems of the world's largest companies. This film also describes wired and wireless security precautions necessary for protecting information systems and computerized devices.		

INDEX

Note that **boldface** page numbers refer to entries in the encyclopedia.

ABOUT THE EDITOR
AND CONTRIBUTORS

THE EDITOR

Samuel C. McQuade, III currently serves as the Professional Studies Graduate Program Coordinator at the Rochester Institute of Technology (RIT). He is a former Air National Guard security officer, deputy sheriff and police officer, police organizational change consultant, National Institute of Justice Program Manager for the U.S. Department of Justice, and Study Director for the Committee on Law and Justice at the National Research Council of the National Academies of Sciences. Dr. McQuade has received numerous honors and awards, including a Presidential Management Internship award that placed him at NIJ in 1994 where he managed computer crime and other technology-related social science and criminal justice research projects. While in Washington, D.C., he also provided independent consulting services to the Urban Institute, among other clients, and taught criminal justice courses at the University of Maryland (College Park), at George Mason University, and at the FBI National Academy on behalf of the Office of Justice Programs. He currently teaches and conducts research at RIT in areas inclusive of computer crime, security technology administration, and career options in technology-oriented societies. Dr. McQuade also oversees a professional course concentration in Security Technology Administration offered through RIT's Professional Studies Master of Science Degree program. His last book titled *Understanding and Managing Cybercrime* was published in 2006.

THE CONTRIBUTORS

Sara E. Berg is a doctoral student and graduate assistant in the Criminal Justice program at the State University of New York (SUNY Albany). Her primary research involves examining the intersection of information technology (IT) and crime, specifically how IT shapes criminal offending behaviors, victimization, and crime prevention. Berg has previously published works on identity theft victimization and Internet fraud. She has also taught courses in Computer Crime, Victims of Crime, and Criminology at SUNY Albany or Rochester Institute of Technology.

Marianne Buehler has been involved with and has taught various aspects of library technologies for over 20 years. She is currently Wallace Library's Head of Publishing and Scholarship Support Services at Rochester Institute of Technology (RIT). The Publishing and Scholarship Support Center provides advice and assistance in the scholarly communication process that includes print on demand self-publishing, editing services, the RIT Digital Media Library, open access journal publishing, copyright consultations, and other related services. She is the Managing Editor of the *Journal of Applied Science and Engineering Technology*, the Scholarship@RIT newsletter, and is RIT's Turnitin Administrator. Marianne has presented at national/regional conferences and has published various articles regarding distance learning information literacy, copyright and plagiarism issues, library information technologies, and open access institutional repositories.

Daniel Cator is currently employed as an emergency dispatch operator (EDO) with ADT Security Services in Rochester, New York. His primary position has been supplemented by assisting with new hire training. He has also served on a task force assembled to transition customer accounts to a more user friendly system. He is currently finalizing a Master's Degree in Professional Studies that consists of concentrations in Security Technology and Human Resource Development at Rochester Institute of Technology.

James P. Colt is the Coordinator of School Safety and Security for the Monroe 1 BOCES school district, and has over 15 years of experience in the fields of law enforcement and security. He is a former police officer employed by the State University of New York. Colt is also a certified public school teacher and school administrator in New York State. He is currently a doctoral candidate at St. John Fisher College completing his dissertation on the topic of cyber bullying.

Nathan Fisk is a doctoral student and teaching assistant in the Science and Technology Studies program at Rensselaer Polytechnic Institute (RPI) of New York State. He is currently writing a reference book titled "Understanding Illegal File Sharing" for Greenwood Publishing. Prior to beginning the degree program at RPI, Nathan was an integral part of the Rochester Regional Cyber Safety and Ethics Initiative of Monroe County, New York, lending both technical and research expertise to the project. Previously, he worked on a variety of technical and communications projects, including the development and administration of a hands-on computer security training course for the faculty and staff of the Rochester Institute of Technology (RIT). Nathan currently holds a Master's Degree in Communication and Media Technologies and a Bachelor's Degree in Information Technology, both from RIT. He is also now completing a second Master's Degree in Professional Studies with a concentration in Security Technology Management from RIT.

Joseph F. Hennekey is currently employed as a Security Manager in the Security Department of the Bausch & Lomb Corporation. In this capacity he performs investigations, forensic examinations, and analysis of digital information. Joe was previously employed by the County of Monroe, New York, first as the Radiological and Chemical Defense Officer and then as a deputy sheriff. During his 25-year career with the County of Monroe, he worked in a variety of assignments including emergency preparedness, road patrol, crime analysis, and criminal investigations. He developed and implemented the first Computer Forensic Unit in Monroe County and became a Certified Forensic Computer Examiner through the International Association of Computer Investigative Specialists. Joe received additional forensic data recovery and computer crime investigation training through the National White Collar Crime Center (NW3C), the New York State Division of Criminal Justice Services, the SEARCH Consortium, and the U.S. Secret Service. He holds a BA degree in Criminal Justice and a Master's degree of Strategic Studies and serves as an adjunct professor and lecturer in areas of computer crime and security technology for many schools, colleges, and professional organizations. Joe is also an active member of InfraGard and the International Association of Computer Information Systems, as well as a 32-year veteran of the U.S. Army Reserve (Colonel-Ret.).

Shaun M. Jamison is an assistant director of the Center for Student Development at the University of Massachusetts Amherst. He holds a B.S. in Professional and Technical Communication from Rochester Institute of Technology and a M.Ed. from UMass Amherst. Shaun currently works advising students, student organizations, and student governments. Research interests include using social networks for student activism, using technology to enhance student governance, and the relationship between campus judicial systems and student use of technology.

Michael J. Kozak is a 21-year law enforcement veteran, retired lieutenant from the City of Rochester, New York Police Department. As a former officer of the Rochester Chapter of FBI InfraGard, he most recently served as the chief information officer for the Rochester Police Department overseeing public safety technology implementations involving encrypted wireless mobile data computing platforms, evidence quality automated field-reporting systems, real-time audio gunshot detection systems, and U.S. Department of Justice standards for police databases management. Mr. Kozak helped integrate military Operations Security (OPSEC) principles with police network operations and security policies, and facilitated implementation of a model network intrusion detection perimeter that has since been adopted by policing agencies across New York State. Michael has extensive experience as an OPSEC practitioner in network security policy, computer forensics, remote mobile computing, wireless encryption standards, information assurance, and ethics in information technology operations. He currently owns and operates the technology consulting firm NetForce Logistics, LLC, and serves as the Western New York corporate liaison for eForensix, LLC, specializing in highly confidential criminal and civil computer forensics investigations.

Paul Lepkowski, CISSP, has been active in the networking and security industry for 16 years. He has held key architectural and strategic positions in multiple large enterprises and universities. Information security is both his profession and his hobby. Paul is an active member of the FBI's InfraGard program dedicated to sharing public information about critical information infrastructure protection, the International Systems Security Association (ISSA), and the Institute of Electrical and Electronics Engineers. He has also been involved in planning the Rochester Security Summit, an annual event sponsored by the Rochester, New York, chapter of the ISSA.

James Lippard is Director of Information Security at Global Crossing, where he manages the groups responsible for the internal and customer-facing network security of the global telecommunications company. He began his career in information technology at Honeywell, where he was a systems developer on the Multics operating system. He also participated in the reviews and testing that led to Multics receiving the first B2 security rating from the National Computer Security Center. He has held senior security operations positions at Primenet, a national ISP, GlobalCenter, a large web-hosting provider, and Frontier Communications, a national telecom provider. Jim has also worked as a "research philosopher" for Genuity when it was part of the Bechtel Corporation, reporting to the Chief Technical Officer (CTO). He was the technical editor for the book of Victor Oppleman, Oliver Friedrichs, and Brett Watson, *Extreme Exploits: Advanced Defenses Against Hardcore Hacks* (2005, McGraw-Hill). He has a master's degree in philosophy with a minor in cognitive science from the University of Arizona and a bachelor's degree in philosophy from Arizona State University.

Kevin J. McCarthy currently works for the Louisiana Department of Health and Hospitals, at the East Louisiana Mental Health System facility in Jackson, Louisiana. In addition to working with an adult inpatient forensic population, he maintains a private practice as a clinical psychologist in rural Western Mississippi and along the Gulf Coast. He has held a clinical faculty appointment at Louisiana School of Medicine (New Orleans) in the Department of Psychiatry and continues to teach at community colleges. He has authored a variety of publications on the practical applications of psychology to diverse or traumatizing situations. In addition, he has conducted numerous workshops and training sessions for local, state, and federal law enforcement personnel in the area of Critical Incident Stress Management and

Post-Traumatic Stress Disorder. More recently he has expanded these activities to emergency services workers through presentations at various national conferences. Dr. McCarthy has provided consultation services to major corporate entities including Procter and Gamble; Cingular Telephone; Harrah's Casino; The State of Louisiana Governor's Conference, The City of New Orleans, The City of Hammond, and others in response to the aftermath of Hurricane Katrina. These activities also included volunteer efforts in conjunction with post-disaster services offered on the Mississippi Gulf Coast. He holds an earned doctorate degree in Clinical Psychology from United States International University in San Diego; a Master of Arts degree in Counseling Psychology from Pepperdine University; and a Bachelor of Arts degree in Psychology from Antioch University–San Francisco. He has clinical interests in neuropsychology, substance abuse, institutionally induced PTSD, and chronic mental illness as related to effective community reintegration. Dr. McCarthy and his wife, Quinta, a dentist, have developed and funded the Dismas Project, a nonprofit organization with an educational outreach to offenders, to their family members, and to community members. They are also been involved in international relief efforts through the provision of health care services in Thailand, Indonesia, and Dominican Republic.

Jim Moore started his security career at Xerox's Corporate Information Security group where he developed its first operating system security standard, architected and led their internal Computer Emergency Response Team, and applied for a patent on a time-stamp nonrepudiation process for electronic documents and files, among other major accomplishments. Jim also championed the use of the Creative Commons share-alike license for information security awareness communications. Currently the Information Security Officer at Rochester Institute of Technology, he is a member of the EDUCAUSE Security Task Force working groups on Effective Practices and Security Metrics. Jim's commitment to collaboration and synergy is also seen in his work with technology vendors—his suggestions have inspired new commercial products while enhancing information security innovations. As an "out-of-the-box" thinker well known in information security professional circles, Jim has assisted firms such as Tripwire®, Proventsure®, and Wetstone Technologies®. Being a loving and effective father is Jim's first priority. He is currently writing a book for Christian single dads.

Rob Paisley is a software engineer for ITT Industries in Rome, New York. He holds a B.S. in Computer Science from Rochester Institute of Technology. His current work in information assurance is in audit review and analysis applications for cross boundary deployments.

Dave Pecora is the Associate Director of Customer Support Services for Information and Technology Services at the Rochester Institute of Technology. Dave has over 20 years of experience in the IT profession, holding positions in the management of technology support, applications development, project management, and IT consulting. He currently oversees the RIT ITS Customer Support function, which includes the central university Help Desk as well as the Desktop Engineering, Residential Network Computing (Resnet), and Distributed Support Services teams. He served as lead for the RIT Anti-Piracy Task Force, and led the communication and training efforts for RIT's ID card replacement initiative. Dave was previously a consultant with SAP America and Apex Consulting, assisting clients such as Kodak and Lucent Technologies with major ERP initiatives. He held IT management and project management positions at Bausch & Lomb, where he managed a multimillion dollar initiative to replace several legacy operations applications with state-of-the-art technology. Dave currently holds a BS in Chemical Engineering and a Master's Degree in Business Administration, both from Syracuse University. He is completing a second Master's Degree in Professional Studies with course concentrations in Security Technology Management and Technical Communications from RIT.

Andrew Perry is an adventurer, author, consultant, public speaker, and technologist who provides services to businesses in need of executive, sales, and technology leadership. Mr. Perry has been involved in technology since the early 1970s and is currently focused on providing leadership to small businesses with a desire for growth. Additionally, he is helping to drive a national volunteer effort originating in Rochester, New York, to create a center for the ethical use of technology.

Neel Sampat is currently a graduate student in the Professional Studies Master's of Science Degree program at the Rochester Institute of Technology. With course concentrations in Security Technology Management and Public Policy, Neel also serves as a graduate research assistant. Through the 2007–2008 academic year he provided project management, community training, and lead statistical analysis support for a major computer crime and victimization survey study undertaken by the Rochester Regional Cyber Safety and Ethics Initiative of Monroe County, New York. Neel holds a Bachelor of Science Degree in Criminal Justice from RIT and is seeking enterprise security career opportunities.

Allen Scalise is president of Great Lakes Networks LLC and has created strong relationships with customers over the past 20 years. His unique experience in information technology enterprise solutions, management, telecommunications, and distribution makes him an ideal leader for Great Lakes Networks, the company he founded in 2005. Previously, Allen worked for two San Francisco based security start-ups, nCircle Network Security and CoSine Communications, held a national sales position at Frontier Communications, and was Regional Director at SBC DataComm (now AT&T Enterprise Solutions) where he managed profit and loss (P&L), six multistate offices, and a remote sales force. Allen is an avid radio hobbyist. Allen graduated with a bachelor's degree from Allegheny College in Pennsylvania, is co-founder and president of the Rochester Chapter of ISSA (2005–2008), co-founder of the Rochester Security Summit, is a member of InfraGard, is an executive committee member of the Rochester Regional Cyber Safety, Security, and Ethics Initiative, and is on the Board of Directors at Brighton Volunteer Ambulance.

Gary Scarborough is a systems administrator for the Information Technology Department at the Rochester Institute of Technology. He earned his Master's degree in Information Technology from RIT. He specializes in the use of Linux and virtualization in the classroom. Gary also advises the Security Practices and Research Student Association (www.sparsa.org). Each year he works with SPARSA members on numerous campus and community activities, including the annual Information Security Talent Search, in which a secure lab affords opportunities for teams of RIT students and information security professionals to compete in a series of red/blue exercises. Many of Gary's students are now employed as information security professionals in government and in the private sector.

Thomas Schiller is a consultant for the Division of Public Safety Leadership at the Johns Hopkins University School of Professional Studies in Business and Education, where he has collaborated on research in the field of transportation security. He also is a lecturer as part of the MS in Intelligence Analysis Program at the Division of Public Safety Leadership. Previously, he spent seven years supporting the international activities of the National Institute of Justice of the U.S. Department of Justice in Washington, D.C. Tom has extensive experience in the research and analysis of terrorism and counterterrorism, dating back to 1982. He has written on terrorism, maritime security issues, international law enforcement, and solar energy. His research has—over the years—examined numerous international conventions governing maritime conflict, terrorism, aviation and maritime security, international organized crime, and now cybercrime. Tom holds an M.Litt. Degree in International Relations from the University of Aberdeen in Scotland.